ARIZONA!

ARIZONA!

JAY J. WAGONER

Peregrine Smith, Inc.
SANTA BARBARA AND SALT LAKE CITY

1979

Copyright © 1979 by Peregrine Smith, Inc.

Library of Congress Cataloging in Publication Data
Wagoner, Jay J   1923–
    Arizona.

    1. Arizona—Juvenile literature.   I. Title.
F811.3.W32   979.1   79-15183
ISBN 0-87905-105-1

All rights reserved for all countries, including the right of translation. No part of this book may be used or reproduced in any manner whatsoever without written permission from the publishers.

Book design by Richard A. Firmage
Cover design by Larry Winborg

Manufactured in the United States of America

INTRODUCTION

Arizona is a beautiful state! It has *many kinds of scenery*. There are warm deserts and cool mountain forests. One can see both canyons and flat, fertile river valleys. The state has lots of lakes and streams.

Arizona has an *exciting history* too! People from many places have come here to live. Indians, Spaniards, Mexicans, Blacks, Anglo-Americans, and Orientals—all are a part of Arizona's history.

A study of Arizona's past teaches us many things. We learn that *change is always going on*. We see that the lives of people in Arizona have changed. A knowledge of history shows us how things used to be. It helps us to understand the present. We can see that the future has already begun.

We gain many *values* from studying the lives of Arizona's pioneers. We share some of their experiences. We see how they were successful in their jobs and daily living. And maybe we can avoid the mistakes they made.

Navajo boy with his mother's sheep on the northern desert in winter.

TABLE OF CONTENTS

UNIT I: GEOLOGY AND GEOGRAPHY OF ARIZONA	8-41
1. GEOLOGY OF ARIZONA	11
2. GEOGRAPHIC ZONES	14
3. CLIMATES	21
4. PLANT LIFE	25
5. WILDLIFE	31
UNIT II: INDIANS OF ARIZONA	42-70
6. ANCIENT INDIANS	43
7. INDIANS IN RECENT TIMES	54
UNIT III: ARIZONA UNDER SPANISH AND MEXICAN RULE	71-97
8. SPANISH EXPLORERS	73
9. THE MISSIONARY ERA: ARIZONA IN THE 1700S	80
10. ARIZONA AS A PART OF MEXICO (1821-1854)	89
UNIT IV: PIONEER DAYS	98-157
11. FUR TRAPPERS	99
12. MINING	105
13. RANCHING	113
14. FARMING	121
15. THE FIRST SCHOOLS	127
16. TRANSPORTATION	132

17. COMMUNICATION	**143**
18. LIFE IN PIONEER TOWNS	**150**
UNIT V: ARIZONA AS A STATE	158-192
19. ARIZONA IN TWO BIG WARS	**159**
20. ARIZONA'S INDUSTRIES SINCE WORLD WAR II	**168**
21. RECREATION	**175**
22. THE ARTS	**180**
23. RAPID GROWTH AND PROBLEMS OF THE CITIES	**186**
UNIT VI: ARIZONA COUNTIES	193-220
24. THE FIRST COUNTIES	**194**
25. THE FOURTEEN COUNTIES	**199**
UNIT VII: ARIZONA GOVERNMENT	221-241
26. HOW GOVERNMENTS CONTROL, HELP, AND PROTECT	**222**
27. THE CONSTITUTION OF ARIZONA	**226**
28. THE THREE BRANCHES OF STATE GOVERNMENT	**229**
29. COUNTY AND TOWN GOVERNMENTS	**235**
30. ELECTIONS	**239**
ACKNOWLEDGEMENTS	243-244
PICTURE CREDITS	243-244
INDEX	245-251

UNIT 1
GEOLOGY AND GEOGRAPHY OF ARIZONA

Arizona is the sixth largest state. Only Alaska, Texas, California, Montana, and New Mexico are bigger in size.

Arizona is a state that a person has to see to believe. The state has great variety in scenery and climate. Elevations vary greatly.

The low point south of Yuma is only 137 feet above sea level. The highest place in Arizona is on top of Humphreys Peak near Flagstaff. It is 12,670 feet high. In between these points there are many kinds of plants and animals.

In Arizona there are both dry, sunny deserts and tall pine forests. Lakes, streams, and deep canyons are part of the beautiful scenery. The Grand Canyon is one of the most scenic natural wonders of the world.

The warm winter climate is attracting many people to Arizona. The population zoomed from 500,000 in 1940 to 1,000,000 people in 1956. The two million mark was reached in 1973.

It is predicted that Arizona will have three million people by 1985. More than four million people will be calling Arizona their home by the year 2000.

A famous drawing of the Grand Canyon by W. H. Holmes.

San Francisco Peaks near Flagstaff.

1. GEOLOGY OF ARIZONA

THE LAND SURFACE OF ARIZONA HAS BEEN CHANGING FOR BILLIONS OF YEARS.

How old is Arizona? Scientists say the earth was formed four billion (4,000,000,000) years ago. It has been changing all that time. Dry land sank below water. Sea floors rose to become land. Earthquakes cracked the surface. Volcanoes erupted and spread hot lava over the land. Wind and water wore away the earth's crust. All of these forces have been at work in Arizona for a long time.

Changes in the earth can be seen at the Grand Canyon. This deep gorge was cut by the Colorado River. Layers of the earth were exposed as the river slowly cut away. Geologists study these layers. They can tell us what the earth was like long ago.

What was Arizona like millions of years ago? It was covered with water much of the time. Seas left sediment that later turned into stone. A good example is the Kaibab limestone. It can be seen along the rim of the Grand Canyon.

All kinds of fish lived in the seas. There were clams, crabs, and a fish that looked like a shark. Slowly some of the sea life began to creep out of the water. To survive on land they developed lungs and legs. These first land animals were ancestors of the dinosaurs.

Dinosaurs were huge reptiles. They once roamed through the swamps in northern Arizona. The *diplodocus* and the *brontosaurus* were the biggest dinosaurs. These plant eaters had a long neck and a small brain. In a fight, the plant eaters were no match for the meat-eating *tyrannosaurus*. This beast could stand on its hind legs. It was able to bite and claw the huge clumsy plant eaters to death. All the huge dinosaurs died off as dry land rose up.

Grand Canyon.

Shallow seas covered much of Arizona during prehistoric times.

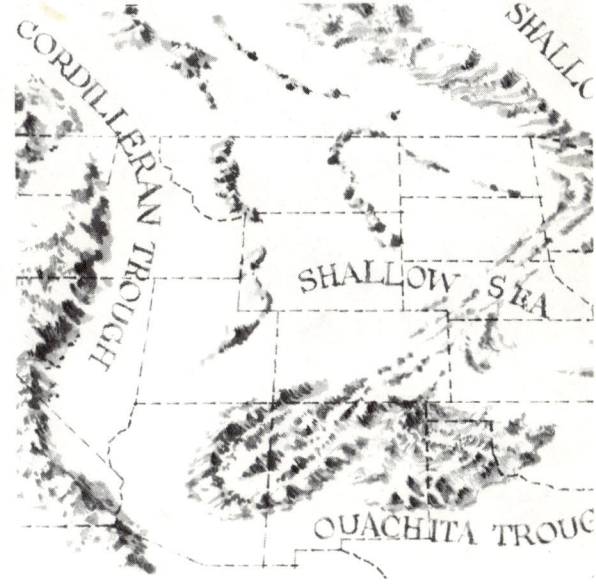

Diorama at the Arizona State Museum in Tucson showing hunters attacking a mammoth.

Dinosaurs such as these once roamed through swamps of Northern Arizona. Painting by Ernest Unterman.

Today, tracks of a three-toed dinosaur can be seen on the Hopi Indian Reservation.

How did the Ice Age affect Arizona? Four times a huge ice cap, or glacier, covered most of North America. The first glacier started forming about a million years ago. The last one melted about 10,000 years ago. The ice caps pushed up mountains and scooped out lakes like a giant bulldozer.

The ice caps did not reach as far south as Arizona. But they brought cooler weather to this region. And more rain fell then. There was plenty of lush green vegetation for wild animals.

Bones of huge mammoths (elephants) have been found in southern Arizona. Camels and antelopes ate tall grass in the Prescott area. Small horses galloped over the plateau north of Payson.

The first humans came to Arizona to hunt the wild animals. That was over 11,000 years ago.

Words and Terms to Know

earthquake　　　　　geologist
volcano　　　　　　dinosaur
gorge

Number a sheet of paper from 1 to 5. After each number write the word from the list above that fits its meaning below.

1. A scientist who knows about the earth.
2. A sudden split in the surface of the earth.
3. An opening in the earth from which melted rock erupts.
4. A huge ditch cut in the earth by a flowing river.
5. A huge reptile that was the earth's largest animal.

Finding the Facts

Complete each of the sentences below on a separate sheet of paper.

1. The earth is at least _____ billion years old.
2. A good place to see changes in the earth is at the _____ _____.
3. Arizona was covered with _____ during much of its history.
4. To survive on land, sea animals developed _____ and _____.
5. The biggest dinosaurs were the _____ and the _____.
6. _____ times a huge glacier covered most of North America.

2. GEOGRAPHIC ZONES

Desert near Yuma.

Arizona can be divided into three large land areas. They are (1) the *plateau,* (2) the *mountain belt,* and (3) the *low desert.* Each is unlike the others.

PLATEAU ZONE

What are the main physical features of the plateau zone? A plateau is a large area of elevated, fairly-level land. The plateau zone in northern Arizona is part of the huge Colorado Plateau. It was lifted up millions of years ago.

The Colorado Plateau includes the Four Corners. This is the only place in the United States where four states touch each other. These states are Arizona, Utah, New Mexico, and Colorado.

The plateau is the largest of the three land areas in Arizona. It makes up 42 per cent of the state. In general the surface is level. But there are mountains which rise above the plateau. Also, great canyons have been cut into the plateau by the Colorado and Little Colorado rivers.

The Mogollon Rim marks part of the southern edge of the plateau. The Rim is a

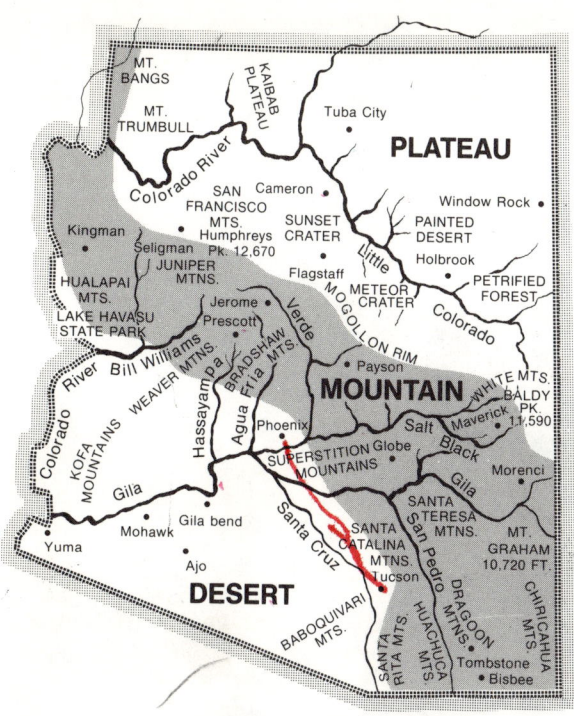

The three physiographic zones of Arizona.

Navajos in the Monument Valley.

steep rock cliff 200 miles long. One of the world's largest ponderosa pine forests is north of the Rim.

How do people make a living on the plateau? Lumbering is an important industry in the plateau zone. Other kinds of work are cattle ranching, sheep raising, and tourism. Flagstaff is the chief city in the plateau zone. It depends on all these ways of making a living. Flagstaff is a trade center. Northern Arizona University is there too.

Tourist attractions. People go to see many natural wonders in the plateau zone. Some of these wonders are the Grand Canyon, Sunset Crater, Meteor Crater, the Petrified Forest, and Monument Valley.

Sunset Crater is near Flagstaff. It was Arizona's last active volcano. The last time Sunset Crater erupted was in 1065. Hot lava was spewed over hundreds of square miles.

Meteor Crater is a well-known landmark

Meteor crater.
Sunset crater.

close to Flagstaff. This crater was not a volcano. It was formed when a giant meteor crashed against the earth. The meteor weighed nearly two million tons. It was buried 600 feet below the surface. The rim of rock around Meteor Crater is almost a mile across.

The Petrified Forest east of Holbrook is a popular sight. The trees here were hardened into stone millions of years ago when much of Arizona was under water. Uprooted trees were covered with silt before they could decay. The tree cells were filled with mineral waters and turned to stone.

Monument Valley is on the Navajo Indian Reservation. Beautiful red sandstone pillars and buttes make this valley a great place for photographers. Many western movies have been filmed there. One of the most famous was "Stagecoach." It starred John Wayne.

Tree in the petrified forest.

Skiing at Mt. Lemmon.

MOUNTAIN ZONE

As you can see on the map, the mountain zone is roughly in the shape of an "S." It stretches from the northwest to the southeast. Most of the mountain ranges in this zone are 25 to 75 miles long and 5 to 15 miles wide. The average mountain top is between 4,000 and 6,000 feet high. Many of the peaks are higher.

The highest peak in the mountain zone is Mount Graham near Safford. It is 10,713 feet above sea level. Another high one is Mount Lemmon in the Santa Catalina

Mountains. Mount Lemmon is forty miles by winding road from Tucson. That makes it a popular vacation area in both summer and winter.

Why is the mountain zone important? Branches of the Gila River flow down many of the fertile mountain valleys. Today most of the river water is stored behind dams. Lakes provide fishing and boating. The lakes also provide water for desert valleys.

Many copper, gold, and silver mines have been found in the mountain zone. Towns were started near these mines. Bisbee, Tombstone, Morenci, Clifton, Globe, and Jerome are just a few of these towns.

Ranching is also important. Many valleys in the mountain zone have good grass. Cattle ranches in these valleys are some of the best in the United States.

LOW DESERT ZONE

The low desert zone is in the southwest part of Arizona. This zone has broad, level *valleys* bordered by mountains.

Most of the *desert mountains* appear to be buried. In fact, they are. For millions of years, loose soil on the mountains has been washed down into the valleys. Now some of the desert mountains look like great slabs of upended rock.

The valleys of the desert zone are not sandy wasteland. The valleys are river plains. They have deep, fertile soil. Only water is needed to turn dry desert land into good farms. Where water flows, Arizona grows!

The Hohokam Indians were the first people in Arizona to farm in the desert. The Hohokams dug canals to divert water from the Gila and Salt rivers. They irrigated crops in this manner for hundreds of years.

Water is still the key to progress and growth in the desert zone. More than half the people of the state live in the big desert cities of Phoenix and Tucson. There is not enough river water to supply all the needs of farms, factories, and homes. Groundwater is being pumped faster than rains replace it.

The desert in Southwestern Arizona.

Water is released from Horseshoe Dam on the Verde River. The water is used by people of the Salt River Valley.

Contrast between desert and irrigated citrus orchard.

An irrigated farm in the Salt River Valley.

More water is needed if Arizona is to keep growing. Where do we get more water?

Words and Terms to Know

plateau
crater
petrified
butte
groundwater

Write the word from the list above that fits the meaning below.

1. Water that is beneath the surface of the earth.
2. Condition of a tree which has turned to stone.
3. A large area of flat elevated land.
4. A bowl-shaped hole at the outlet of a volcano.
5. A hill with steep sides and a flat top.

Finding the Facts

1. Arizona's three land areas are the _____, _____ belt, and the low _____.
2. The largest land area is the _____.
3. The southern edge of the plateau is the _____ _____.
4. _____ is the main trade center of northern Arizona.
5. _____ _____ was the last volcano in Arizona to erupt.
6. The _____ _____ is east of Holbrook.
7. The highest peak in the mountain zone is _____ _____.
8. _____ and _____ are two important industries in the mountain zone.
9. Only _____ is needed to turn the desert into good farmland.
10. More than half the people of Arizona live in the desert cities of _____ and _____.

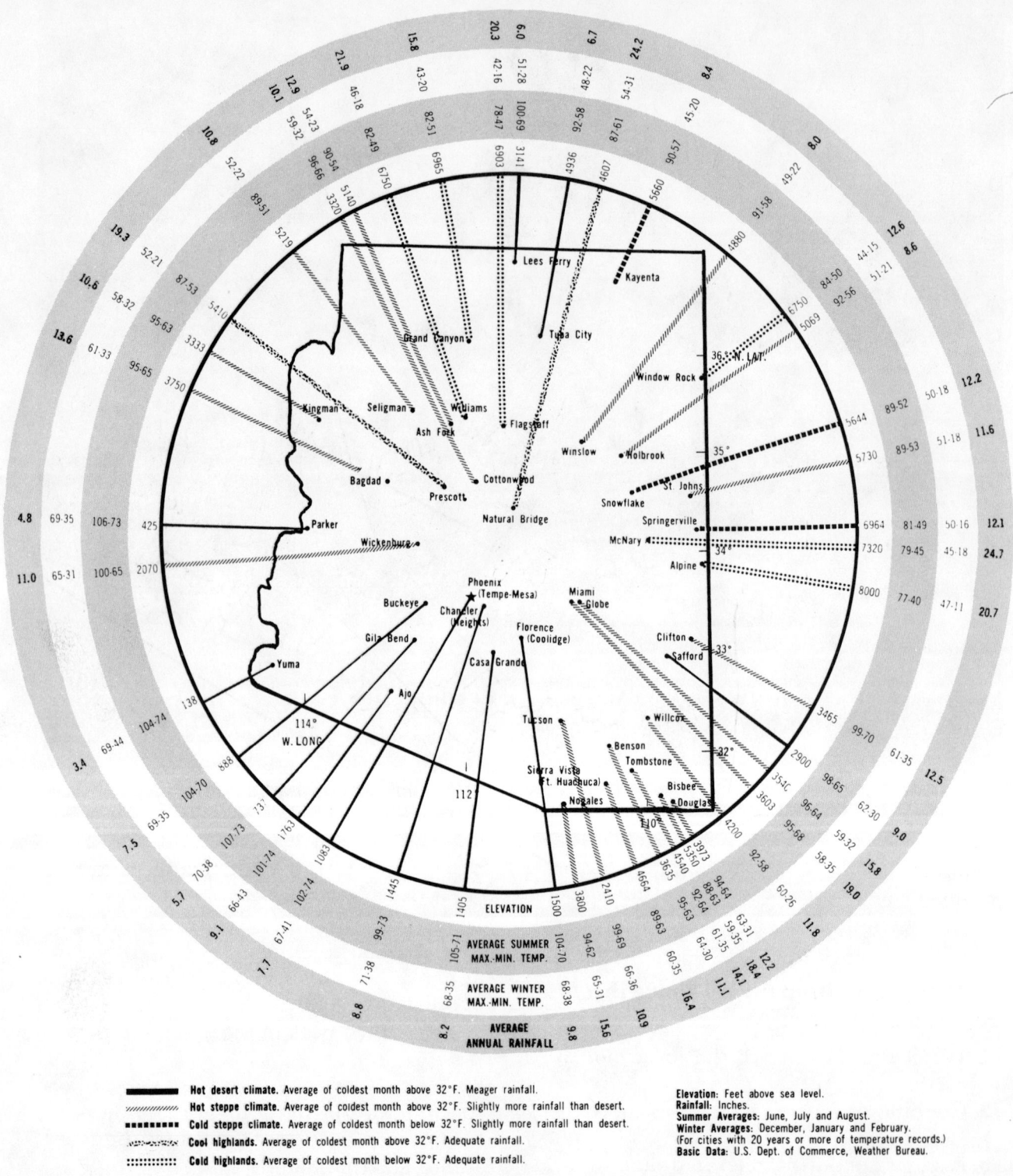

Chart showing range of climate in Arizona.

3. CLIMATES

Humphreys Peak north of Flagstaff.

Why can most kinds of climate be found in Arizona? For one reason, Arizona is the sixth largest state. It measures nearly 400 miles north-to-south.

Even more important, the state is not flat. The low point near Yuma is only 137 feet above sea level. At the other extreme, Humphreys Peak near Flagstaff is 12,670 feet high. The higher up one goes, the cooler the temperature. There is more rain in the mountains.

Temperature. Arizona sometimes has the coldest and hottest places in the nation on the same day. Maverick, in the White Mountains, is one of the state's coldest spots. The record low there was 33 degrees below zero. Desert towns near the Colorado River are often the hottest places.

There is a great difference in day and night temperatures in Arizona. On the dry desert, summer days are hot. There are few clouds to block off the sun. But the night

21

Flood waters in the Salt River at Tempe 1978.

Flash flood on New River northwest of Phoenix in 1978.

brings refreshing coolness. Why? Because the air is dry and there are seldom any clouds to keep daytime heat from rising.

Rainfall. Much of Arizona is dry. It does not rain much or often in the desert. The average annual rainfall in Phoenix, for example, is less than eight inches.

The driest time of the year in Arizona is in the spring. During April, May, and June the humidity is very low. The sun shines all day long.

There are two rainy seasons. Gentle rains come in the winter months of December, January, and February. During this season clouds can get over the mountains in California. Winds from the West bring in moisture from the Pacific Ocean.

The second rainy season is during July, August, and September. The heaviest rains fall during this so-called "monsoon" season. Great cumulus clouds float in from the southeast. A late afternoon thunderstorm often follows a sandstorm in the desert. A cloudburst may drop several inches of rain in a few minutes. Streets are flooded. Severe damage is done to roads. Poorly-located homes or stalled automobiles may be damaged.

Snowfall. Snow and winter rains provide most of the water to fill Arizona's man-made lakes. It has snowed in nearly every part of Arizona—even in the desert. But only places above 4,500 feet get enough snow for it to stay on the ground. The record annual snowfall was in Flagstaff in 1949. Nearly 132 inches fell during January and February. The average in Flagstaff, however, is only 55 inches a year.

In what ways is the warm desert climate an advantage to Arizona? One is a long growing season. Farmers can raise vegetables in the winter time. These crops and citrus fruits are shipped to markets all over the nation.

Arizona's good climate also attracts a skilled labor force. Manufacturing is Arizona's number one industry.

But tourism brings in the most money. Winter visitors like Arizona's warm climate. Many jobs in the state depend on the tourist trade. Can you name some?

Arizona is a good place to retire. Sun City, near Phoenix, is one retirement town. A lot of new residents also come for health reasons—a member of the family has some ailment that is helped by warm, dry air.

Words and Terms to Know

elevation   humidity
temperature   cloudburst
cumulus

Match the words above with the following definitions:

1. Moisture or dampness in the air.
2. The degree of heat or cold.
3. Height above sea level.
4. A dense, usually white cloud.
5. A sudden, heavy downpour.

Finding the Facts

1. Arizona varies in elevation from _____ feet near Yuma to _____ feet on Humphreys Peak.
2. At night, the desert is much _____ because there are usually no _____ to keep the daytime heat from rising.
3. The driest time of the year in Arizona is during the months of _____, _____, and _____.
4. Gentle rains come during the _____ season and cloudbursts are during the _____ season.
5. Flagstaff's annual snowfall average is _____ inches.
6. In the desert area, Arizona has a long _____ _____.
7. Arizona's good climate attracts a skilled _____ _____.
8. _____ is Arizona's number one basic industry.
9. _____ brings in a lot of money for the state's businesses.
10. An example of a retirement community is _____ _____.

Sun City, a fast growing retirement community northwest of Phoenix.

Saguaro cactus and palo verde trees.

4. PLANT LIFE

Ponderosa pines.

Ponderosa pines provide most of wood for lumber mills in northern and eastern Arizona.

At least 3,500 kinds of plants can be found in Arizona. These plants are classified into three main types: trees, grasses, and desert plants.

TREES

Outside the desert, there are three types of native trees in Arizona. They are: (1) tall timber trees, (2) pinyon and juniper, and (3) chaparral.

The main tall timber tree is the ponderosa pine. It grows 200 feet tall. The lumber from the ponderosa pine is soft and durable. Ponderosa beams that were found in a 500 year old Hopi house are still good.

The ponderosa pines grow on mountains and on the plateau north of the Mogollon Rim. The pines live at elevations between 5,500 and 8,500 feet. Higher up, trees like the Douglas fir grow.

Pinyon and juniper. At levels below 5,500 feet, the trees are smaller. A good way to see this is to drive north of Flagstaff to Cameron. Between these towns, the annual rainfall drops from twenty inches to six inches. Large pines at Flagstaff give way first to smaller conifer trees—pinyons and junipers. Still lower in elevation are the grasslands and the northern desert plants.

The pinyon tree is a member of the pine family. Pinyon nuts are valuable. Indians gather tons of nuts in the early winter.

There are many kinds of junipers. The most common is the "stringybark" Utah juniper. It makes good fence posts and firewood.

The chaparral is the third group of trees. It is a thorny brush thicket. It is found on the foothills below the ponderosa pine forests.

There are many types of chaparral south of the Mogollon Rim. Some are scrub oak, manzanita, and sumac.

In places closer to the desert, the evergreen jojoba grows. Jojoba nuts were used by some pioneers to make a drink like coffee. Jojoba may someday be a good domestic crop. The nut of the female jojoba has a number of uses. The oil can be used in cosmetics. The rest of the nut is high in protein and nitrogen. It makes good animal feed.

GRASSES

There are two main types of grasslands in Arizona. *Short grasses* grow on the northern plateau. *Desert grasses* are the second type. The largest desert grasslands are in Cochise County in southeast Arizona. The valley floors in this county are covered with rolling seas of grama and other desert grasses. Cattle do well on the ranches there.

Pinyon and juniper.

Cattle ranch in Cochise County.

DESERT VEGETATION

There are many desert plants. But the *high northern desert* on the plateau is covered mainly by sagebrush. One species, the "big sagebrush," grows three to six feet high. Sheep graze on it, especially in the winter.

The *low southern desert* has more kinds of plant life. Cacti and the palo verde tree are found on the rougher terrain.

The palo verde is the state tree of Arizona. The name means "green stick." The young palo verde has a smooth green bark. In spring the palo verde is covered with beautiful yellow flowers.

Cacti come in all sizes, shapes, and colors. The largest is the *saguaro*. Its white blossom is the state flower. The saguaro grows slowly. A 50 foot plant might be 150 years old. The saguaro survives in the desert on water stored in its large, fluted column. Elf owls nest in holes drilled in the saguaro by woodpeckers.

Riders look at a huge saguaro cactus. The horse stands beside an ocotillo.

Navajo sheep grazing near Window Rock on the northern desert.

An early day Arizona man standing beside a cholla cactus.

Papago Indians pick the sweet saguaro fruit to eat.

The *barrel* cactus can grow to a height of four to six feet. The barrel is called the "compass cactus" because it leans to the south. Ground squirrels love the rich seeds of the barrel cactus fruit. Somehow they manage to climb over the thorns without harming their soft-padded feet.

The *ocotillo* is a strong and graceful cactus. It has long stems called "monkey tails." In the spring each stem has a beautiful orange flower. The stems are covered with tiny green leaves after some good rains.

The *prickly pear* is one of the best known cacti. It grows in most parts of the United States. Fruit from the prickly pear makes a delicious jam.

The *cholla,* or jumping cactus, is the fierce touch-me-not of the desert. The sharp cholla spines easily pierce shoes. The cholla is a problem to animals like sheep. Many birds, however, like the cholla's thorny protection. The cactus wren is the Arizona state bird. It likes the cholla better than any other nesting place.

There are many other cacti, including the pincushion, organ pipe, hedgehog, and night-blooming cereus.

Other desert plants. The *agave,* or century plant, is not a cactus. But it is often mistaken for one. The agave sends out thick leaves. Each leaf has a sharp barb that can be used for a needle. The leaf's fiber provides the thread. Indians used to eat the cabbage-like head of the agave. When the head is allowed to send up a flower stalk, it may reach 25 feet in height. The stalk contains water that could save the life of a person lost in the desert.

The *yucca* is another plant that is often mistaken for a cactus. The yucca has sharp pointed leaves and is called "Spanish dagger" or "the Lord's candlestick." Indians use the leaves to make baskets. They crush the roots and trunks to make soap.

Many kinds of *wildflowers* grow on the desert. Some flower seeds lie on the ground for years before they bloom. When rains come, the flowers seem to jump out of the ground. For a short time the flowers carpet the desert. On a hillside they can be seen for miles.

Mesquite and *ironwood* trees are two kinds of desert trees. Like the palo verde, they are members of the pea family. Ironwood looks a lot like the mesquite. But ironwood has grayer bark and heavier thorns. Its pods have dark round peas. Mesquite pods have flat beans.

Mesquite trees grow best in bottomlands where water collects. With deep soil and underground water, a mesquite may grow 30 or 40 feet tall. Mesquite trees can be a problem on ranches. They may take over grasslands which have been overgrazed by cattle.

The Indians and pioneers made good use of the mesquite. Indians ground the mesquite beans into flour. Pioneers used the wood for fence posts, roofs, corrals, bridges, and fuel. Have you ever tasted mesquite honey? Honey bees like the mesquite flowers.

A pin cushion cactus in bloom.

Wild flowers on a desert mountain.

Words and Terms to Know

species	vegetation
chaparral	bottomland
fluted column	overgrazed

Match the words above with the following definitions:

1. A category or group of plants.
2. Another word for plant life in general.
3. A low, thorny tree or thicket.
4. The grooved, main stem of a cactus.
5. Condition of land where too many cattle or sheep have been feeding.
6. Lowland along a river.

Finding the Facts

1. At least _____ species or varieties of plants can be found in Arizona.
2. The ponderosa is a tall _____ tree used for _____.
3. _____ and _____ are smaller conifer trees which are found at lower elevations than the ponderosa pine forests.
4. The _____ is a smaller thorny tree found below the ponderosas.
5. Some of the best desert grasslands are in _____ County.
6. The northern desert is covered mainly with _____.
7. Arizona's state tree is the _____ _____.
8. The state flower is the white blossom of the _____ cactus.
9. "Compass cactus" is another name for the _____ cactus.
10. One of the country's best known cacti is the _____ _____.
11. Some desert plants which are not cacti are the _____ (century plant) and the _____ (Spanish dagger).
12. Indians used to grind beans from the _____ tree into flour.

A yucca plant, prickly pear cactus, and chaparral on banks of an Arizona lake.

5. WILDLIFE

Elk.

Arizona has many kinds of wildlife. Lots of mammals, birds, fish, reptiles, and amphibians are found in Arizona. In fact, the state has 60 per cent of all the types of wildlife found in North America. Most of them are harmless. They are more afraid of you than you are of them.

MAMMALS

Mammals are animals that have hair. Young mammals are born alive. They are not hatched from an egg. They are fed milk from the mother's body. Mammals are warm-blooded.

What "big game" mammals are found in Arizona? There are nine species: elk (wapiti), antelope (pronghorn), mule deer, white-tailed deer, black bear, mountain lion, javalina, bighorn sheep, and the bison (buffalo).

The *elk* is the largest game animal in Arizona. Today's elk are not the native Merriam elk. The Merriam elk was killed off before 1900. The present herds go back to animals that were imported from Wyoming. Today the Arizona Game and Fish Department issues elk hunting permits. Just enough permits are issued to keep the elk from overbalancing the food supply. The elk are found on the national forest lands.

The beautiful *pronghorn antelope* is one of the world's fastest animals. It is called an antelope, but it is really more closely related to the sheep family. It stands about three feet high. Both the male and female have horns which curve a little. Each horn has a prong,

31

Pronghorn antelope.

or stub, that grows forward. The pronghorn is light tan in color. It has white undersides and two white bands on the throat. When frightened, the pronghorn shows a snow-white rump patch. This signal is a danger warning to other pronghorns.

The pronghorn antelope almost became extinct in pioneer days. They once roamed over most of Arizona. Today the pronghorn are found in the open grassy country in northern and central Arizona.

Mule deer are an important game animal. They are found in both mountain forests and desert country. Mule deer are large, handsome animals. They have wider antlers than most deer. Long ears give them their name. The deer browse instead of graze. That means they eat mostly leaves and shrubs instead of grass.

Arizona's *white-tailed deer* are small, graceful animals. Shy and nervous, these deer prefer the mountains. There they can hide in the brush. The adult is tan in color with white underparts. Its broad tail rises and looks like a white flag when the deer runs or is frightened. Young fawns have white spots on their cinnamon-colored coats for six months after birth. This coat helps the fawns to hide from predators. They are born about the time of the July and August rains. Browse food is easy to find at that time of year.

Arizona once had two species of *bears*. They were the grizzly and the black bear. The grizzly is now extinct. Today the black bear is legally a game animal—not a predator. This means that the animal is protected by certain laws. By state law, however, a rancher can kill a bear he suspects of killing his livestock. Only a few bear hunting permits are issued each year.

The *mountain lion* is the largest wildcat in the United States. It is called a cougar or puma. The mountain lion prefers the rough mountain country. The huge cat stalks its prey and can leap great distances. It eats mule deer and other wildlife. The porcupine is a special treat.

Ranchers sometimes report that mountain lions kill their cattle or sheep. Like the black bear, however, the mountain lion is protected as a game animal. This keeps people from causing a species to become extinct.

The *javalina* is a wild pig. Though not large, it is classified as a big game animal. The javalina has a sturdy body, powerful neck, short legs, long snout, and large ears. Its sharp tusks can cut deeply. The javalina is nearsighted. But it can detect danger with its good sense of smell.

Mountain lion.

Javalina with twin babies at Arizona Sonora Desert Museum.

Bighorn sheep.
Bison.

The wild pigs run in herds. They like desert washes with the shelter of trees. The javalinas eat cactus fruit, mesquite beans, roots, insects, and reptiles, including snakes. The javalina is a popular game animal for hunters.

The *bighorn sheep* live in desert mountains near the Colorado River. Two federal refuges are there to protect them. The bighorn sheep are large, heavy animals. They have hair, like deer, instead of wool coats. Adult rams have huge horns. These horns curve back, down, and then up at the tip. The sure-footed sheep climb rocky ridges. Early in the morning they come down for water. Lambs of the bighorn sheep are sometimes carried away by golden eagles.

The *bison,* better known as the *buffalo,* is not native to Arizona. Herds are kept on two ranches. One is Houserock Ranch north of the Grand Canyon. The other is Raymond Ranch east of Flagstaff. The Game and Fish Department sponsors a buffalo hunt once a year. Permits are given to only a few hunters.

OTHER MAMMALS

Not all the mammals in Arizona are big game animals. There are smaller mammals all over the state. These include the jackrabbit and the cottontail rabbit. Other small mammals are the bobcat, both striped and

Coatimundi.

spotted skunks, the gray fox, the badger, the porcupine, the raccoon, the ringtail (raccoon family), the kangaroo rat, and the coyote.

The coyote's name means "barking dog." The *coyote* is a very adaptable animal. It can live almost anywhere. The coyote sleeps in the shade by day. At night it looks for food. It eats smaller animals, insects, carrion, plants, or city garbage. Coyotes sometimes kill sheep and calves. For that reason, they are hunted, trapped, and poisoned. But the coyote keeps increasing.

Squirrels live in the forests. The Abert, Kaibab, Arizona Gray, and Red are the main kinds in Arizona. Another mammal, the *beaver*, lives along streams close to trees.

The long, slender *coatimundi* is found in southeastern Arizona. It has a long tail that usually sticks straight up. A long snout comes in handy to dig out roots, insects, lizards, and rodents. The coatimundi also eats birds' eggs and berries. Sharp claws and padded feet enable it to climb trees. It is a native of Mexico. The coatimundi is one of the least known desert animals in Arizona.

BIRDS

Arizona has many kinds of birds. Some live in the state the year round. Others come and go. The birds range in size from the small hummingbird to the Merriam wild turkey.

Hummingbirds are visitors in Arizona. Only three inches long, these birds can fly backwards and straight up. They hover like a helicopter to sip nectar from a flower. One kind, the *black-chinned hummingbird,* is seen mainly in cities with trees. This "hummer" likes red. It is attracted to hummingbird feeders filled with red-colored sugar water.

Another kind, the *Costa's hummingbird,* is found in the desert. The Costa's is violet on top of the head and on the throat. It feeds on red-orange ocotillo cactus blossoms in the spring. Then it migrates to California for the summer.

The *wild turkey* is the state's largest game bird. It is found in the pine forests of central Arizona and north of the Grand Canyon. Wild turkeys once thrived on the desert mountains of southern Arizona. Today the Game and Fish Department is trying to get them started in these mountains again.

Another game bird is the *Gambel's quail.* This bird is easy to identify. It has a black plume that curves to the front. Quail eggs are laid in nests on the ground in brushy desert country.

The quail have large families. They like to be together. A covey looking for food may include dozens of quail. Their soft voices can sometimes be heard in movies made in the Arizona desert. The quail's song sounds like this, "keee-ow, keee-ow!"

The *white-winged dove* and the smaller *mourning dove* are visiting game birds. The white-winged doves come north from Mexico for the summer. The mourning doves fly south from Canada for the winter.

The doves build shallow, flimsy nests in desert trees. One popular nesting place is the green mesquite belt along the Gila River west of Buckeye. Dove sounds—a kind of "coo kuk, coo cooah"—might be heard coming from a

Hummingbirds.

Wild turkeys.

Gambel's quail.

saguaro cactus. Doves like the fruit and seed of this cactus. Many mourning doves can be seen in the cities too.

Some unusual birds of Arizona. Many birds live in Arizona the whole year. *Mockingbirds* like to be around farms or homes with lawns. These graceful, long-tailed birds are fun to watch. It is not uncommon to see them dart down from trees or rooftops. They imitate the calls of other birds and scold anyone who gets close to their nests.

The *roadrunner* is Arizona's most comical bird. The roadrunner would rather run than fly. It sometimes races cars on desert roads. The roadrunner has a long tail which it raises and lowers. It has a strong, curved bill and playfully pecks at almost everything. Unlike most birds, the roadrunner eats lizards and snakes.

Many birds live around cactus. The *cac-*

White-winged dove.

Roadrunner.

Vulture.

tus wren is the state bird. It nests in the cholla cactus. The cactus wren's ratchety song is heard all day long in many desert areas.

The *Gila woodpecker* is another noisy bird. It cries "hu-it, hu-it" while perching or flying. The Gila woodpecker and its cousin, the *Flicker,* drill nesting holes in saguaro cacti.

Did you ever see a *turkey vulture*? Called a buzzard, this large bird can soar and glide on air currents. Good eyesight enables the vulture to see dead animals from high up. Carrion is its chief food.

Hundreds of other bird species are found in Arizona. Hawks, owls, thrashers, ravens, orioles, and verdins are a few examples. Early morning is usually the best time to see birds. They become less active as the day warms up.

FISH

More than 60 species of fish live in Arizona's waters. But only about half of them are native. There is only one native game fish. It is the *Arizona trout.*

The Arizona trout has a beautiful yellow-golden color. In its pure form it is found in Eagle Creek in Greenlee County. Elsewhere in Arizona the native Arizona trout is crossed with the imported rainbow trout.

Other *trout species* in the state are the brown, cutthroat, and eastern brook. The trout are found in lakes and streams.

In warmer waters, the bigmouthed black bass is an important game fish. Other *warm water fish* are the striped and the smallmouthed bass. The channel catfish, yellow

This fisherman landed a four pound rainbow trout on the Colorado River.

Crappie.

A happy fisherman with a large catfish.

perch, white crappie, walleye, green sunfish, and bluegill also live in warm waters.

Arizona has several unusual kinds of *minnows*. The Gila topminnow and the desert pupfish are among the smallest fish in North America. At the other extreme, the Colorado squawfish is one of the world's largest minnows. It can be five feet long and weigh 100 pounds. The squawfish is almost extinct.

A third unusual minnow is the bonytail. It can weigh about two pounds. Fishermen have fun catching the bonytail in Arizona's rivers. But it is too bony to eat.

REPTILES

Reptiles are animals such as snakes, lizards, and turtles. Reptiles are cold-blooded. That means their body temperature is the same as the temperature around them.

Reptiles can survive in the desert because they *estivate*. In other words, they stay in the shade or go underground during the heat of the day. Many reptiles hunt food in the coolness of the early morning or at night.

During the cold months reptiles *hibernate*. This means they crawl into a cave or hole and sleep all winter. Their hearts beat slowly in hibernation. Their breathing almost stops.

For scientists who study reptiles, Arizona is a good place to work. There are nearly 100 species of reptiles in the state. About half of these are snakes.

The snakes vary in size, colors, markings, and in other ways. Some are rare and hard to find. Others, like the gopher snake, are found in most parts of the state.

The *gopher snake* is known as the *bull snake*. It is more active in daytime than most snakes. Like the rattlesnake, the bull snake vibrates its tail and makes a hissing sound. But it is not poisonous. The bull snake is a real value to farmers. It devours large numbers of mice, rats, and gophers which eat crops. Gopher snakes lay eggs.

Which snakes should be avoided? The only poisonous snakes in Arizona are the rattlesnakes and the coral snake. The *diamond-backed rattlesnake* is the kind which has caused the most human deaths. Its bite can kill.

All rattlesnakes are poisonous. The *sidewinder* is found in sandy desert areas. This snake is small. It has horns on its head. It leaves a pattern on the sand as it wiggles along in an "S" shape.

Other rattlesnakes found in Arizona are the Mojave, black-tailed, tiger, rock, twin-spotted, ridge-nosed, and western species. Rattlesnakes do not lay eggs. Young rattlers are born alive.

The *Arizona coral snake* has beautiful red, whitish-yellow, and black bands. The coral snake is shy and tries to avoid humans. It is unlikely to bite unless cornered or picked up. Its small black head can be mistaken for the tail. A Marana man made this mistake. A coral snake was found in his house. It bit

Arizona coral snake.

Diamond-backed rattlesnake.

him on the hand when he grabbed it at the wrong end. The coral's venom affected the man's nervous system. He was taken to a Tucson hospital for treatment.

The *Sonora king snake* looks a lot like the coral snake. But the king snake is harmless to people. It kills other reptiles by squeezing them to death. It can kill rattlesnakes. The king snake usually hides under logs or rocks in the daytime.

Other kinds of snakes are found on the desert. Lots of snakes live in the mountains.

Lizards. Many kinds of lizards are found in the deserts and mountains of Arizona. The lizards are well-equipped to survive. Their coloring blends into the landscape. Most of them have clawed toes. These toes enable them to run on the loose sand and to climb. Their diet is bugs, spiders, and other insects. All lizards are harmless except the Gila monster.

The *Gila monster* is the only poisonous lizard in the United States. The adult is large, slow-moving, and about a foot long. Its back looks like a pattern of black and yellowish beads. The tail stores fat for future use.

The Gila monster minds its own business if left alone. But when handled, it may bite. The Gila monster does not have fangs like a rattlesnake. It has to bite and chew in its poison. This poison comes from glands in the animal's jaw. Today the Gila monster is protected by state law.

The *chuckwalla* is another lizard. It is found in rocky country. The chuckwalla can change colors. It also has an unusual way to hide. The body is wedged in a rock crevice

Chuckwalla.

Gila monster on Arizona desert near Superstition Mountains.

and inflated with air. Indians got the chuckwalla out with a pointed stick. The lizard's tender flesh was good eating.

Horned lizards are wrongly called "horny toads." They have little horn-like scales behind the head. The body is oval-shaped. It is not long like many lizards. The horned lizard is often found near ant dens. Ants are their favorite food. When frightened, the horned lizard can hold blood in its head and squirt it from the eyes.

The horned lizard has been used in movies. A camera enlarges it to giant size. It then looks like a prehistoric monster. The little "horny toad" does not scare children. It is often made a pet. The horned lizard is protected by state law.

Lizards of many kinds, like birds, give a sense of motion to the quiet desert. These scaly, beady-eyed reptiles are some of the most-seen animals. They streak across the

39

A mother horned toad with babies.

Colorado River toad.

sands or along the backyard fence. They stop quickly and sometimes appear to be doing push-ups. When frightened, they dash off.

AMPHIBIANS

Amphibians live both in water and on land. They are not like the scaly reptiles. Amphibians have soft, porous skin. The amphibian life cycle starts with an egg laid in water. From an egg a small fish is hatched. The fish then changes into an adult land animal. Frogs, toads, and salamanders are amphibians.

There are over twenty kinds of frogs and toads in Arizona. But there is only one kind of salamander—the *tiger salamander*. It is found in northern Arizona. The tiger salamander looks like a lizard. But its skin is smooth. The life of the salamander has three stages: the egg, the larva, and the adult. The larva is called a water dog. The water dog is hatched with legs, teeth, and gills. It is used for fish bait.

What is the difference between a frog and a toad? A frog usually has smooth skin. It stays in or near water. A toad has warts and rough, dry skin. It lives mainly on land. Most frogs and toads hibernate. But frogs winter in the mud of stream beds. Toads dig nests in dry ground.

The *bullfrog* is the largest western frog. It is not native to Arizona. It was imported from the southeastern part of the United States. The bullfrog is a game animal. It is prized for its legs.

The *spadefoot toads* become active during the summer rains. They seem to "explode" out of the ground. The toads breed in rain-formed ponds. Eggs hatch in a day or two. Tadpoles become toads in about two weeks.

The *Colorado River toad* is the largest western toad. It is the most poisonous toad in Arizona. Its skin has large poison glands. A Colorado River toad can be deadly to a dog that mouths it.

Amphibians are helpful to us. They eat insects. They catch the insects with long, darting, sticky tongues.

Words and Terms to Know

mammal	carrion
game animal	migrate
predator	covey
extinct	reptile
browse	estivate
to stalk	hibernate
refuge	venom
adaptable	amphibian

Match the words above with the following definitions:

1. An animal that is hunted.
2. Warm-blooded animals whose females nourish their young.
3. Animal that kills other animals for food.
4. To feed on leaves, shrubs, or shoots.
5. No longer existing.

6. Decaying flesh of a dead animal.
7. To move from one place to another.
8. A safe place where animals are protected.
9. To creep up quietly on prey.
10. Able to change or adjust to new things.
11. A flock of quails.
12. A cold-blooded scaly animal.
13. To stay out of the heat in the summer time.
14. To stay warm and inactive in the winter time.
15. Poison in the glands of certain reptiles or scorpions.
16. A cold-blooded animal that is adapted to both land and water.

Finding the Facts

1. The _____ _____ is one of the world's fastest animals.
2. _____ _____ have wider antlers than most deer.
3. The black bear is legally a _____ _____, not a _____.
4. A _____ is a wild pig.
5. _____ _____ are protected on refuges near the Colorado River.
6. _____ means "barking dog."
7. The _____ _____ is Arizona's largest game bird.
8. A black plume on its head makes the _____ _____ easy to identify.
9. The _____ is a bird that would rather run than fly.
10. Arizona's state bird is the _____ _____.
11. The state's only native game fish is the _____ _____.
12. An important warm water game fish in Arizona is the _____ _____ _____.
13. The _____ snake helps farmers by eating rats and mice.
14. Poisonous snakes in Arizona are the _____ and the _____ snake.
15. The _____ _____ is the only poisonous lizard in the United States.
16. _____ are the favorite food of horned lizards.
17. The larva of the salamander is called a _____ _____.
18. _____ _____ increase their numbers during the summer rains.

UNIT 2

INDIANS OF ARIZONA

Indians were living in Arizona a long time before Europeans came. Their food, clothing, and shelter came from the plants and animals around them. The Indians lived in harmony with nature. They neither spoiled nor wasted nature.

The early Indians did not have a written language. No written record was made of their daily life. To learn about the prehistoric Indians we must study the things they left at campsites, in caves, or in cliff dwellings.

We do not know as much about early Indian life as we would like. But there is no doubt about one thing—the Indians were here first. They are deserving of our study.

Today Arizona is Indian country. There are more Indians and more reservations in Arizona than in any other state.

Hohokam building canals to bring water to the barren desert.

6. ANCIENT INDIANS

Diorama of a mammoth being killed at the Lehner site.

PEOPLE HAVE LIVED IN ARIZONA FOR AT LEAST 11,000 YEARS.

Indians have been living in Arizona for a long time. The first people in Arizona hunted animals for a living. They also ate berries and other wild foods. After thousands of years, the Indians began to farm.

Elephant hunters. The first Indians most likely came from Asia by way of Alaska. They found Arizona cooler and wetter than it is now. Land that is now desert had thick grass, streams, and lakes.

There were many wild animals in Arizona. The largest were the *mammoths*. They looked like elephants. The big mammoths stood thirteen feet high at the shoulder.

The first Indians in Arizona hunted the mammoths. They would wait for their prey at a watering place. They worked together to kill it. The Indians hunted with a spear. This weapon had a stone head and a detachable

Part of a prehistoric animal skeleton is observed by curious children at the Museum of Northern Arizona near Flagstaff.

43

wooden shaft. The hunter stuck his spear into the mammoth. He then removed the shaft. This way the wounded animal could not easily get rid of the stone point.

Elephant bones have been found along the San Pedro River near Naco. Scientists say these elephants were killed about 11,000 years ago. Some of the meat was cooked over open fires.

Cochise food gatherers. When Arizona's climate became drier, the big game animals disappeared. The Indians had to learn new ways to make a living. Food gathering became more important. The Indians ate more berries and wild grains. Of course, they still hunted smaller animals.

By 2000 B.C. the Indians learned to raise an unusual corn. Each kernal had its own husk. This corn and wild seeds were ground into flour. For grinding, the Indians used a crude stone. It is called a *metate*.

A few metates and other Indian artifacts have been found along creek beds in Cochise County. For that reason, the Indian food gatherers are called "Cochise people." They were a link between the elephant hunters and later Indians.

Three major Indian cultures. The Indians learned to farm. That made it possible for them to live in one place. They no longer had to spend all their time searching for food. Their lives became more comfortable. They built houses, made pottery, and played games. The Indians learned to live and work together in a community.

A higher civilization arose in each of the three geographic zones. The *Hohokam* occupied the desert river valleys. The *Mogollon* lived in the mountain belt. The *Anasazi* were on the plateau.

HOHOKAM

Irrigation farming. The Hohokam were the first irrigation farmers in the Southwest. They most likely came from Mexico. Their civilization in the desert lasted about 1700 years.

The Hohokam dug a system of canals along the Gila and Salt rivers. This irrigation system was a great feat. The Hohokam had no machines. They used stone and wooden tools to dig. Baskets were used to haul dirt. With these simple methods over 200 miles of canals were dug in the Salt River Valley. Modern engineers are amazed.

How did the irrigation system work? First, the Hohokam built a dirt or rock dam across the river. This dam held back water. The level of water was raised high enough to

Location of prehistoric Indian cultures in Arizona.

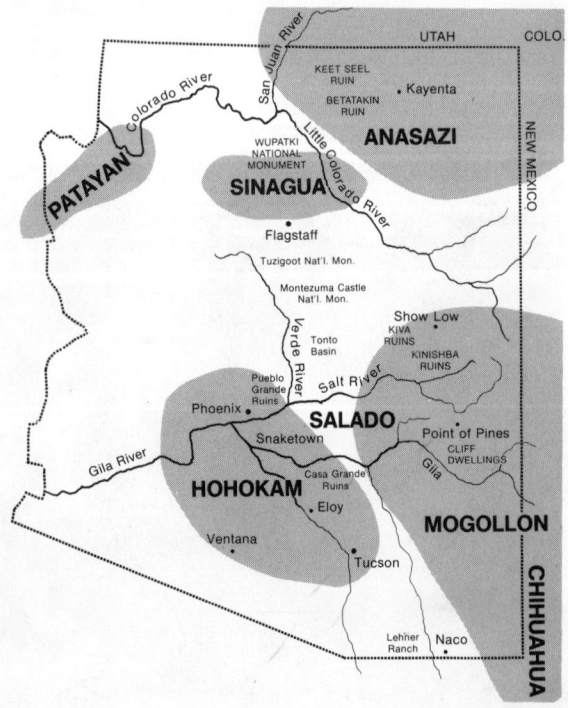

The main canal at Snaketown. A Pima Indian stands in a lateral canal.

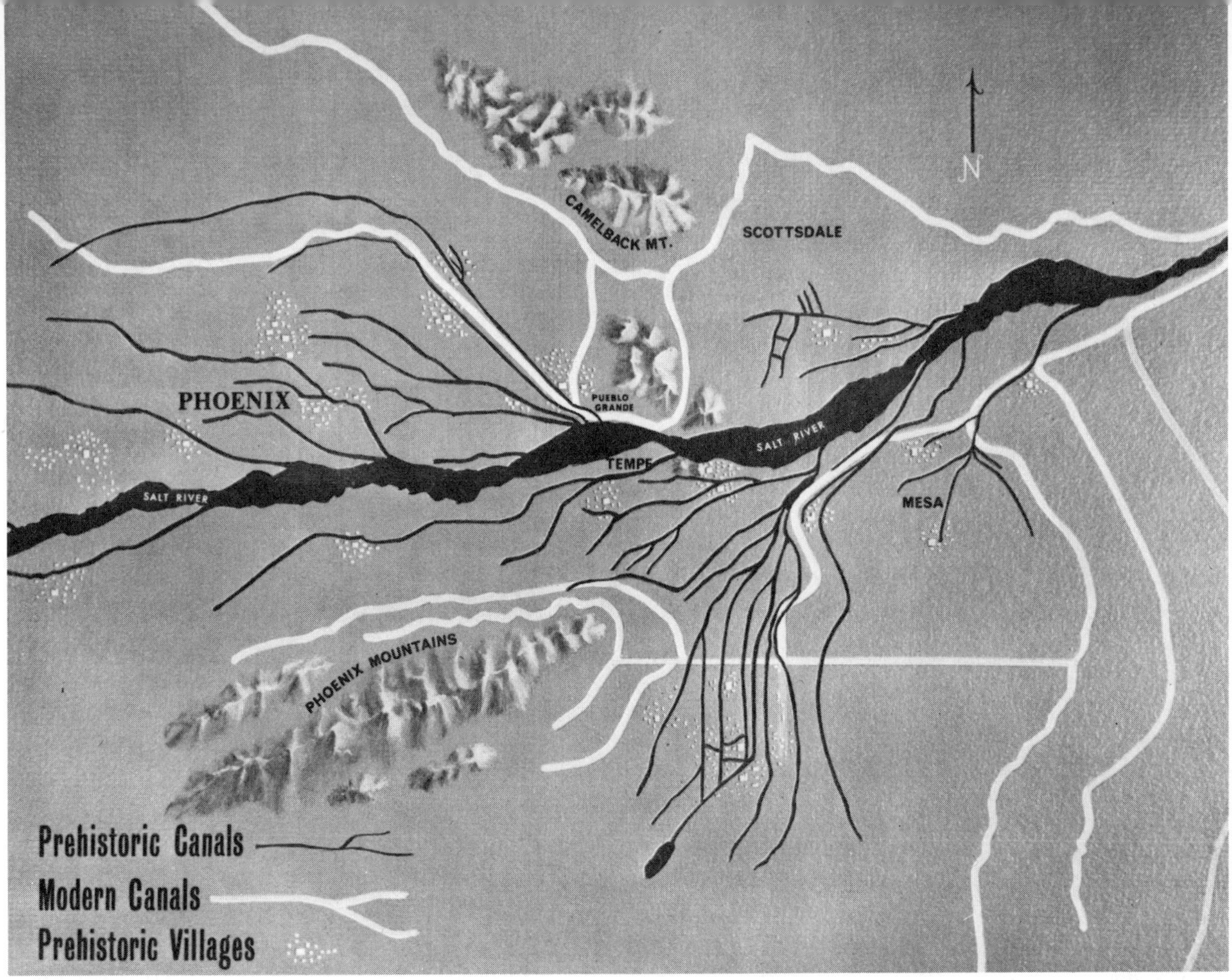

This map by Charles O. Kemper shows similarities between the Hohokam and modern Salt River Project canals.

flow into canals. The Hohokam did not have water pumps. They graded the canals so that water flowed slowly to their fields.

Arts. Farming enabled the Hohokam to settle in permanent villages. With a surplus of food stored away, they had time to learn new things. The Hohokam were artistic people. Potters made beautiful jars and bowls. Others wove cotton into cloth. Figurines were made of clay. Carved bone jewelry was popular.

The Hohokam learned to do etching before it was done in Europe. How? A design was drawn on a shell with pitch or tar. The shell was then soaked in a weak acid. The part of the shell around the pitch was eaten away. The design was usually of an animal such as a toad.

A Hohokam etched shell from Snaketown.

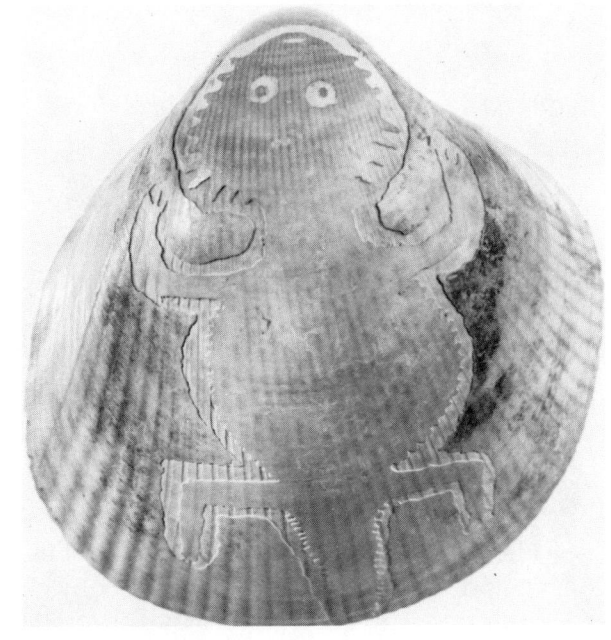

Hohokam pottery from Snaketown and Grewe sites.

A Hohokam ball game at Snaketown. Painting by Peter Bianchi, courtesy of National Geographic Society.

The Hohokam also played ball. The court was dug below ground level. The object of the game was to get a rubber ball through one of the rings on the sides of the court. Players could use only their elbows, knees, and hips. When someone scored, the winning

Casa Grande National Monument near Coolidge.

players could claim the jewelry and clothing of the spectators—if they could catch them!

Houses. At first the Hohokam built pithouses for homes. The house was partly below ground. This style gave protection against hot and cold weather. The walls and roof were made of tree poles. Cracks were filled with mud.

Later the Hohokam built pueblo-style apartment houses. The four-story Casa Grande (big house), near Coolidge, can be seen today. Pueblo Grande in East Phoenix is another example.

Disappearance. For some reason, the Hohokam left their villages in the 15th century. No one knows why. The farmland may have been waterlogged. That means the irrigation water seeped underground and slowly raised the water table too high. There may be other reasons. Maybe the soil just became worn out.

Whatever happened, the Hohokam likely never went very far away. They may be the ancestors of present-day Pimas and Papagos. Hohokam is a Pima Indian word meaning "all used up" or "those who have vanished."

The Hohokam cremated their dead. This practice makes it hard for scientists to learn what the Hohokam looked like.

ANASAZI

The name "Anasazi" means "the ancient ones." They were ancient. The Anasazi came to the Four Corners area about 2,000 years ago.

Physical appearance. What did the Anasazi look like? They were a short, slender, long-headed, and broad-nosed people. The men sometimes shaved the top of the head. They wore a braid down the back and a bob of hair on each side. The women wore their hair short. They had a reason. Their hair was used to weave ropes.

At one time the Anasazi made their heads flat in back. How? They fastened babies tightly against a hard cradleboard. In this way, the baby's skull was deformed. The head became wide and flat in back.

Economy. The first Anasazi in Arizona made a living by hunting. They also gathered

Farming brought many changes in the lives of Indians. The security of a stable food supply made it possible for them to remain in one place. Diorama in the Arizona State Museum of Tucson.

wild foods. Early hunters used the *atlatl*. This was a notched stick. It was used to hurl a spear with great force. Later the bow and arrow became the main hunting weapon.

The Anasazi became farmers slowly. They learned to raise corn, squash, and beans. The turkey was raised for food.

Crafts. The early Anasazi are called "basketmakers." They wove baskets and sandals from yucca plant fibers. Later the Anasazi learned to make pottery. Their pots were gray or white with a black design for decoration.

Houses. The Anasazi farmers built round *pithouses*. The one-room houses were partly underground. The cone-shaped roof was made of poles. The dirt or stone floor always had a small hole. This hole was called a "sipapu." To the Anasazi it was a symbol of the place where their first ancestors came out

Anasazi pottery from various sites in northern Arizona.

of the earth. The dead were sometimes buried under the floor.

Beginning about 1050 A.D. the Anasazi life style changed. They began to build large apartment-style *cliff houses*. These houses were located in out-of-the-way canyons near good farmland.

Two impressive cliff houses can be seen

48

Interior of Keet Seel.

today on the Navajo National Monument. Keet Seel once had 350 rooms. Keet Seel means "broken pottery" in Navajo. A second house, Betatakin, had 200 rooms. The name means "side hill house."

Disappearance. The cliff houses were deserted in the 13th century. Why? The main cause was likely a 23-year *drought*. The Anasazi were dry farmers. That means they needed rain to raise crops. With no rain, the Anasazi had to move away from the Four Corners area. Later groups of Anasazi moved back to the plateau. They became ancestors of the modern Hopi Indians.

MOGOLLON

Mountain Indians. The Mogollon lived in the mountain zone. For food they hunted wild game. Their diet included berries, roots, nuts, and seeds. They did not rely on farming to survive.

The Mogollon, however, were the first people in Arizona to grow a good kind of corn. They were also the first to make pottery. Their pots were made by coiling a rope of clay into the desired shape. The sides were scraped. Then the brown or reddish pot was fired in a kiln.

Villages. Related families of Mogollon banded together in a clan. The clan had its own village. Pithouses were built on a mountainside with the doors facing east.

A *kiva* was built in the center of the village. The kiva was an underground room. It was used for ceremonies.

Several Mogollon villages have been dug up. One example is Point of Pines. This village is on the San Carlos Apache Reservation in eastern Arizona. Crude *metates* and stone plows have been found there. Other artifacts include pottery and simple tools made of bone.

Golden Age. In later years the Mogollon came into contact with other Indians. From the Hohokam they got cotton fiber for cloth. The Anasazi taught them how to build better houses using stone and adobe. The Mogollon made more progress. Their "golden age" was

49

Mogollon black-on-white pottery.

This Mogollon plate shows an Indian spearing a fish.

from 1000 to 1200 A.D. Designs on their pottery give us a picture of Mogollon life-style at that time.

Life-style. Scenes on the pottery show men picking bugs from corn plants. Other people are setting snares to catch birds. Some are killing a deer with bow and arrow. Some are dancing. The men are shown wearing a breechcloth. Women are dressed in a fringed sash and sandals. Sometimes they also wore a blanket.

Some pottery was buried with a person who died. But it was a custom to punch a "kill hole" in each pot before it was put in the grave. The Mogollon believed that each pot housed the spirit of its owner. The spirit was freed through the hole after the pot was "killed." This was done at a ceremony in the kiva.

Disappearance. About 1200 A.D. the Mogollon left their mountain villages. Archaeologists believe they went south to Chihuahua in Mexico. No modern Arizona Indian tribe is descended from the Mogollon.

OTHER PREHISTORIC INDIANS

Sinagua. The word Sinagua means "without water." It is a good name for the early Indians who lived north of Flagstaff. The Sinagua were dry farmers. They had to depend on rain to water crops.

For 500 years the Sinagua farmed in peace. Then disaster struck! In 1064 A.D. a volcano erupted. Hot lava flowed down and covered a large area. The people were scared. They fled their homes. The volcano which forced them to move has never erupted again. Today it is called Sunset Crater.

Later, the Sinagua moved back. They had reason to be happy. The soil was enriched by the volcanic overflow. Word of the fertile fields soon spread. Other Indian groups moved in. They brought their customs and skills with them.

The style of Sinagua houses changed. Before the eruption, the people lived in pithouses. These homes were built with timber. The logs were covered with grass or bark and dirt.

Wupatki.

Montezuma Castle.

After the eruption, the Sinagua built new homes. Their villages were now surface pueblos with many rooms. Ruins of these stone pueblos can be seen on the Wupatki National Monument north of Flagstaff. Wupatki is a Hopi word meaning "tall house."

Late in the 13th century the Sinagua had to leave again. This time the cause was a long dry spell. The people moved to the Verde

Salado cliff house ruin on the Tonto National Monument.

Valley. There the Sinagua learned to irrigate crops.

They built stone pueblos in the Verde Valley. One pueblo is known today as Montezuma Castle. It is a cliff house overlooking the Verde River. Another pueblo was Tuzigoot. It was built on a hilltop near present-day Clarkdale.

The Sinagua planted and irrigated their fields. They hunted wild game and gathered wild foods. There was time to weave cloth, mine salt, and fire finely-polished red pottery. The Sinagua seemed happy in their life-style.

But about 1400 A.D. the Sinagua suddenly left the Verde Valley. The reason is still a mystery. Was it another dry spell? Disease? Water pollution? No one knows for sure.

Patayan. This name means "old people" or "ancient ones." It is a Yuma Indian word. In fact, the Patayan Indians were ancestors of the modern Yuma-speaking tribes. Among these are the Yuma, Cocopah, Maricopa, and Mojave. Others are the three Pais: Walapai, Yavapai, and Havasupai.

The Patayan lived along the Colorado River in northwestern Arizona. They farmed along the river banks. Their crops grew well in the rich silt left by flood waters. The Patayan looked for more food in the desert.

Little remains of the Patayan civilization. Flood waters long ago washed away their villages. Some gray-brown pottery and shell jewelry has been found.

There were sub-groups of the Patayan. Among these were the Cerbats and Cohoninas. They lived south of the Grand Canyon and west of Flagstaff.

Salado. The Salado Indians were distant cousins of the Anasazi. Their cliff houses can be seen today. The houses are on the Tonto

National Monument near Roosevelt Dam.

The Salado farmed in the Salt River flood plain. But they built their pueblo-style houses several miles away in the cliffs. The cliffs gave them safety and a good place to store food.

Words and Terms to Know

- mammoth
- *metate*
- irrigate
- etching
- pueblo
- waterlogged
- *atlatl*
- pithouse
- *sipapu*
- drought
- kiva
- artifact

Match the words above with the following definitions:

1. An Indian apartment-like building.
2. A home that is built partly underground.
3. An underground room for Indian ceremonies.
4. A long dry spell.
5. A stone used for grinding corn.
6. Anything made by human work, such as art.
7. A way of engraving a design on shell or metal.
8. To supply water to land by means of ditches.
9. Condition of land that has too much water.
10. An elephant that is now extinct.
11. A notched stick used to throw a spear.
12. Hole in the floor of an Anasazi home.

Finding the Facts

1. The first Indians in Arizona hunted elephants known as _____.
2. _____ people were food gatherers who came after the elephant hunters.
3. The _____ dug a system of irrigation canals in the Gila and Salt river valleys.
4. _____ _____ and _____ _____ are examples of Hohokam pueblos.
5. Basketmakers is another name for the early _____.
6. _____ _____ is an example of an Anasazi cliff house.
7. The _____ lived in the desert zone, the _____ on the plateau, and the _____ in the mountain zone.
8. An example of a Mogollon village is _____ _____ _____ on the San Carlos Apache Reservation.
9. The Sinagua lived near a volcano now called _____ _____.
10. Sinagua pueblo ruins can be seen on the _____ _____ _____.
11. _____ _____ and _____ are Sinagua pueblos in the Verde River Valley.
12. The _____ were ancestors of the modern Yuma-speaking tribes.
13. The Patayan lived along the _____ _____.

7. INDIANS IN RECENT TIMES

Navajo rug weaver.

Who is an Indian? An Indian is a person whose ancestors lived in America when Columbus came in 1492. Not every Indian is a full-blood, of course.

Most Indians belong to a tribe. A tribe usually has its own language, customs, and land.

Arizona is Indian country. Arizona has more Indians than any other state. More than one-fourth of the land in Arizona is set aside for Indian reservations.

Many Indians live in Arizona's towns and cities. The largest number of urban Indians live in Phoenix. Other cities with many Indians are Tucson, Flagstaff, and Winslow.

Where are the reservations? Most of Arizona's Indian tribes live in the homelands of their ancestors.

The Hopis are on the plateau in northeast Arizona. The Pimas and Papagos are

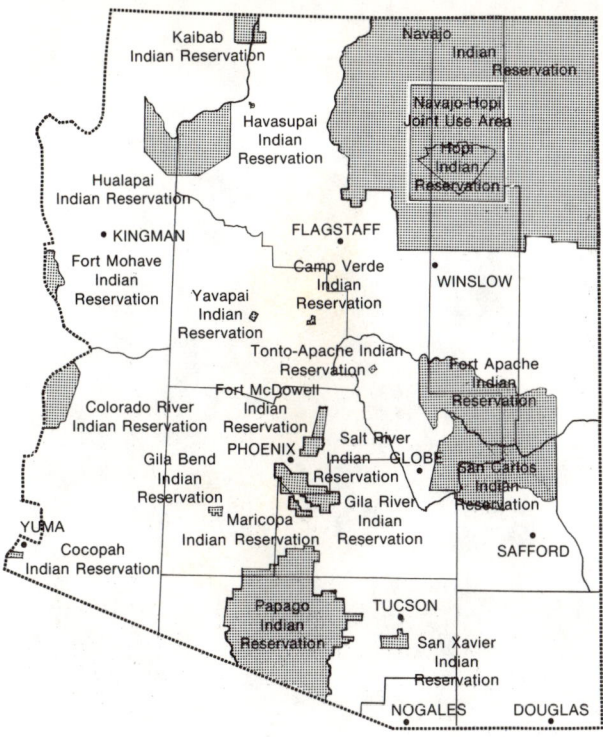

Indian Reservations.

Navajo girl with sheep. The house is a hogan.

The Hopi village of Old Oraibi is the oldest continuously-occupied town in the United States.

Havasupai Indians at Havasupai Falls.

living in the southern desert. Most Yuma tribes are on reservations along the Colorado River.

Even the Indian "newcomers"—the Navajos and Apaches — have been on the same lands for hundreds of years.

Arizona's Indians can be divided into four major cultural groups. The tribes in each group have a similar history and life-style.

(1) **Athapascan tribes** include the *Navajos* and *Apaches*. These tribes came from Canada. For centuries they were nomads and warriors.

(2) **Pueblo Indians.** The only pueblo Indians now in Arizona are the *Hopis*. They have lived on the same mesas for over a thousand years. The Hopi village of Old Oraibi has been lived in all that time.

(3) **Plateau tribes.** Most of the plateau tribes in northern Arizona were hunters and food gatherers. Only the *Havasupais* were farmers when the Spanish came. The Havasupais now live at the bottom of the Grand

Indian basket display.

Canyon. Waterfalls and other beautiful scenery can be seen there. The reservation can be reached by an eight-mile long trail. The Havasupais rent horses and mules to visitors.

Another plateau tribe is the *Hualapai* (Walapai). These Indians raise cattle and sell timber.

Today most *Yavapais* earn a living by working in or near Prescott. Some Yavapais live on reservations at Camp Verde and Fort McDowell.

The *Paiutes* live on the Kaibab Reservation near the Utah border. They were once called the "Digger Tribe." Why? Because they got their food by digging up edible roots.

(4) **Desert farming tribes.** There are two main sub-groups of desert farming Indians in Arizona.

The Piman tribes are the *Pimas, Papagos,* and *Yaquis.*

The Yuman tribes are the *Yumas, Mohaves, Maricopas,* and *Cocopahs.*

Except for the Yaquis, all these Indians were living in Arizona when the Spanish first came. The Yaquis came from Mexico after 1880. The United States government does not treat the Yaquis as native Indians.

NAVAJOS

The Navajos are the biggest Indian tribe in the United States. More than half the Indians in Arizona are Navajo.

The Navajos have the largest reservation. In size it is larger than the whole state of West Virginia.

History. The Navajos call themselves "*Dineh.*" This word means "the people." They came from Canada 600 to 1,000 years ago. At

Canyon de Chelly on the Navajo Reservation.

first the Navajos were nomads. They did not stay in one place. The early Navajos were also warlike.

After the United States took over the Southwest, the U.S. Army rounded up the Navajos. Colonel Kit Carson's soldiers marched the Navajos to a reservation in New Mexico. This journey was called the "long walk."

The Navajos were unhappy. They had to share the land in New Mexico with some Apaches. Many of the Navajos died of disease or starved to death. In 1868, they were finally given their own reservation. It is in the Four Corners area. From time to time the U.S. Congress gave more land to the Navajos.

Sheepherding became the Navajo way of life. They did not live in villages. The Navajos spread out over the country with their flocks of sheep.

The Navajo herders lived in *hogans*. This style of house was built of logs and mud. The roof was covered with dirt. All the hogans face the rising sun. Hogans are still used. But now

The Hubbell Trading Post on the Navajo Reservation is an example of a national historic site.

many Navajos live in wood frame houses. They have modern appliances.

Blankets and rugs. Navajo women became famous for their wool blankets and rugs. The women spun their own thread. Some thread was colored with dyes. The dyes were made from roots, berries, sage plants, and earth.

Blankets and rugs were woven on upright looms. But the Navajos quit making blankets long ago. Now rug weaving is a disappearing art. A rug takes many days to make. Fewer Navajo women can afford to spend their time on rugs. The Navajo people, however, are proud of their crafts. The art of rug weaving is taught at the Navajo Community College.

Silversmithing is a craft at which Navajo men excel. They began putting designs on silver in the 1860s. At first they used silver coins to fashion discs for horse bridles. Soon they were making silver crosses, buttons, concha belts, necklaces, and other jewelry. Some turquoise and other stones were used to ornament the silver.

Now Navajo and other Indian silversmiths are as good as the world has seen anywhere.

Clothes. The Navajos like to wear bright clothes. The old-style dress for women is a long velvet blouse over a pleated skirt.

The men dress cowboy style. They wear levis, a bright shirt, hat, and boots.

Religion and social events. The Navajos are very religious. They have many chants, dances, and sand paintings to honor the gods. There are chants to cure sickness, to bless a new home, or to keep dangers away. Medicine men spend years learning the chants and sand paintings.

Ceremonial dances are usually held at night around a bonfire. The dances keep the Navajos in harmony with nature and the gods. The ceremonies are also social events. People come together.

The Navajo tribal fair is the biggest social event on the reservation. It is held once a year in September at Window Rock. Navajos and tourists come to see a rodeo. They can see horse races, dances, and a "Miss Navajo" pageant. The fair also has food stalls, livestock shows, and booths for craft works.

World War II changed Navajo life. Thousands of Navajos got jobs in the cities.

Peshlakai, a famous Navajo silversmith, in 1885.

Navajo woman.

They worked in war plants, at shipyards, on railroads, and in mines. Many Navajos had jobs at the Navajo Ordnance Depot west of Flagstaff. Ammunition was stored at the depot after 1942. The Indians lived in two villages built near the gates of the depot.

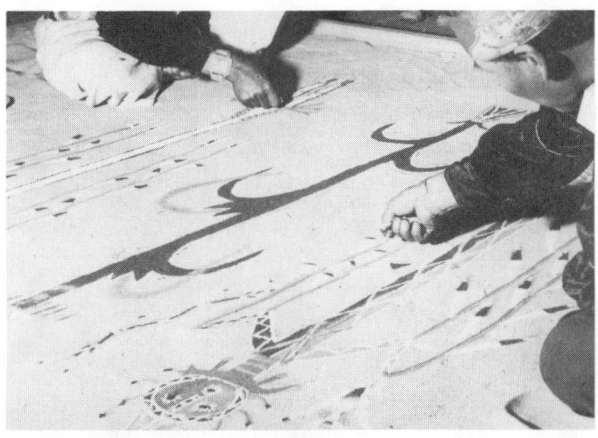
Navajos doing a sand painting.

Navajo medicine man.

A Navajo uranium miner.

the Signal Corps became famous. They were used in the Pacific to send and receive messages in Navajo. The Japanese were never able to understand it.

After the war many changes took place. Outside companies were invited to build factories on the reservation. Large deposits of coal and uranium are now bringing in wealth. About half of Arizona's electricity comes from power plants fired by Navajo coal.

Who runs the Navajo tribe? An elected tribal council meets at Window Rock. The councilmen pass laws. They make sure the tribe's money is spent wisely.

A tribal chairman is chosen from the whole reservation. He speaks for the council and for the people.

Navajo code talkers in the Pacific during World War II.

Meeting of the Navajo tribal council.

A lot of Navajo young men were in the armed services in World War II. Navajos in

Apache wickiups.

APACHES

The Apaches are cousins of the Navajos. Both came from Canada. The Apaches and Navajos split after they got to the Southwest.

What were the first Apaches like? When the Spaniards came to the Southwest in the 1500s, the Apaches were living in the mountains. The Apaches were not united as one tribe. They were divided into bands. The bands were made up of related families. Each band had a chief.

The Apaches were said to be kind and gentle to their families. But they could be cruel to their enemies.

The Apaches were a hunting and fighting people. They did not like to stay in one spot. The bands liked to roam from place to place. When the Apaches stayed in one place for awhile, they lived in *wickiups*. These huts were made of poles. They were covered with bear grass or brush. The top was dome-shaped.

The Apaches were strong and untiring. They could walk for miles day after day. Apaches had keen senses. They knew all the plants and water holes. Few Apaches ever died a desert death.

Apaches lived off the land. Meat was their favorite food. The men hunted for deer, antelope, and smaller game. The women gathered wild plant foods. The Apache diet included piñon nuts, juniper berries, mesquite beans, and cactus fruit. The diet must have been all right. The Apaches were healthy. They could live in freezing weather with just a few clothes.

Every day the young boys and girls practiced with bows and arrows, slings, and spears. When the Apaches got horses from the Spaniards, the children were taught to ride. They learned how to mount an unsaddled horse without help.

Spanish cattle and sheep gave the Apaches a new source of food. The Indians made hit-and-run raids on Spanish settlements. They drove off the livestock.

When chased by soldiers, the Apaches moved fast. They crossed mountains and deserts to hidden camps. The soldiers who chased them seldom caught up. The soldiers were slowed down by pack mules. And they stayed on the trails. The men were willing to fight. But they had trouble seeing the Apaches.

Apache children after the Indians were put on reservations.

Apache warrior on the reservation. The Indians began to wear some of the white man's style of clothing.

Apache warriors knew how to hide themselves. They tied brush on their heads. Dirt was rubbed on the body. Sometimes the Apaches crawled on the ground to get close to the enemy. At first the Apaches used bows and arrows. Later they got guns when they could. Apaches never fought unless they had the advantage.

The Apaches did not like outsiders coming into their land. They fought the Spaniards, the Mexicans, and the people who came from the United States.

Apaches were put on reservations. After Arizona became part of the United States, soldiers were sent to Arizona. Forts were built to protect the pioneers.

During the 1870s and the 1880s the U.S. Army forced the Apaches to live on reservations. But some of the Apaches refused to stay.

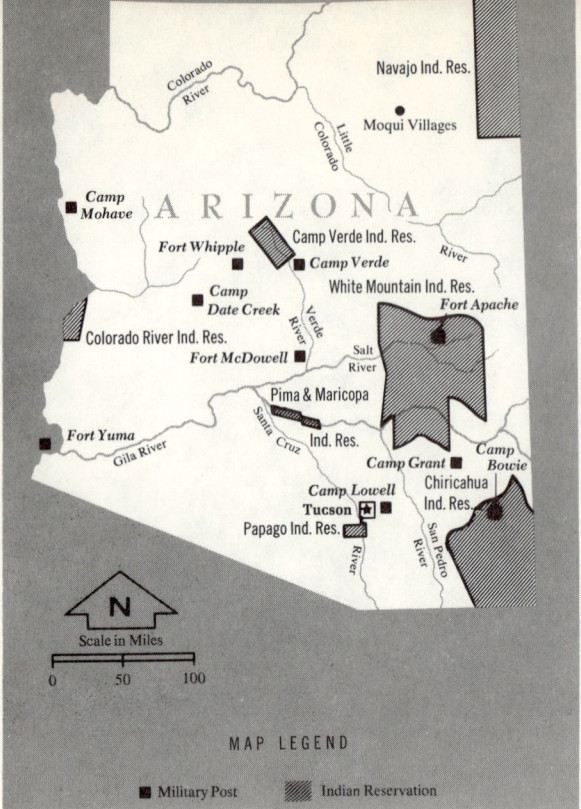

Arizona Indian Reservations and Main Military Posts —1874.

Apache warriors. Geronimo is on the right.

Led by Geronimo and other chiefs, some Chiricahua Apaches escaped. They went on the warpath.

The soldiers who searched for Geronimo set up a signal system. It was called the *heliograph* system. Messages were sent by mirrors from station to station.

In 1886, Geronimo surrendered to General Nelson Miles in Mexico. The Chiricahua Apaches were put on trains. They were sent to Florida. Later, Geronimo was moved to Fort Sill in Oklahoma. He never came back to Arizona.

San Carlos Reservation. Most of the Apaches in Arizona now live on two reservations. They are the San Carlos and the Fort Apache.

The San Carlos Apaches are called the "cowboy Indians of the West." The men dress, look, and act like cowboys. Cattle raising is important at San Carlos. But there are only a few hundred real cowboys.

Many Apaches work for the government. Some work in copper mines. Some have jobs

Apache cowboys at work.

as forest fire fighters. Others work in the lumber and tourist industries.

San Carlos Apaches also make peridot jewelry. Peridot is a yellowish-green gemstone.

The White Mountain Reservation is well-known as a recreational area. Trout streams, lakes, and forests attract tourists. Ski slopes are popular in the winter time.

Lumbering is done on the White Mountain Reservation. The Fort Apache Timber Company (FATCO) employs hundreds of Apaches. They work at logging or in the sawmills. Cattle are raised on the White Mountain Reservation.

A fun event on both the Apache reservations is the annual rodeo and fair. Apache cowboys compete for prizes. Apache dances are performed. They do the famous *Crown Dance*.

Apache crown dancers.

63

An Apache girl becomes a woman in this puberty ceremony. Many Indian religious customs are still practiced.

The most popular Apache dance is part of the *Sunrise ceremony*. This dance is for teenage Apache girls. The purpose of the ceremony is to help the girls have long, happy lives.

The Apaches are one of the most colorful Indian tribes.

Hopi kachina dancers.

HOPIS

The Hopis can trace their ancestry back to the Anasazis. For centuries they have lived on high mesas in northeastern Arizona.

The name Hopi means "peaceful people." But the Hopis have not always been at peace. In fact, they built their villages high on the mesas for protection from other Indians.

The Hopis did not like the Spaniards. They tore down Spanish missions. They drove out or killed the Spanish priests. They had reasons for their anger. Contact with the white man nearly destroyed the Hopis. Smallpox was brought in by the Spaniards. This disease nearly killed off the Hopis. A population of 14,000 was reduced to 900 by the late 1700s.

Now the Hopi Reservation is surrounded by the Navajo Nation. For years the Hopis and Navajos have fought over lands.

Hopi religion. The Hopis are held together by their religion. More than anything else, their religion helps them keep the old way of life.

The Hopis have many ceremonials. Some parts of their ceremonies are held in underground *kivas*. Outsiders cannot go into the

Hopi kachina dolls.

kivas. But some parts are done in the *village plazas.* Visitors can watch there.

The *Snake Dance* is popular with tourists. To the Hopis it is a serious and sacred rain dance. Live snakes are used in the dance. The snakes are messengers to the gods. Hopis believe that the gods who make things grow live underground.

Snakes are caught and brought to the kiva. On the morning of the dance the snakes are sprinkled with sacred water. When it is time for the dance, the snakes are put in a brush shed in the plaza.

As each snake priest passes the shed, he is given a snake. He holds the snake in his mouth and goes on dancing. The snakes are then put in a circle on the plaza. The women and girls put sacred meal on them.

Then the snakes are turned loose. The priests talk to the snakes. "Go back to the gods," they say. "Tell them the Hopis are good and need rain."

Kachinas are important to the Hopis and other pueblo tribes. What is a kachina? A kachina is a spirit (god) who lives in the spirit world. There are hundreds of kachinas. The ones that seem to help the people are kept. The others are dropped and new ones made up.

A *kachina dancer* is an Indian who acts like the kachina spirit. The kachina dancer wears a mask. He paints his body and chants. The dancer then must tell the people's needs to the kachina spirit. The dancers give gifts to the children. These gifts include sweets and dolls.

Kachina dolls are made to teach children about the spirits. The dolls are *not* idols. They are hung from the rafters of houses to be seen at all times.

PIMAS

The Pima Indians can trace their ancestry back to the Hohokam. The Pimas were living in southern Arizona when the Spaniards came. They called themselves *o-odham.* This word means "people" in the Pima language.

The Spanish described the Pimas as

Pima Indian woman grinding corn on a metate, about 1900.

Pima Indian children listen to Mrs. Anna Moore Shaw read from her book, *Pima Indian Legends*.

Avery Lewis, a Pima Indian, and his son in dance costume at the St. John's Indian fair.

dark-skinned and sometimes fat. The men wore a light breechcloth. The male hair-do was long. It was twisted into a crown. It was decorated with feathers and sticks.

The women wore cloth or deerskin clothes. Their hair was long down the back. In front it was cut in bangs at eyebrow level.

The Pimas have lived near the desert rivers for centuries. They made a living by farming. The Pimas grew good corn. They used a pointed stick to make a hole for seed. For cloth the Pimas grew wild cotton.

Father Kino taught them to grow wheat. The Pimas also raised sheep and chickens after the Spaniards came to Arizona.

The Pimas were peaceful and hard-working. They were doing well when the first Americans came to Arizona. Pima farmers sold grain and livestock to the U.S. Army. They had surplus food for the "forty-niners." These travelers stopped at the Pima villages on the Gila River.

Three Pima Reservations. Today the Pima Indians have three reservations in Arizona. The *Gila Reservation* is on the Gila River south of Phoenix. It was created in 1859 and was the first Indian reservation in Arizona.

The *Salt River Reservation* is east of Scottsdale. The *Ak-Chin Reservation* is near the town of Maricopa. The farmers at Ak-Chin are mainly Papagos, not Pima.

Interstate 10 runs through the Gila Reservation. The desert land by the highway is very valuable. Like other Indian tribes, the Pimas have started industrial parks. They hope to bring in industries to create jobs for Indians.

The Gila Arts and Crafts Center is near Interstate 10. The center has a museum, gift shop, and restaurant. The gift shop has Indian crafts for sale.

Firebird Lake is on the north edge of the Gila Reservation. Boat races are held there.

The St. John's Indian Fair draws visitors to the Gila Reservation. It is held at Komatke, southwest of Phoenix. The students at the St.

Carlos Montezuma at eight years of age.

Dr. Carlos Montezuma as a young man.

John's mission school do dances. There is an Indian-style barbecue.

The Pimas have long been loyal citizens of the United States. One Pima Indian, Mathew B. Juan, was the first Arizona soldier killed in World War I. The most famous Pima hero was Ira H. Hayes. He was one of six marines who raised the American flag on Mount Suribachi during World War II.

Old Fort McDowell is on the *Salt River Reservation.* A famous Yavapai Indian is buried near the old fort. His adult name was Carlos Montezuma. But he was called Wassaja as a youth. When a small child, he survived a battle between two Indian groups. But the woman who looked after the boy sold him to a Chicago photographer for 30 dollars. The photographer thought he would be a good model.

Maricopa Indian girls with water ollas on their heads.

Carlos went to school in Chicago. He became a rich medical doctor. He spent a lot of time helping Indians win their rights.

Near the end of his life Carlos got tuberculosis. He returned to Arizona. His home was a wickiup on the Salt River Reservation. His message to the people who came to see him was simple. "Learn and make something of yourself," he said.

Maricopa Indians. The Maricopas live on the Gila and Salt reservations with the Pimas. But they are a Yuman tribe. Long ago they were driven away from the Colorado River by Mohaves and other unfriendly tribes.

The Maricopas are famous for their good pottery. Years ago they had a pot for every use. Women carried large water jars on their heads. There was a long-necked pot for syrup. Another jar was made just for scalps taken from enemies.

An old painting of Papagos harvesting cactus fruit.

PAPAGOS

The Papagos are related to the Pimas. Long ago the Papagos moved to the desert. Their reservation is there now.

The Papagos call themselves "Desert People." But the word Papago means "Bean People." The first Papagos farmed in the summer time. They built dams in gulleys to hold back rain water. The water spread out over their fields of beans, squash, and maize.

The Papago Reservation is one of the largest in the country. But much of it is wasteland. The people have a hard time making a living.

It is not easy to grow crops on the desert. Even now Papagos gather wild desert foods. In summers they harvest the bright red fruit of the saguaro cactus. The Papagos cook the fruit. Then they pour off a thick syrup. This is used for making jam or wine. The seeds are ground into flour.

Now the Papagos are cattlemen, too. They have a large tribal herd. In very dry years, however, hundreds of cattle die.

Tourist attractions. The Kitt Peak National Observatory is on the Papago Reservation. It is one of the world's largest centers for research in astronomy.

The annual All-Indian Papago Tribal Fair and Rodeo is the biggest event on the reservation. Besides the rodeo, it has a Miss Papago contest, dances, and games. It is a happy get-together time for the Papagos.

Outside visitors come to the fair to shop for baskets. The Papagos make coiled baskets in many shapes. They use yucca fiber, beargrass, devil's claw, and willow.

INDIAN CULTURES WILL SURVIVE

Indians on the reservations have been able to keep their languages and life-style. They may use the "things" of the outside world. Indians might drive pickups, eat canned foods, and dress like outsiders. But they still have pride in their Indian culture. They are proud to be Indians—and should be!

Papago woman grinding corn (1916).

Words and Terms to Know

tribe
reservation
custom
cultural group
nomads
hogan
chant
medicine man
band
wickiup
heliograph
plaza
kachina
Dineh
o-odham

Match the words above with the following definitions:

1. A kind of hut built by nomadic Indians.
2. A Navajo house which is built out of timbers and earth.
3. A signaling system which uses mirrors.
4. A spirit or god of the Hopis and other pueblo tribes.
5. Land that is set aside for Indians.
6. The Pima word for "people."
7. The Navajo word for "people."
8. An Indian group which is usually made up of related families.
9. A larger group of Indians who usually have a common ancestry as well as the same language and reservation.
10. A song.
11. People who have no permanent home.
12. An Indian who has a special power to cure disease.
13. An open, public place where people can assemble.
14. A usual practice, habit, or social convention which people in a group accept.
15. A group which has a common culture—skills, religion, arts, and habits.

Finding the Facts

1. The Navajos and Apaches are _____ tribes.
2. The _____ are the only pueblo Indians now in Arizona.
3. The _____ are the largest Indian tribe in the United States.
4. Navajo men excel in the craft of _____.
5. During World War II many Navajos served in the _____ _____ branch of the U.S. Army.

6. The Apaches got horses from the _____.
7. _____ was an Apache chief captured by General Miles.
8. Apaches on the _____ _____ Reservation are called the "cowboy Indians of the West."
9. The _____ _____ Apache Reservation is a well-known recreational area.
10. The most popular Apache dance is part of the _____ _____.
11. The Hopis are surrounded by the _____ Reservation.
12. Hopis hold some religious ceremonies in underground _____.
13. A _____ _____ acts lika a kachina spirit.
14. _____ _____ taught the Pimas how to grow wheat.
15. The _____ _____ was the first Indian reservation created in Arizona.
16. Boat races are held at _____ _____ on the Gila Reservation.
17. A Pima hero of World Was II was _____ _____ _____.
18. _____ _____ was a famous Indian doctor.
19. The _____ Indians are a Yuman tribe but share two reservations with the Pimas.
20. The _____ _____ National Observatory is on the Papago Reservation.

Papago woman making baskets (1916 photo).

UNIT 3

ARIZONA UNDER SPANISH AND MEXICAN RULE

The Spanish were the first Europeans to see the Indians of Arizona. For nearly 300 years they were the only non-Indians in Arizona.

How did Arizona become a part of Spain's empire? The story began with Columbus. He sailed from Spain to the New World in 1492. Other Spanish explorers followed him. One of them, Hernán Cortés, conquered Mexico City.

From that city other Spaniards went north to what is now the United States. During the 1500s Spanish explorers claimed most of the Southwest. This area includes Arizona, California, New Mexico, Texas, and other states.

Why did Spain want to control so much land? The three g's—gold, God, and glory—kept the Spaniards going. The Spanish greed for gold caused them to explore many lands. But it was not the gold seekers who built the big Spanish empire. That was done by the ranchers, miners, merchants, soldiers, priests —and the Indians!

The whole Spanish system rested on the Indians. The natives worked in mines. They herded cattle and did farm work. Indian girls married the Spaniards. Very few Spanish women came to the New World.

The gold seeking explorers rushed through Arizona in the 1500s. The king of Spain then turned this area over to the priests. Until the late 1700s the missionaries were about the only contact the Indians had with Spanish culture.

In 1821 Mexico won its independence from Spain. The new government in Mexico City paid little attention to Arizona. The Apache Indians raided the Mexican ranches. Many white men left. Arizona was nearly deserted except for Tucson and Tubac.

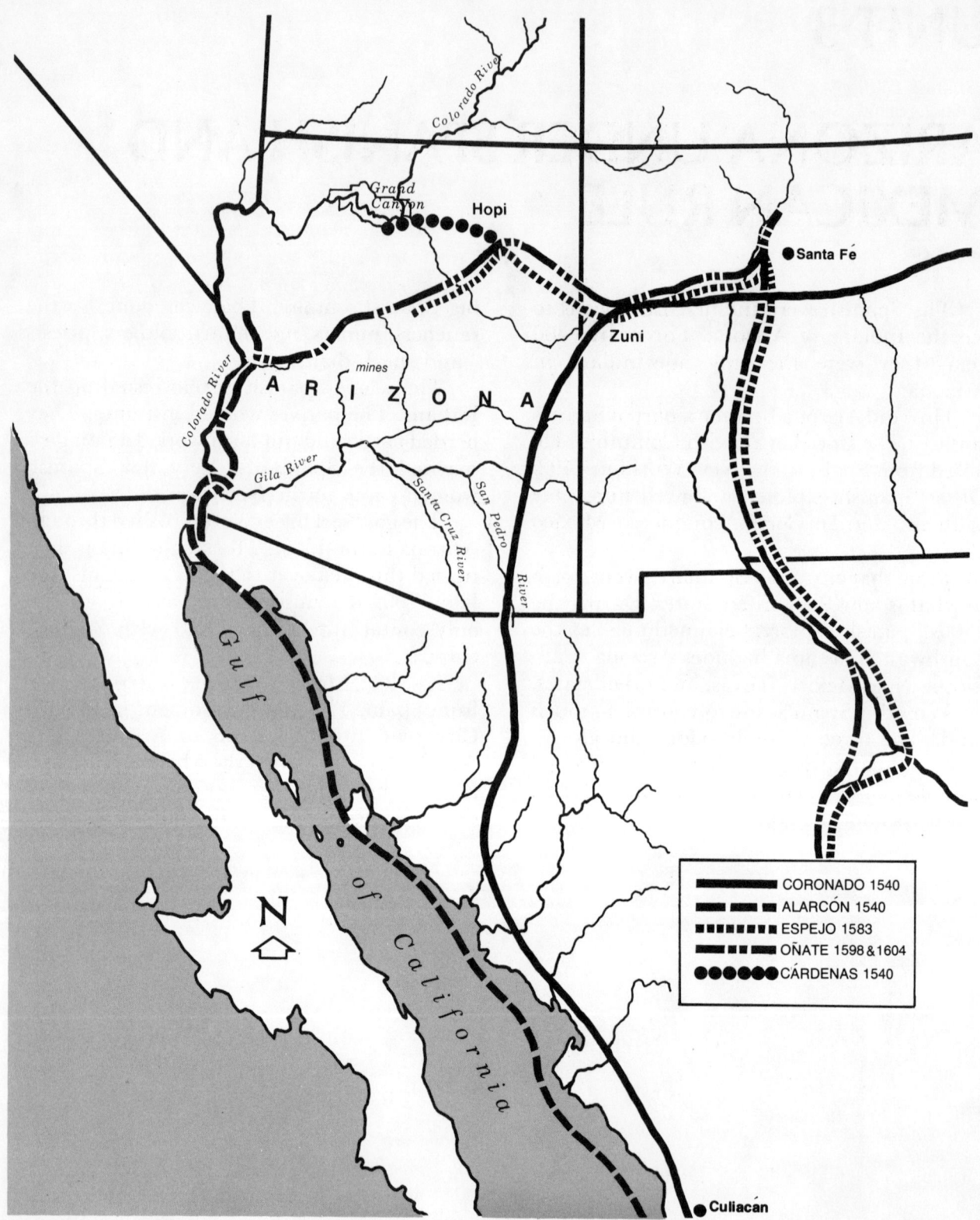

Spanish Explorations in the Southwest.

8. SPANISH EXPLORERS

A Spanish soldier wore a leather jacket and carried a heavy bullhide shield.

CABEZA DE VACA

Maybe Cabeza de Vaca was never in Arizona. But he had a great influence on Arizona's history.

Cabeza made an exciting journey from Florida to western Mexico. He was with Spanish explorers in Florida. Indians drove them away. The men crossed the Gulf of Mexico in log boats. Only a few survived. Some of them were killed in a gulf storm. Others died of disease or at the hands of unfriendly Indians in Texas.

Cabeza was made a slave by the Indians. But he soon won fame as a medicine man. Cabeza performed minor surgery. He also cured the sick with magic. He did this by rattling a gourd and making the sign of a cross. His Indian captors were pleased. After awhile they let him visit other tribes.

Cabeza and three other men slowly made their way across Texas. On their way to Mexico, they came close to New Mexico and Arizona. They heard rumors of rich Indian cities there.

Cabeza and his friends were taken to Mexico City. There they told the fantastic story of the journey to Viceroy Mendoza. The viceroy was the king's head man in Mexico. He was very interested in the rumors of golden cities.

Mendoza formed a group to find the cities. A scouting party was sent out first. It was led by a priest named Marcos de Niza. The guide was one of the three men who came to Mexico with Cabeza de Vaca. He was a black Moor named Estevan.

FRAY MARCOS DE NIZA AND ESTEVAN

Fray Marcos de Niza had seen rich cities in Peru. His job now was to find riches in the north. He sent Estevan ahead on the trail.

Estevan could not read or write. So a

73

The Spanish in Arizona is the subject of this mural by Jay Datus in the state capitol. Only two figures represent definite persons—Estevan the Moor on the right and Fray Marcos de Niza next to him. A *conquistador* rides a horse and carries the banner of Spain. Priests work with the Indians.

simple system of communication was worked out. When there was news, Estevan would send back a cross with an Indian runner. The bigger the cross, the better the news about riches.

Fray Marcos must have been excited one day. A cross as big as a man arrived. Estevan had heard more rumors about rich cities. He was urging Fray Marcos to hurry.

Why is Estevan important in Arizona history? He was the first non-Indian to touch Arizona. As he traveled, he played the part of a medicine man. No one could be a better showman. Estevan was a giant, dark-skinned man. His body was decorated. Bells jangled from his knees and arms. He rattled a magic gourd adorned with feathers.

Indians were impressed by Estevan. A large number followed him. Estevan was treated like a king until he got to the Zuñi villages. The Zuñis killed Estevan. They shot him with arrows.

Fray Marcos de Niza heard the bad news from Indian runners. He was stunned. Fray Marcos later claimed that he went on to see a rich Zuñi village. He said it was one of the "Seven Cities of Cíbola."

Fray Marcos returned to Mexico City. He told Viceroy Mendoza about a huge Indian city. There were high buildings with turquoise doors. Fray Marcos said the Indians wore giant pearls, gold beads, and emeralds. Whether he was lying or dreaming may never be known. But one thing is certain. His description of Cíbola excited the king's officials in Mexico City.

CORONADO

Viceroy Mendoza chose Francisco Coronado to lead another group to Cíbola. Coronado was a young, handsome Spanish noble.

Coronado is shown ready for battle in this painting.

His wife, Beatríz, was beautiful and wealthy.

The viceroy and Coronado put up much of the money to equip the group. They wanted to get most of the profits. The king of Spain would get only the royal *quinto* (one-fifth).

The expedition. Many men were eager to go on the journey. They were lured by riches and glory. Some 225 *caballeros* (horsemen) were chosen. These men were mainly young nobles. A few wore coats of armor. But most of them had only a helmet or a breastplate.

The expedition was formed at Compostela. This town is on the west coast of Mexico. Viceroy Mendoza was there to see the expedition move out in February, 1540.

First in line were the men on horses. Then came more than 60 foot soldiers. They carried swords, long pikes (spears), and shields. About a thousand Indians with native weapons were next in line of march. Indian and Negro slaves brought up the rear. They looked after the pack animals. They herded thousands of cattle, sheep, and goats.

The Spaniards were in the New World over 300 years. But this was their largest exploring trip.

Coronado passed through Arizona. Coronado left the main body of his army at Culiacán. He moved on into Arizona with a small force of about 100 men and a large group of Indian friends. Coronado followed the San Pedro Valley to a point near what is now Benson, Arizona. From the San Pedro he went northeast. Traveling between mountain ranges he came to Eagle Pass. This pass is in modern-day Graham County.

Coronado led his men through the rugged mountain country of eastern Arizona. The gold seekers ran out of food. They were half-starved by the time they got to one of the "cities of Cíbola" on July 7, 1540.

Spanish soldiers. The lance was a good weapon.

It was the Zuñi village of Hawikuh. This village is in New Mexico.

Golden cities? The Spaniards were in for quite a shock. Here they were at the end of the rainbow. But there was no pot of gold!

Zuñi warriors met the Spaniards at the edge of town. The Zuñis raised their weapons and yelled threats. They drew lines on the ground with cornmeal. They ordered the Spaniards not to cross the lines. The Indians had no fear of Coronado's tired-looking soldiers.

Coronado ordered an attack. The soldiers spurred their horses. With swords flashing in the sun, they rushed toward the Zuñis. In the battle, Coronado's gilded armor made him a special target. Twice he was knocked off his horse by rocks hurled from atop the pueblo. He was wounded in the leg by an arrow.

In less than an hour the Zuñis were forced to flee the pueblo. The hungry Spaniards gorged themselves on food left in the homes. They had their first good meal in weeks. At that moment the beans, maize, and fowl were more welcome than gold or silver.

In the weeks that followed, Coronado met with Zuñi chiefs from the other "cities of Cíbola." They had no gold. Coronado wrote the sad news in a letter to Viceroy Mendoza.

Fray Marcos took the letter to Mexico City. He was happy to go. By this time, the men were mad at Fray Marcos. All his stories of rich cities were false.

Coronado found no gold, no silver, and no jewels. But he went on searching. It took him awhile to catch on to an Indian trick. The Indians quickly learned how to get rid of the Spaniards. They told the visitors about riches to be found "somewhere else." Then the Spaniards rushed away to chase the next rainbow.

Hopis visited. Coronado sent two side expeditions into Arizona. Pedro de Tovar, with the help of Zuñi guides, took a small company of men to the Hopi villages. At Awátovi the Hopis were not friendly. Like the Zuñis, they drew cornmeal lines. But Tovar was not bluffed. He attacked Awátovi and forced the Hopis to surrender. Indians in the other mesa-top Hopi villages also asked for peace.

Tovar was pleased with the Hopi peace offerings. These gifts included cotton cloth, cornmeal, and pinyon nuts. Tovar was interested in what the Hopis had to say. They told him about a great river and rich Indians to the west. Tovar hurried back to the Zuñi villages to report the Hopi stories to Coronado.

Grand Canyon viewed. Coronado was excited. He sent Captain García López de Cárdenas, his toughest officer, to check out the Hopi rumors. Cárdenas and 25 horsemen stopped at the Hopi villages.

The Spaniards then traveled over the plateau of northern Arizona to the Grand Canyon. They were the first non-Indians to

Zuni Indians at Hawikuk. Mural by Gerald Cassidy in the Santa Fe post office.

Captain Cardenas at the Grand Canyon.

Most of the time, the Spanish soldiers carried their armor, especially when crossing the hot deserts of the Southwest.

see this great wonder of the world. But the men were not able to go down the canyon walls to the Colorado River. They returned to the Zuñi villages. No gold was found.

First non-Indians on the Colorado River. A Spanish navy officer was the first non-Indian to explore part of the Colorado River. Captain Hernando de Alarcón was supposed to bring supplies by water for Coronado. But the Colorado River was a lot farther from the Zuñi villages than the Spaniards thought.

Alarcón anchored his ships at the mouth of the river. With twenty men he went upstream by boat. Alarcón visited a Yuma tribe and gave them gifts. From the Yumas he learned that Coronado had reached the Zuñi villages. Alarcón saw no hope of reaching Coronado's army. He returned to Mexico.

Coronado's journey to Gran Quivira. From the Zuñi villages Coronado went east to the Rio Grande Valley to spend the winter. The Indians in this valley were like the Zuñis and the Hopis. They knew how to get rid of the Spaniards. They had a slave named "El Turco" tell a story about the rich city of Gran Quivira. Coronado took the bait.

He let El Turco lead the Spaniards on a wild goose chase. They crossed the Texas plains to a mud and straw village near Wichita, Kansas. The only metal in the village was a copper amulet worn by the chief. El Turco confessed to lying. The Spaniards strangled him and returned to the Rio Grande Valley.

Was Coronado a success or failure? In 1542 Coronado led his tired army back to Mexico. His report to the viceroy was discouraging. It was 40 years before another Spanish explorer entered Arizona.

Coronado was not a complete failure. He brought back knowledge of the geography and Indians of the Southwest.

Today the Coronado National Monument and the Coronado National Forest honor him.

ESPEJO

Three other Spaniards explored Arizona in the 1500s. All of them came from New Mexico.

In 1583 Antonio de Espejo led a few soldiers and friendly Zuñis to the Hopi villages. The Hopis gave Espejo gifts. The gifts included blankets, cotton towels, shawls, and some blue and green ores.

From the Hopi villages Espejo went west. He found some ores near present-day Jerome. Espejo took samples back to Mexico. But the Spaniards never came back to develop mines in the Jerome area.

OÑATE AND FARFÁN

Governor Juan de Oñate of New Mexico traveled more in Arizona than any other Spanish explorer. He was a wealthy man. Oñate spent his own money to bring colonists to New Mexico. In 1598 he led an exploring group to the Hopi villages. It was winter time. His men and horses suffered from the cold weather.

Farfán. Governor Onate decided to take most of his men back to New Mexico. But first he formed a smaller group to explore west of the Hopi villages.

Hopi village of Walpi.

Oñate sent Captain Marcos Farfán with eight men to look for Espejo's mines. Farfán located some rich ore near what is now Prescott. Oñate was pleased when he heard about the discovery. But he never got around to sending miners to dig the ore.

Why did Governor Oñate return to Arizona? In 1604-1605 Oñate crossed northern Arizona to the Colorado River. He went down the river to its mouth. He wanted to find the Pacific Ocean. His idea was to open up trade for the New Mexico colony with Peru and China. But he did not reach the Pacific Ocean.

On this trip Oñate heard some strange stories. His diarist, a Franciscan priest, wrote them down. The Mojave Indians told the Spaniards about a great lake. They said the people at the lake all wore gold bracelets.

There was another tall tale about a rich island of bald-headed men. They were ruled by a fat woman with big feet. The Indians told a story about a tribe of one-legged people. One tribe slept in trees and another slept under water. No one, of course, believed these stories.

Oñate had bad luck. In his Arizona travels he found no gold. And, of course, he did not reach the Pacific Ocean. But Oñate—like Coronado and Espejo—did succeed in one way. He helped to make the Southwest better known to Europeans.

Words and Terms to Know

explorer
medicine man
scouting party
communication
expedition
quinto
caballero
coat of armor
gilded
amulet
diarist

Match the words above with the following definitions:

1. Spanish word for a man who rides horses.
2. Spanish word meaning one-fifth or 20 per cent.
3. A person who travels to a new or strange region.
4. A person who writes down a record of experiences.
5. A person who claims to have magical powers to heal the sick.
6. Anything, such as a charm, worn on the body for protection against evil.
7. A metal suit worn for protection.
8. Coated with a layer of gold.
9. A word meaning either a journey for a specific purpose, or the group of people who make the journey.
10. A group of persons who are sent ahead of an army or expedition to observe and get information.
11. Any means of getting a message or information between places or persons.

Finding the Facts

1. The three "g's" _____, _____, and _____ were the Spanish motives for building an empire.
2. _____ _____ _____ brought rumors of rich Indian cities to Mexico.
3. _____ _____ _____ was the priest who headed a scouting party to look for rich cities.
4. A black Moor named _____ was the first non-Indian to touch Arizona soil.
5. Viceroy _____ chose _____ to head an expedition to find the rich "Cities of Cíbola."
6. Coronado entered Arizona by way of the _____ _____ Valley.
7. The _____ Indians at Hawikuh did not welcome the Spaniards.
8. Indians sometimes got rid of the Spaniards by telling them of riches to be found _____ _____.
9. _____ _____ _____ conquered the Hopi villages.
10. Captain _____ led the first group of non-Indians to see the Grand Canyon.
11. Captain _____ was the first non-Indian to explore the Colorado River.
12. Coronado was taken on a wild goose chase to the village of _____ _____ by a slave named _____ _____.
13. Espejo discovered rich ores near the present city of _____.
14. Farfán discovered rich ores near the present city of _____.
15. The second time Governor Oñate passed through Arizona he hoped to reach the _____ _____.

79

9. THE MISSIONARY ERA: ARIZONA IN THE 1700s

Father Kino with cattle.

Why were missionaries (priests) sent to New Spain? There were several reasons. The main goal of the missionary, of course, was to tell Indians about Christ. Spain was a strong Catholic country.

Another reason was that the priests also kept good diaries for the explorers. They were educated and trained to observe.

Priests helped the Spanish king win an empire. They had a strong influence with some Indian tribes. Sometimes priests could go where soldiers were not welcome.

There were two religious orders which had priests in Arizona. The *Jesuits* (Society of Jesus) worked mainly with the Pima Indians before 1767. The *Franciscans* were the first priests to visit the Hopis. After 1767 the Franciscans also worked with the Pimas and Yumas.

The Hopis wanted nothing to do with Spanish rule and religion. They were not friendly to the priests.

Franciscan friars came to the Hopi villages in 1629. The friars were sent from missions in New Mexico. The Hopis showed no interest at first. Then came a miracle. Fray Porras healed a blind boy. For awhile a few Hopis became Christians. But jealous medicine men poisoned Father Porras.

Other Franciscans came to live among the Hopis. But the friars had little success. At least three friars were killed in the Hopi vil-

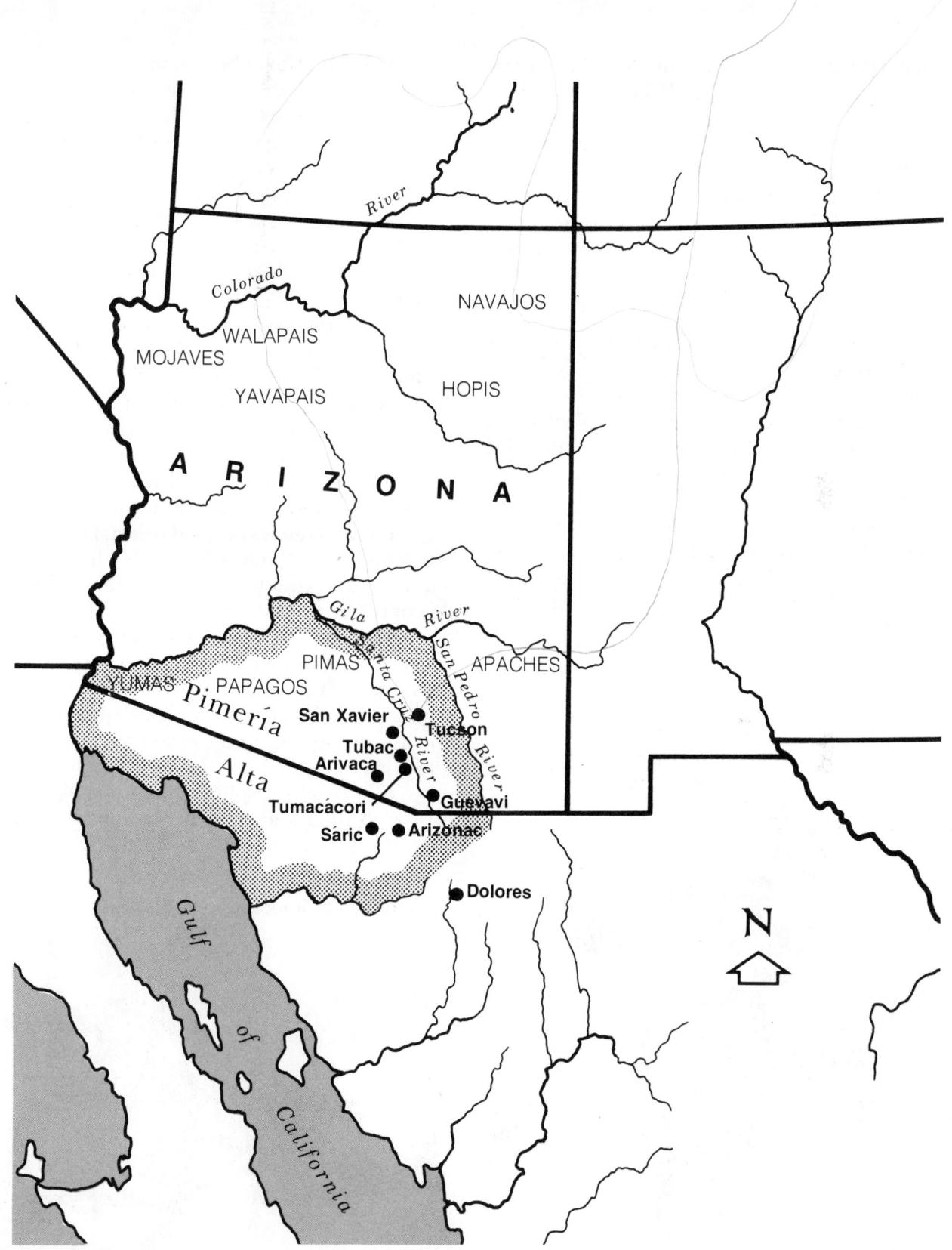

Arizona in the 1700s.

lages during the rebellion in 1680. The Hopis had their own religion. They wanted their own way of life.

How did Hopi defiance of the Spaniards affect Arizona history? It meant that Arizona would not be colonized from New Mexico. Instead, Arizona became a part of the Mexican state of Sonora. Priests, soldiers, and settlers came from the south.

PADRE KINO (1645-1711)

Padre Kino was Arizona's first successful missionary. He was one of the most important men in all Arizona history.

Kino was born in Italy. He was educated in Austrian and German schools. He decided to join the Jesuits while recovering from a serious illness.

Kino was sent to Mexico. After a few years he was appointed a missionary to the Pimas. His head mission was at Dolores. This town is about 75 miles south of present-day Nogales.

Father Kino.

Pimería Alta. The region in which Kino lived and worked was called Pimería Alta. The name means "land of the Upper Pimas." It included what is now southern Arizona and part of the Mexican state of Sonora.

Kino started three missions in Arizona. All were in the Santa Cruz Valley. The first was built in 1700 at the Indian village of Bac. It was named San Xavier del Bac. There have been several different church buildings at San Xavier. The present mission building near Tucson was not Kino's. It was built by Franciscans in the late 1700s.

Kino had a second mission at Guevavi. There was also a temporary mission, called a *visita*, at Tumacácori. Like San Xavier, the church now at Tumacácori is Franciscan. It is near the highway north of Nogales.

Padre Kino was a good priest. He taught religion to the Pima Indians. But he wanted to do more. Kino tried to make each mission a complete community.

The Indians were taught the best way to farm. New grains and fruit trees were planted. Kino also started ranching in Arizona. His Indian cowboys rounded up cattle, sheep, and horses at Dolores and herded them to missions in Arizona.

Kino was an explorer and mapmaker. He traveled thousands of miles in southern Ari-

Tumacácori as it looked in the 1920s.

zona. A Spanish lieutenant named Juan Mateo Manje often rode with Kino.

Kino died as he had lived—with extreme humility and poverty. His deathbed consisted of two calfskins for a mattress and two Indian blankets for covers. His pillow was a pack saddle. Kino was buried in a church at Magdalena. This town is in Mexico south of Nogales.

In 1961 the Arizona legislature honored Padre Kino. The members voted to have his statue placed in the capitol in Washington, D.C. The honor is great because each state can have only two statues in the capitol.

ARIZONA AFTER KINO

For twenty years after Kino's death, Arizona was ignored by Spanish officials. But in the 1730s more Jesuit priests were sent to the Pimas. Some of the new padres were German. They had names like Grazhoffer, Segesser, Stiger, Keller, Sedelmayr, Pauer, Pfefferkorn, and Middendorff.

The name "Arizona." In 1736 an event happened that gave Arizona its name. A Yaqui Indian miner found chunks of silver near Arissona. This place was a Spanish *visita* southwest of present-day Nogales in Mexico.

News of the silver discovery spread. Hundreds of people rushed in to search the hills. Silver could be picked up from the ground. It was in the form of large balls and slabs. About 4,000 pounds of silver was found.

Future generations were told the story of the silver boom. The musical word "Arissona" was remembered. After Arizona became a part of the United States, the Anglo-American settlers liked the name. So "Arizona" became the name of the 48th state.

It is believed that Arizona is a softened spelling of two Papago words. *Ali* means "small" and *shonak* is "place of the spring."

The Pima Rebellion of 1751. The Pimas were usually peaceful. But in 1751 they rebelled against Spanish rule. Luis, one of their leaders, was eager to drive out the white men and rule Pimería Alta himself.

The rebellion started at Sáric. This village was south of the present Mexican border. Within a few days, more than a hundred people were killed. Among the dead were miners, herdsmen, farmers, and two priests.

Drawing of the Tubac presidio.

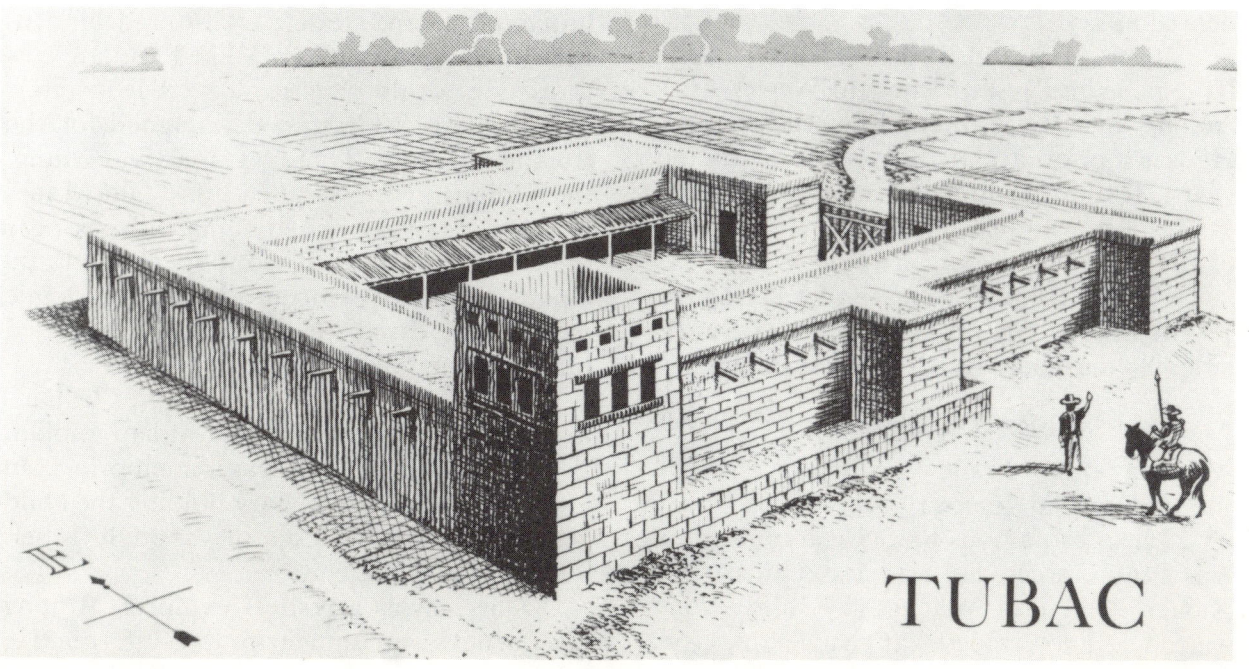

The Arizona missions and ranches did not escape the killing and looting. Missions in the Santa Cruz Valley were destroyed. At the Arivaca farms a number of Spaniards and loyal Indians were murdered. These farms were west of Nogales.

Luckily, the Jesuit priests at San Xavier and Guevavi had guessed trouble was coming. They were safe at the presidio (fort) of Terrenate.

Spanish soldiers at Terrenate took to the field. After three months Luis was captured in the Catalina Mountains north of Tucson. He agreed to live in peace.

Presidio of Tubac. The Spaniards made plans to prevent more Indian uprisings. Two new presidios were built in 1752. One of them, Tubac, was in Arizona.

Fifty Spanish soldiers were assigned to Tubac. A settlement soon grew up around the fort. The first white women to touch Arizona soil came to Tubac in 1752.

The main job of the soldiers at Tubac was to protect Spaniards from the Apaches. These Indians made hit-and-run raids to drive off livestock. When chased, the Apaches knew how to avoid capture. They fled swiftly across rugged mountains or waterless deserts to hidden camps.

Jesuits expelled. In 1767 King Charles III expelled all Jesuits from the New World. Among them was Father Alphonso Espinosa. He was a priest at San Xavier for nearly ten years. He built a church there. The roof beams of Espinosa's church were later used in a wing of the present San Xavier mission.

Charles III gave no reason for taking the Jesuits back to Spain. He was an autocratic king. No one could question what he did.

FRAY GARCÉS

Gray-robed Franciscan priests replaced the black-robed Jesuits.

The most famous Franciscan in Arizona was Fray Garcés. He was assigned to San Xavier. A band of Apaches gave him a rude welcome. They raided San Xavier in 1768.

Fray Garcés.

Espinosa's adobe church was partly destroyed.

Garcés was only 30 years of age and a native of Spain. He was well-suited by attitude for his work. Garcés liked Indian customs. He would sit cross-legged in a circle with Indians. Indian food was good for the stomach, he said. Though Garcés was young, the Indians lovingly called him "Old Man."

Garcés often visited Pima villages near the Gila River. He learned to speak the Pima language fluently. During a measles epidemic in 1770, he cared for the sick. He baptized many of the Gila Pimas.

Garcés was always searching for Indians to convert. He used a visual aid to explain the plan of salvation. It was a linen print. On one side was a Virgin Mary holding the child Jesus. A picture of a lost soul was on the other. The choice was clear.

Garcés was a restless explorer. Among his journeys were some trips to California. He

Father Garcés talks to Yuma Indians. They were scared by his picture of "Hell."

Royal presidio of Tucson as it looked about 1790.

Captain Anza (right) inspects Spanish soldiers in this 1975 bicentennial re-enactment of the Anza expedition.

worked with Captain Juan Bautista de Anza in forming two expeditions to the Pacific. Anza was the commander at Tubac.

In 1775-1776 Anza's soldiers escorted colonists to northern California. An important stop was made at the Yuma crossing on the Colorado River. Anza presented Chief Palma of the Yumas with a fancy suit of clothes. It consisted of a decorated jacket, blue trousers, a blue cape with gold braid, and a black velvet cap. The Yumas treated their Spanish guests with watermelons. They also helped them across the river.

While Anza was busy with the colony, Garcés explored. He tried to find a good trade route between the Pacific coast and Santa Fe, New Mexico. That is one reason why he visited the Hopis. In fact, he was at the Hopi village of Oraibi on July 4, 1776.

The Hopis did not make Garcés feel welcome. At night he tried to sleep in a dark corner of the village. But he was frightened. Some of the Hopis danced all night. The dancers were painted red and wore feathers. They danced to the beat of a drum. The next morning one Hopi leader asked Garcés to leave.

Garcés felt sad. As a missionary, he failed with the Hopis. But he was pleased in other ways. His journey proved that a trade route could be opened across northern Arizona to the coast. Also, as Garcés rode out of town he saw signs of Spanish culture. He passed a peach orchard. There were flocks of sheep near the trail.

Tucson presidio. Garcés was happy when soldiers at the Tubac presidio were moved to Tucson in 1776. He had helped a Spanish officer pick out the new site. It was well-located to defend the San Xavier mission.

Yuma massacre. The career of Fray Garcés was ended by the Yuma massacre.

San Xavier Mission at night.

At first, the Yumas wanted to be friends with the Spaniards. For years Chief Palma of the Yumas waited for Spanish missions. Captain Anza promised to help. He even took Palma to Mexico City. Palma was baptized in the National Cathedral there.

Finally, in 1780, two Spanish colonies were started at the Yuma crossing on the Colorado River. Each colony had a mission with two priests. There were also Spanish soldiers and settlers. The Spaniards hoped to control the Yuma crossing. It was the only good place to cross the river.

Some of the soldiers and settlers were not kind to the Yumas. They took the best farmland. They made fun of the Yuma way of planting—punching a hole in the soil for seeds with a stick. They crowded the Indians out of the missions.

The soldiers overused the whipping post, hurting Indian pride. Worst of all, the Spaniards grazed their horses and cattle on mesquite beans. The beans were an important food. The Yumas ground them into flour.

The Yumas finally became hostile. On July 17, 1781 they rebelled. About fifty Spanish men were killed. There were 48 captives, mostly women and children. All four of the priests, including Father Garcés, were murdered.

Troops from Sonora came to the Yuma crossing. They traded blankets, beads, and tobacco for the captives. But the Yumas were never punished.

The Spaniards gave up trying to control the Yuma crossing.

Golden Age of Spanish rule (1790 to 1821). Peace and well-being came to the Spanish frontier in the 1790s. Why? The Spaniards gave up trying to kill all the Apaches. They changed to a peace policy.

Spanish officials offered gifts to Apache

Interior view of San Xavier del Bac.

Indians to surrender. And the Apaches were given food rations if they settled near a presidio. The ration system quieted the Apaches who took part.

The last thirty years of Spanish rule in Arizona was a "golden age." More mines were opened than in the previous 250 years. Ranchers brought vast herds of cattle to southern Arizona.

New church buildings were a symbol of "golden age" peace and prosperity. At San Xavier the Franciscans built a beautiful church. It still stands. It is sometimes called the "white dove in the desert."

At Tumacácori a large church with a beautiful dome was built. It can still be seen near the highway north of Nogales.

Words and Terms to Know

missionary	rebellion
friar	defiance
visita	to convert
humility	salvation
presidio	hybrid
autocrat	rations
fluent	"golden age"

Match the words above with the following definitions:

1. The Spanish word for fort.
2. The Spanish word for a temporary mission where a priest came once in awhile.
3. A person who is sent to another country or region to teach a religion or to help the people.
4. A man who is a member of the Franciscan religious order.
5. To change a person from one religion or set of beliefs to another.
6. The quality of being modest or meek.
7. The process or state of being saved from sin.

8. Resistance or opposition.
9. Allowances of food or other goods.
10. Anything made up of different elements.
11. A supreme ruler with unlimited power.
12. Able to speak or write well.
13. Armed resistance against a government or authority.
14. A time of peace, prosperity, and achievements in the arts.

Finding the Facts

1. The two religious orders which had priests in Arizona were the _____ and _____.
2. Padre _____ was Arizona's first successful missionary.
3. The three Spanish missions in Arizona were _____ _____ del Bac, _____, and _____.
4. Discovery of _____ at a place near Nogales gave Arizona its name.
5. The Pima rebellion of 1751 led to the founding of a presidio at _____.
6. King Charles III expelled the _____ from the New World in 1767.
7. The most famous Franciscan priest in Arizona was Fray _____.
8. Soldiers at Tubac moved to a new presidio at _____ in 1776.
9. _____ was chief of the Yumas.
10. Captain _____ was the Tubac commander who escorted Spanish colonists to California.
11. The last thirty years of Spanish rule is called the _____ _____.
12. The San Xavier mission is known as the "_____ _____ _____ _____ _____."

10. ARIZONA AS A PART OF MEXICO
(1821 to 1854)

Mexico and the United States, 1821.

Most people in the New World wanted their freedom. You may know that the 13 English colonies fought the American Revolution to be free. England gave the colonies independence in 1783. Six years later George Washington became the first president of the United States. At that time Arizona was still under Spanish rule.

When did Mexico win its independence? The people in Mexico waited until the 1800s to revolt. Mexico has a national holiday to celebrate its first revolution in 1810. On September 16 of that year Father Miguel Hidalgo called the Mexican people to arms. But Hidalgo was killed. His revolution failed.

At last, in 1821, Mexico won its indepen-

89

These young students dance at a Mexican Independence Day celebration.

dence from Spain.

Who was Captain José Romero? When Mexico got its independence, a new flag was raised over Tucson. The presidio commander, Captain José Romero, took an oath of loyalty to the new government of Mexico.

Romero was the "Mexican Anza." In 1823 he set out to locate a good route to California. He had bad luck. On the return trip his small party got lost in the Mojave Desert. Romero was not back in Tucson until December, 1825.

Missions abandoned. Spain had put great faith in missions. The priests had some success working with the Indians.

The new government of Mexico did not feel a great need for missionaries. Priests were given a choice—take an oath of loyalty to Mexico or leave the country. All foreign missionaries were sent back to Europe.

San Xavier did not have a priest for years. At one time the church and mission buildings were used as barns, horse stables, and soldier barracks.

The mission at Tumacácori was deserted. Farm and ranch lands belonging to the mission were sold at an auction.

MEXICAN CATTLE RANCHES

Arizona had some big cattle ranches in the 1820s. The ranchers got huge land grants from the Mexican government. A typical land grant had 27 square miles. A rancher could also buy the surplus lands around his ranch. These lands were known as "overplus."

Most of the big ranches were in the valleys of the Santa Cruz, San Pedro, and their tributaries.

A cowboy on a Mexican ranch was called a *vaquero*. Much of his range language was later adopted by American cowboys.

Take these words, for examples: bronco, lasso, rodeo, corral, stampede, remuda, and lariat. All are of Spanish or Mexican origin. From the vaquero also came the horned saddle as well as roping and branding techniques.

Mexican ranches deserted. Nearly all the Mexican ranchers left their lands in the 1830s and 1840s. The main cause was Apache

Sketch of a Mexican vaquero roping a longhorn.

raids. For safety the ranchers moved to Tucson, Tubac, or to towns and ranches south of the present border.

The cattle became wild. Soldiers in the U.S. Army saw them during the Mexican War. The Mexican cattle were described as "mealy-nosed" because their faces were covered with coarse hair. They were all colors—black, brown, blue, and red. Black was the main color. Their trim horns were white. The long-legged wild cattle were quick and easily excited. They were always sniffing the air and watching for danger.

APACHES ON THE WARPATH

How did many Apaches make a living? During the 1820s, the Apaches waited to see how they would be treated by the new Republic of Mexico. They wanted the Mexican leaders to keep Spain's ration system. But the Indians were not given rations to remain at peace. As a result, many Apaches took to the warpath again.

The Apaches lived mainly in what is now eastern Arizona and western New Mexico. On their raids, they followed trails into Chihuahua and Sonora. The Apaches raided Mexican ranches and drove away livestock. Sometimes they carried away women and children.

"Help!" That is the cry that came from presidio commanders. They needed more soldiers to stop the Apache raids. But leaders in Mexico City said "no." They thought the northern frontier was a wasteland.

Scalp-hunters. Some governors of the frontier states took matters in their own hands. They offered bounties for Apache scalps. This bounty system attracted some bad men—both from the United States and Mexico.

The scalp-hunters got up to $100 for a head of hair. They were greedy as well as cruel. Not all the scalps which the bounty hunters brought in belonged to raiding Apaches. Some came from the heads of innocent Mexicans and peaceful Indians.

The only result of the bounty system was to make the Apaches hate non-Indians even more. The Apache raids continued. Little growth or progress was possible on the frontier of Mexico after the 1820s.

MEXICAN WAR

What were some causes of the Mexican War? Many pioneers moved west from the 13 colonies. By the 1840s one thing was clear. The United States was about to push its western boundary all the way to the Pacific Ocean.

In 1836 Texas won independence from Mexico. The United States made Texas a state in 1845.

President James K. Polk was not satisfied with only Texas. He wanted to buy California and other Mexican land. Polk sent John Slidell to Mexico City to make an offer. But Mexico said "no sale."

Mexican leaders were angry over the loss of Texas. They would not accept the Rio Grande River as the border between the United States and Mexico. But when Mexican troops crossed the Rio Grande, President Polk asked Congress to declare war.

General Stephen W. Kearny.

During the Mexican War (1846 to 1848), two army expeditions crossed what is now Arizona. They were on the way to California.

Kearny's Army of the West. Stephen W. Kearny led the "Army of the West" across the Kansas plains to Santa Fe. The Mexican army deserted the town before Kearny arrived.

Kearny left most of his army in Santa Fe. He took about 100 mounted soldiers along the Gila River route across Arizona. Supplies were carried on pack mules.

At the Pima villages General Kearny traded for cornmeal, flour, beans, pumpkins, and melons. Farther downstream he was able to get cattle from the Maricopa Indians.

The war was not quite over in California. About a third of Kearny's small force were killed by Mexican lancers near San Diego. Not long after this skirmish, the Mexican army in California surrendered near present-day Hollywood.

Kearny, Arizona is named after General Kearny.

The Mormon Battalion was the second army group to travel across Arizona during the Mexican War.

This battalion was formed in Iowa by leaders of the Latter-day Saints (Mormon) Church. Mormons had been persecuted for their beliefs. They wanted to prove their patriotism. They also wanted to learn more about the West. The Mormons hoped to settle in the West.

From Iowa the Mormon Battalion marched to Santa Fe. The commander, Captain Philip St. George Cooke, picked out the men unfit for service. He sent them and most of the women and children to Pueblo in present-day Colorado.

Cooke took a route south of the Gila Trail. His army blazed a wagon road across southern Arizona. It was used after the war by people going to California.

The Mormon Battalion got to fight only one battle. Near the San Pedro River they were attacked by a herd of wild bulls. These bulls gored the mules, damaged a few wagons,

Wild bulls attacked the Mormon Battalion.

and injured some soldiers. One private wrote in his diary that the bulls "would run off with a half dozen balls in them unless they were shot in the heart."

The battalion entered Tucson without firing a shot. They raised the United States flag over Tucson for the first time.

The Mexicans in Tucson were friendly. They sold tortillas and pomegranates to the Mormons. The tortillas were made from local flour. Most Tucson homes had a burro flour mill. A blindfolded burro went round and round, turning a rough stone that ground wheat.

From Tucson the Mormon Battalion traveled by way of the Pima villages on the Gila River. When the soldiers got to San Diego, the war was over in California.

Treaty of Guadalupe Hidalgo. The Mexican War ended soon after an American army entered Mexico City. The peace terms were signed in 1848 at Guadalupe Hidalgo, a small town near Mexico City.

Mexican leaders signed a treaty giving almost half their country to the United States.

A burro flour mill, called a *molino*.

The land that Mexico gave up in 1848 was called the *Mexican Cession*.

Most of the states in the American southwest were later carved out of the Mexican Cession. The part of Arizona north of the Gila River and most of New Mexico were included. The United States also got all of California, Utah, and Nevada. Parts of Colorado and Wyoming were in the cession too.

In effect Mexico was forced to sell the Mexican Cession for less than President Polk offered for it in 1845. The United States paid Mexico $15,000,000. Our country also agreed to pay debts owed by Mexico to American citizens. This bill came to $3,250,000.

ON THE ROAD TO CALIFORNIA

Who were the Forty-niners? Just two weeks before Mexico signed away California, gold was discovered. The news spread to the East. Gold seekers rushed to California. The greatest number went in 1849.

Thousands of "Forty-niners" followed Cooke's wagon road through Mexican land to California. Travel over the desert between Tucson (still a part of Mexico) and the Colorado River was difficult. Signs of hardship were visible. Beside the trail were graves of those who died of sickness or thirst. There were skeletons of horses and oxen and abandoned baggage. Large caravans of people usually had little mishap. But small parties were often in trouble.

Oatman Massacre. A terrible tragedy struck a California-bound family in 1851. Royse Oatman, his wife, and seven children were attacked by Yavapais about 100 miles east of Yuma. The adults and four children were murdered. A son, Lorenzo, was also left for dead.

Two teenage Oatman sisters, Olive and Mary Ann, were taken as slaves. They were traded to the Mojaves for horses and blankets. The girls were tatooed on the chin with five vertical blue lines. Mary Ann starved to death. But in 1856 Olive was turned over to a Yuma carpenter who paid a ransom for her. Olive was reunited with her brother Lorenzo.

MEXICAN BOUNDARY SURVEY

After the Mexican War, the boundary between the United States and Mexico was surveyed. The survey was supervised by two commissioners. One man was from the United States. One man was from Mexico.

Both countries agreed in the 1848 treaty to use the Disturnell map. But it was not accurate. El Paso, a key city in the survey, was

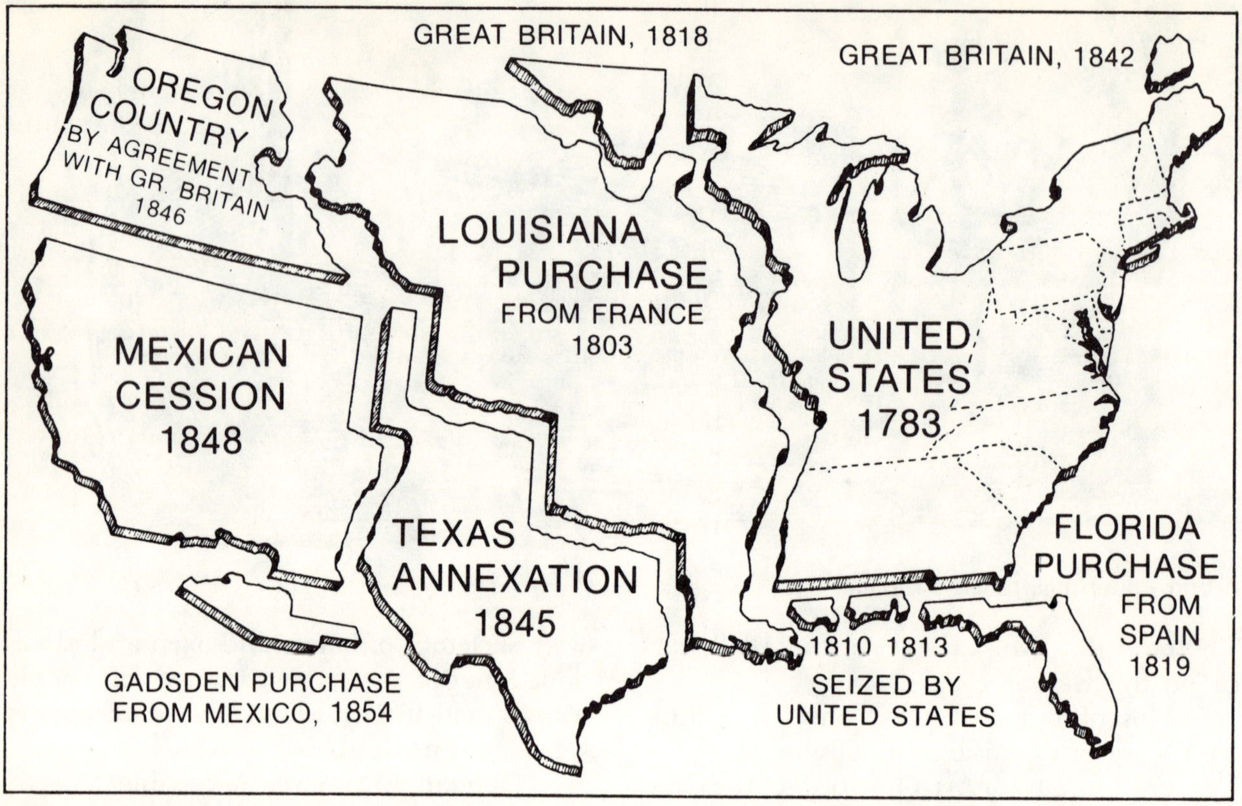

Territorial Growth of the United States.

in the wrong place on the map.

John R. Bartlett. The American commissioner, John R. Bartlett, did not insist on using a correct map. He gave up a strip of land 35 miles wide and 175 miles long in southern New Mexico. Another war almost started over this land.

Bartlett was a political appointee. He knew little about surveying. And too much of his time was spent on side trips in a mule-drawn ambulance. In 1851, for example, he insisted on returning a 14-year old Mexican girl to her family in Santa Cruz, Sonora.

Inez Gonzales had been kidnapped by Apaches. She was sold to traders in New Mexico. When Bartlett rescued her, Inez was working as a slave. General Condé, the Mexican commissioner, offered to take Inez to her family. He had to go to Santa Cruz anyway. But Bartlett wanted to take her home himself. He did.

John Russell Bartlett.

On the way to Santa Cruz with Inez, Bartlett's party stopped at the deserted Babocomari Ranch. Bartlett saw herds of wild cattle and mustangs on the ranch. The huge Babocomari is located north of the present-day town of Sierra Vista.

Bartlett left Inez in Santa Cruz. He then took a whirlwind tour of Mexican cities. Next, his party went by sea to San Diego, California. Not until 1852, almost a year after he left New Mexico, did Bartlett return to his survey job.

His engineers were not yet done with the Gila River boundary survey. But Bartlett took off for El Paso, Texas. He stopped in Tucson long enough to sketch a picture of that town.

A new commissioner was appointed to complete the survey. But it didn't matter. After the Gadsden Purchase in 1854, a new boundary had to be surveyed farther south.

Bartlett was a failure as a commissioner. But he drew many sketches. These pictures show us what the Mexican border country was like in the 1850s.

GADSDEN PURCHASE

In 1854 the United States bought more land from Mexico. The Gadsden Purchase was south of the Gila River. It is now in southern Arizona and New Mexico.

Why did the United States buy this land? For one reason, the boundary errors of the 1848 treaty needed to be corrected. Also, the United States government wanted a level route for a southern railroad to the Pacific Ocean.

President Franklin Pierce sent James Gadsden, a South Carolina railroad promoter, to Mexico City. Gadsden made five different offers to buy land. The biggest offer was $50 million for a huge amount of Mexican land south of the present states of California, Arizona, New Mexico, and Texas.

President Santa Anna, however, was willing to sell only enough land for a railroad route. And he would not sell the United States a sea outlet on the Gulf of California.

The United States Senate changed Gadsden's original treaty. Most of the senators

Bartlett's sketch of Tucson in 1852.

President Antonio López de Santa Anna of Mexico.

thought the desert land was worthless. They reduced the amount of land the United States would get by 9,000 square miles. They also cut the purchase price. The United States paid $10 million for nearly 30,000 square miles. Most of it is in what is now Arizona. Both nations ratified the treaty on June 30, 1854.

Tucson was the main town in the Gadsden Purchase. Mexican soldiers stayed there until March 1856. In November some United States cavalry troops finally rode into Tucson. The American flag was raised.

The Gadsden Purchase filled out the now familiar profile of the United States.

Words and Terms to Know

independence	bounty
revolution	lancer
abandon	to blaze
land grant	tortilla
tributary	cession
vaquero	ratify
lariat	

Match the words above with the following definitions:

1. Land which a government gives to a person, railroad, or school for some specific purpose.
2. Anything, such as land, which is given up by one country or person to another.
3. To approve and make something legal, such as a treaty.
4. To make a trail for other travellers.
5. To desert, forsake, or leave behind.
6. A condition of being free and able to manage one's own affairs.
7. The attempt to overthrow and replace a government by the people who are governed.
8. A reward paid by a government for the capture, killing, or scalping of an outlaw.
9. In Mexico, a flat cake made of coarse cornmeal.
10. A Mexican cowboy.
11. A rope, the name of which comes from the Spanish words *la reata*.
12. A mounted soldier armed with a spear-like weapon.
13. A stream that flows into a larger stream.

Finding the Facts

1. Mexico got its independence in the year _____.
2. Captain _____ _____ was the presidio commander at Tucson who tried to find a new route to California.
3. Most of the big _____ _____ were in the valleys of the Santa Cruz, San Pedro, and their tributaries.
4. Mexican governors tried to stop Apache raids by paying bounties to _____.
5. One cause of the Mexican War was the desire of President _____ to get more Mexican land.
6. General Kearny took the _____ route across Arizona.
7. The Mormon Battalion fought a battle on the San Pedro with _____ _____.
8. The Mexican War was ended in 1848 with the Treaty of _____ _____.

9. All of Arizona north of the Gila River was part of the _____ _____.
10. People who rushed to the California gold fields are called _____-_____.
11. _____ _____ was the American boundary commissioner who made sketches in the Southwest in the early 1850s.
12. The Gadsden Purchase Treaty was ratified in the year _____.
13. All of Arizona south of the _____ River was part of the Gadsden Purchase.

The state museum in Tubac shows how the early Spanish settlers lived in Arizona.

UNIT 4
PIONEER DAYS

The first American pioneers in Arizona were fur trappers—better known as "mountain men." They trapped for beaver along the Gila and other rivers in Arizona. Most of trapping was done between 1824 and 1832. At that time Arizona was still a part of Mexico.

Arizona became a part of the United States by two treaties: the Treaty of Guadalupe Hidalgo in 1848 and the Gadsden Purchase in 1854.

From 1850 to 1863 Arizona was an isolated part of the Territory of New Mexico. There were only a few settlers. They lived in what is now southern Arizona. This region was called a "paradise for devils."

The people had almost no law to keep outlaws in check. Only a few soldiers were sent to Arizona to hold off raiding Apaches. Every man had to carry a gun for protection.

In this setting, the good work done by the pioneers seems amazing. Miners, ranchers, farmers, stage drivers, road builders, merchants, and soldiers—all these pioneers made progress in the 1850s.

Arizona was separated from New Mexico and a made a territory in 1863. It was a territory until 1912—a total of 49 years. During that time a lot of people moved west from the States. The population of Arizona grew. There were only about 10,000 people, including friendly Indians, in Arizona in 1863. This number grew to more than 200,000 in 1912, the year Arizona became a state.

A typical mountain man. Sketch by Frederic Remington.

11. FUR TRAPPERS

Here is a typical trapping party, such as those led by or sent out by Ewing Young. Artist was William Henry Jackson.

The first Americans in Arizona were trappers. They were known as "mountain men." They came to this region while it was still a part of Mexico.

During the 1820s and 1830s the mountain men were looking for beaver. They trapped along the Gila, Salt, Verde, San Pedro, San Francisco, Colorado, and other rivers of Arizona. In those days—long before modern dams were built—there was water flowing in all these rivers.

The beaver. There used to be a big demand for beaver furs. Hairs from the soft underfur made the finest felt. The felt was made into tall-crowned beaver hats. This style of hat was popular in the East and in Europe.

To catch the beaver a mountain man used a strong steel trap with a five-foot chain. The trap was placed in three or four inches of water close to the bank. The chain was fastened to a strong stick. For bait the trapper used a sweet-smelling secretion taken from the musk gland of a beaver. The bait was placed on a twig above the trap.

After the beaver was trapped and drowned, the skin was removed and dried on a willow-hoop. The fur pelt of a full grown beaver weighed up to two pounds.

The cured pelts were packed in bundles by means of a crude press. The bundles were tied with green buckskin thongs. These thongs shrank while drying. They held the bundle like an iron band.

The mountain man was daring, carefree, and independent. He loved adventure. To survive in the wilderness the mountain man adopted Indian ways. He stood, walked, rode, and wore his hair like the Indians. Sometimes he took an Indian woman for his wife.

His clothes were a mixture. Indian things, such as buckskin, were added to the white man's way of dressing.

The favorite weapon of the mountain man was his long-barreled rifle. He carried a powder horn, flints, a bullet pouch, and a hickory ramrod.

His equipment included a short-handled axe or tomahawk, a sharp skinning knife, blankets, cooking gear, and traps.

The beaver pelt was used to make felt for men's hats.

Beavers built dams creating ponds in which they built their lodges.

Mountain man with his ponies.

The trapper carried store-bought flour, salt, tea, and coffee. He lived off the country, however, for most of his food.

Two towns in New Mexico—Taos and Santa Fe—were headquarters for trappers. They could get supplies in these towns. Missouri traders were there to buy furs. The main trade route to the East was the Santa Fe Trail. It ran from Santa Fe to Independence, Missouri.

JAMES OHIO PATTIE

Few of the mountain men kept a diary. James Ohio Pattie did the next best thing. He wrote a book about his experiences. His *Personal Narrative* was one of the first books dealing with the Southwest.

Pattie was only twenty when he came to Santa Fe in 1824. He was with his father, Sylvester, and a caravan of traders and trappers.

While in Santa Fe, the younger Pattie had an exciting experience. He helped a Mexican force rescue Jacova, the beautiful daughter of a former governor of New Mexico. Jacova was a captive of some Comanche Indians. For his part in the rescue, James won both the love of Jacova and a Mexican trapping license.

The Patties joined a party of trappers. These men were the first known Americans to enter Arizona. In 1825 the trappers went west along the Gila River. They went as far as the mouth of the Salt River near present-day Phoenix.

On the way back the party trapped a lot of beaver along the San Pedro River. But the Indians crept into their camp at night and drove away the horses. The trappers hid their furs and went back to New Mexico to get pack horses. When the men returned to the San Pedro, their furs were gone.

Sylvester Pattie got a job in the mines near present-day Silver City, New Mexico. But James was restless. He joined a party of French trappers going to Arizona.

Near the fork of the Gila and Salt rivers, the trappers were attacked by Indians. Only Pattie and two others survived. These three

Mountain man.

men were lucky in a second way too. Another party of 30 trappers led by Ewing Young came by.

Pattie trapped with the Young party along the big rivers of Arizona. After trapping along the Colorado River, they had enough pelts. They headed for Santa Fe across northern Arizona.

The men nearly starved. They were so hungry they ate their dogs. To make matters worse, the Mexican governor seized their furs in Santa Fe. He said the Americans were trapping without a license.

Pattie and his father were in Arizona for the last time in 1827. When Indians stole their horses, the Patties and six other men hollowed out cottonwood logs to make boats. They floated down the Colorado River and hid their furs near the Gulf of California. They then hiked across the desert to San Diego.

The whole party was put in a Mexican jail. Sylvester died in jail. James got the other trappers released as a reward for his services as a doctor. The Mexican governor sent him around California to vaccinate people against smallpox.

In 1830 the governor gave Pattie a passport to the United States. He returned to Kentucky.

"OLD BILL" WILLIAMS

William Shirley ("Old Bill") Williams has a mountain, a stream, and a town in Arizona named after him. He was one of the best-known mountain men.

Williams began his adult life as a Methodist missionary. He worked among Indians and liked them. He married an Osage Indian girl who bore him two daughters. After the death of his wife, he turned to hunting and trapping.

He first came into Arizona in 1826. He was with a group of trappers. In the next few years "Old Bill" wandered over most of Arizona. He liked to go alone.

He was a good trapper. Williams would

show up at Taos with a big bundle of furs. He gambled and drank away his profits. Then he would go again into the wilderness.

What manner of man was "Old Bill?" He was six-feet and one-inch tall. He was lean but tough. He had red hair. His weather-beaten face had been marked by smallpox.

His walk was strange. He staggered like a drunk but never seemed to get tired. He could run along streams all day with five-pound beaver traps on his back.

Williams was a good rider, but looked like a hunchback on his horse. He used short Mexican stirrups which made him lean forward. His buckskin pants were worn so that his legs were bare below the knees.

Williams was a good shot with the rifle. But he was not able to hold the rifle steady to aim it. He squeezed the trigger just as his rifle swept across the target.

In some ways Williams was like an Indian. He did not think it was necessary to cook meat. He believed that dreams could tell the future. Williams said that when he died his soul would come back in the form a buck elk.

PAULINE WEAVER

Another "lone wolf" mountain man was Pauline Weaver. He came to Arizona in about 1830.

Weaver was born in Tennessee. His mother was a Cherokee Indian. He was named Paulino. His name later was changed to Pauline. The spelling did not matter. Weaver never learned to read and write.

Weaver trapped up north until he got tired of the cold winters. Once in Arizona he found plenty of beaver. He stayed even though desert beaver furs were not always of good quality.

Like "Old Bill" Williams, Weaver trapped alone. In time he learned the geography of Arizona. With this knowledge he was able to work as a guide and scout for soldiers, explorers, and prospectors. Weaver was also able to work out treaties with Indian groups.

Drawing of Pauline Weaver.

Though not a miner, Weaver discovered gold placers along the Colorado and Gila rivers. He also guided a party of gold seekers to a mining area known as the Weaver District. In this area, south of present-day Prescott, the richest placer gold deposit ever found in Arizona was discovered.

In his older years Weaver was a scout for the army. When assigned to Camp Lincoln, he refused to live at the fort. His tent was pitched among the willows on the river bottom. That is where he died in 1867.

His body was buried at Fort Whipple. It was later moved to the presidio cemetery in San Francisco. But in 1919 the body was brought back to Prescott. Sharlot Hall, a pioneer historian, collected pennies from Arizona school children to pay the cost. Today a large granite rock marks the grave. It is in front of the old Governor's Mansion at Prescott.

Pauline Weaver's grave marker in Prescott.

Kit Carson.

KIT CARSON

Christopher "Kit" Carson was the most famous mountain man.

Carson was born in Missouri. At age 16 he became an apprentice in a saddle and harness shop. After a year he ran away. He wanted a more exciting life in the Far West.

While Kit was on his way to Santa Fe, his boss ran an insulting ad in the newspaper. A reward of one cent was offered for his return. This was to show that Carson was worthless. During the next forty years, however, Kit Carson became the most admired trapper, guide, and scout in America.

After he got to Santa Fe, the young Carson worked for three years at any job he could get. In his spare time he became an expert rifleman. He learned enough Spanish to serve as an interpreter.

In 1829 Carson joined a group of 40 trappers led by Ewing Young. He trapped the streams of Arizona and northern California. When the trappers got back to New Mexico, they had ten thousand pounds of beaver pelts.

Carson is more famous as a guide than a mountain man. He guided General Kearny across Arizona during the Mexican War. His greatest fame came as a guide for some exploring expeditions in the West led by John C. Frémont.

Carson and the other mountain men were pathfinders. In their search for beaver, the trappers were the first Americans in this region.

Words and Terms to Know

mountain man	placer
pelt	apprentice
ramrod	interpreter
caravan	pathfinder
vaccination	

Match the words above with the following definitions:

1. The skin of an animal with the fur left on.
2. Another name for a beaver trapper who lived in the wilderness.
3. A person skilled in locating a way through unknown regions.
4. A group of traders traveling together for safety.
5. A straight, slim piece of wood or metal used to pack the powder and bullet in a muzzle-loading gun.
6. A deposit of sand or gravel containing particles of gold that can be washed out.
7. A beginner who is bound to a master worker for a fixed period of time to learn a trade.
8. One who translates from one language to another.
9. The process of preventing a disease, such as smallpox, by putting a mild form of the disease into the body.

Finding the Facts:

1. The _____ _____ were the first people from the United States to touch Arizona soil.
2. The beaver fur was made into felt for _____.
3. In many ways the mountain man was like an _____.
4. Beaver pelts were taken to market in the East over the _____ _____ _____.
5. One of the first books about the Southwest was the _____ _____ by James Ohio Pattie.
6. After the Patties lost their horses, they floated their furs down the Colorado River in boats made from _____ _____.
7. _____ is a town with the name of a mountain man who also has a mountain and a stream named after him.
8. _____ _____ used his knowledge of Arizona geography to guide prospectors and soldiers.
9. The _____ District near Prescott is a mining area that is named after a mountain man.
10. _____ _____ was the most famous mountain man.

12. MINING

Gold miners rushed to the new diggings.

Arizona is a mining state. It is rich in minerals. The mining industry pays a big share of state and local taxes. Many people work in the mines. Others have jobs in smelters. Hundreds of businesses depend on income from the mines. They sell goods or services to the mine companies and to the miners.

The history of Arizona mining by Americans begins in the 1850s.

TUBAC SILVER MINING

The first mining boom in Arizona during the American period was in the Tubac region. Silver mines were developed there by eastern companies. The biggest was the Sonora Exploring and Mining Company.

This company was formed in Ohio. The president was Major Sam Heintzelman. The manager was Charles Poston with the title of "colonel." These men met in 1854. Heintzelman was then commander at Fort Yuma. Poston came by the fort with silver ore from the Tubac region.

Poston used the old Tubac fort for the mining company headquarters. Mexicans came there in great numbers. Some were skilled miners. Others came to farm along the

Tubac in 1864.

A *boleta* worth 50¢ in Tubac.

Charles Poston.

Santa Cruz River. By 1860 a thousand people were living near Tubac.

The Sonora company did well. The richest silver came from the Heintzelman mine west of Tubac. The silver ore was smelted. It was then sent to Guaymas, Mexico to be shipped to San Francisco.

Santiago Hubbell, a New Mexico trader, brought the first mine machinery into Arizona. He delivered it to Tubac in 1857. His huge wagons were pulled by twelve-mule teams. On the way back Hubbell hauled silver ore in rawhide bags to Kansas City.

Poston acted as the government in Tubac. Like a justice of the peace, he married young couples. A Mexican peso was used as a seal to stamp their marriage certificate.

There were not enough coins to pay wages and do business in Tubac. Poston solved this money exchange problem. He had pasteboard bills, known as *boletas,* printed in New York. The miners were paid in these *boletas.* Not many of the people could read.

Headquarters and smelter of Mowry's silver-lead mine.

But the bills had pictures. A pig was one bit, or 12½ cents. A calf was worth two bits, or 25 cents. A rooster was 50 cents and a horse one dollar. A bull was five dollars and a lion ten dollars.

Arizona's first newspaper, the *Weekly Arizonian,* was published in Tubac. The first issue was dated March 3, 1859. The *Arizonian* was full of ads for Eastern goods. It had stories about mining and Indian raids.

Sylvester Mowry first came to Arizona as an army officer at Fort Yuma. He later developed the Patagonia mine in southern Arizona. For several years before the Civil War, he worked hard to get Arizona created as a territory. But Congress refused to do this until 1863.

The Civil War (1861 to 1865) ended the Tubac silver boom. Soldiers who were stationed in Arizona were needed elsewhere. They were ordered to leave Fort Buchanan and other posts in Arizona. With the soldiers gone, the Apaches went on the warpath. The miners had to leave. Tubac became a ghost town.

GILA CITY GOLD RUSH

Gila City was Arizona's first wild and wicked gold rush town. In 1858 gold was discovered about twenty miles up the Gila River from Arizona City. That is what Yuma was called then.

Within a year, about a thousand people rushed in to pan gold near the stream. Gila City was the center of activity. It was a village of tents and brush shanties.

Merchants rushed to Gila City to open general stores, saloons, and pool halls. Food prices were high. Flour, for example, sold for a dollar a pound. Beans were fifty cents a pound—a very high price in the 1850s.

Gamblers came with cards and other games. It is said that Gila City had everything but a church and a jail.

The boom was soon over, but not before two million dollars worth of gold was panned.

OTHER EARLY GOLD DISCOVERIES

La Paz gold rush. The danger of Indian attack during the Civil War did not stop prospecting in Arizona.

In 1862 Pauline Weaver and others found gold placers along the Colorado River north of Yuma. People flocked to the spot. A new town, named La Paz, was born.

At its height La Paz had 1,500 people. They lived in tents or in quickly-built houses.

The La Paz gold rush boom lasted two years.

Gold was discovered near present-day Prescott. On Rich Mountain, for example, prospectors were able to dig out surface gold using only knives.

Panning gold. This is the simplest method of separating gold from sand.

Henry Wickenburg, who discovered the Vulture Mine.

A Wells Fargo guard protects a pile of gold ingots from the smelter at Wickenburg.

TOMBSTONE SILVER BOOM

Many rich silver mines were opened in Arizona during the 1870s. The most famous silver strike was at Tombstone. Ed Schieffelin found a rich vein there in 1877. With help from his brother and a mining engineer, he located the Lucky Cuss and Toughnut mines.

Within two years one of the maddest mining rushes in American history was underway. In 1880 the Schieffelin brothers sold out for $600,000. By that time Tombstone was booming. The mines in the region were producing $5 million worth of silver a year.

Most of the Tombstone mines were abandoned after 1888. Underground flooding was the cause. Pumps used in those days could not get the water out of the mines.

COPPER MINES

Copper was first mined in Arizona near present-day Ajo. As early as 1855, copper ore was hauled from Ajo mines to the Gulf of California. It was then shipped to Wales in Great Britain for smelting.

Lack of good transportation held back the copper industry. In the 1870s copper was mined in the Clifton-Morenci area. But transportation was a problem in the rough country of eastern Arizona. The copper ore was hauled in wagons to Kansas City—1,200 miles away.

Wickenburg's Vulture Mine. The richest gold deposit was discovered by Henry Wickenburg in 1863. Ore from his Vulture mine was hauled by wagon to the Hassayampa River for processing.

The town of Wickenburg grew up along the river. The population of 200 included about 80 miners who worked for Wickenburg.

The discovery of gold during the Civil War impressed Congress. Gold mining was one reason why Congress created Arizona as a territory in 1863.

Boys hauling water to the Congress gold mine in the early 1900s.

This picture of Tombstone was taken in 1882, a year after the famous gun battle between the Earps and the Clantons.

The railroad made copper mining easier. Morenci, Arizona.

The first railroad engine in Arizona. Its name was changed later from "Coranada" to "Little Emma."

The transportation problem was partly solved by the Lesinsky brothers, Henry and Charles. They built a smelter at Clifton.

The Lesinskys also built a railroad. It was the first in Arizona. The track ran from Clifton to the Longfellow mine. Mules pulled empty cars about five miles uphill to the mine. The mules rode down on top of the ore. The Lesinskys later used small locomotives. The most famous was the "Little Emma."

There was little profit in copper mining before the railroads connected Arizona to the rest of the country. This was in the 1880s. Inventions, of course, gave the copper industry its biggest boost. A big demand for copper was created by the electric motor, the telephone, and the light bulb.

The Arizona Copper Company's smelter, roundhouse, and shops in Clifton in 1912.

Bonanza copper mines. From 1880 until about 1910 the copper mines in Arizona were "bonanzas." They were high-grade with a lot of copper in the rock.

The Clifton-Morenci mines were bonanzas. Others were the Copper Queen at Bisbee, the Old Dominion at Globe, and the United Verde at Jerome.

The bonanzas were mined underground. The miners followed copper veins through waste rock to rich masses of ore. This kind of mining was profitable as long as the ore was rich and copper prices high.

Some of the most famous people in Arizona history were mine builders in the bonanza days. Dr. James Douglas is a good example. He was one of the geologists who found rich copper deposits at Bisbee. The city of Douglas was named after him. A smelter was built there.

Mules were used to pull ore wagons in this underground copper mine at Bisbee.

Arizona begins to process its own copper. Copper ore contains materials other than copper. The copper needs to be separated out of the ore. Copper ore is brought to the smelter. There it is crushed. Then it is ground into dust as fine as flour. Next the dust is put in flotation tanks. In the tanks copper separates from the dust.

One method of separating copper was discovered by a washerwoman. In washing a miner's greasy clothes she saw that oil and copper stuck together and floated on the water.

Oil was the first of many things used in the flotation process. This process was perfected by Dr. Louis Ricketts. It was first used at the Inspiration mine near Superior in 1915.

The flotation process made it possible to get enough copper out of low-grade ore to make a profit.

In what ways has the copper industry been changing since pioneer days? Most of the copper is now low-grade ore. Most of the mines are open pits. Large-scale methods are used. And it is now against the law for companies to pollute the air. A lot of money is spent to remove pollutants from smoke.

Underground copper miners setting up drills in a drift in the early 1900s.

Open pit copper mine at Morenci. It is the largest copper mine in Arizona.

By the early 1900s most of the rich bonanzas were mined out. Copper companies were forced to mine low-grade ores. The copper in low-grade ore is scattered in a rock mass. There is less copper and more rock.

Open pit strip mining became common. There was no longer a profit in underground mining of low-grade ores. Steam shovels made strip mining possible. They were first used in Arizona at Ajo in 1917. The next year steam shovels were in use at Sacramento Hill near Bisbee.

In the 1920s the big shovels were lifting ore out of the huge open pits into long lines of railroad cars. The trains rolled around great looping spirals of track to the smelters. Today the ore is also hauled in huge trucks.

Words and Terms to Know

boom
smelter
boleta
prospector
ore
bonanza
flotation process
open pit

Match the words above with the following definitions

1. A person who searches for mineral deposits.
2. Rock mass that contains a valuable metal.
3. A rich mine or body of ore.
4. A type of mine where ore is removed from the top rather than underground.
5. A place where pure metal is separated from ore.
6. A method of putting ground copper ore in a solution in which the copper floats and can be separated.
7. A time of rapid growth and prosperity.
8. A pay voucher that had the value of money in Tubac.

Finding the Facts

1. From 1850 to 1863 Arizona was part of the Territory of _____.
2. Arizona's first mining boom during the American period was in the _____ area.
3. The first newspaper in Arizona was the _____.
4. _____ was Arizona's first wild and wicked gold rush town.
5. The Vulture mine was discovered by _____.
6. _____ was the most famous silver boom town in Arizona.
7. The copper industry became profitable after main line _____ were built and copper-using _____ were made.
8. Dr. _____ was a geologist who helped locate rich copper mines in the Bisbee area.
9. Copper can be separated from ground ore in _____ tanks.
10. Most copper mining today is _____ instead of underground.

13. RANCHING

Cattle were herded into Arizona to supply the army posts and Indian reservations.

CATTLE INDUSTRY

There was little ranching in Arizona during the 1850s. Most of the cattle were just passing through. Large herds of Texas longhorns were driven across Arizona to California.

The first American rancher from the States was Bill Kirkland. In 1857 he brought 200 Mexican cattle to the old Canoa Ranch south of Tucson. A few more men soon started small ranches.

The Civil War almost brought ranching to an end. Pete Kitchen was one of the few ranchers not driven away by Apaches. His ranch was north of present-day Nogales.

Why did hundreds of cattle ranchers come to Arizona in the 1870s and 1880s? They were attracted by the grass-filled open spaces and mild climate. One of the most successful pioneer ranchers was Henry Hooker. He drove in large herds of Texas longhorns to sell beef to U.S. Army posts and Indian reservations.

Henry C. Hooker.

113

Vail brands as advertised in the *Arizona Livestock Journal.*

Hooker found a good place for a ranch in the Sulphur Springs Valley in southeastern Arizona. He called it the Sierra Bonita Ranch. In a few years Hooker controlled 800 square miles of public grazing lands.

Success in ranching depended on a water supply. Ranchers, like Hooker, who owned land with streams or springs were lucky. With water they could control the unfenced range. They did not own the land or grass on the public range, but they would only let their own cattle drink the water. Other peoples' cattle could not use the range because they would die of thirst. So people who owned land with water ended up controlling much more land than they actually owned.

There were many big ranches in southern Arizona. One of the most famous was the Empire Ranch near Sonoita. This ranch was started in 1876 by Walter Vail and a partner. The Empire's brand was a heart.

By the end of the 1870s stock raising was one of Arizona's leading industries.

Overstocking the grasslands. Too many cattle were turned loose on the ranges. Before the herds came, Arizona's valleys were covered with grasses. Some grass grew as high as a horse's belly. The grass allowed rains to soak slowly into the ground.

But overgrazing by cattle upset nature's balance. By the 1880s the grasslands were being destroyed. Soil that was once held in place by grass roots began to wash away. Rapid run-off of water eroded the ranges. Instead of a lush carpet of grass, there were now gullies and plants such as mesquite and greasewood.

Ranching methods had to be changed. Cattlemen got rid of their scrub cattle which ate grass but produced little beef. Purebred cattle, like the white-faced Herefords, were put on the ranges.

Breeding good cattle became an important part of ranching. Most of the older animals were sold. Only a breeding herd of cows and a few bulls were kept. The calves were raised and sold as yearlings. These young cows were fattened in feedlots, not on the ranges.

Cattle feeding. In 1888 Henry Hooker and other ranchers began fattening cattle on alfalfa. Thousands of steers were driven to alfalfa fields near Phoenix. By the 1890s, grains and cottonseed products were used in the feeding pens.

Cattle industry in northern Arizona. The A-One was the largest ranch near Flagstaff. It belonged to the Arizona Cattle Company. One of the founders of this company was John W. Young. He was the son of the Mormon leader Brigham Young.

Hashknife cowboys.

Cattle on pasture in the Salt River Valley. Today most cattle are fattened in feedlots.

Holbrook was another center of ranching. Many ranches were started there after the Atlantic and Pacific (Santa Fe) Railroad was built in the 1880s. The largest was the Aztec Land and Cattle Company. It was better known for its brand—the hashknife.

The Hashknife Ranch stretched along the railroad from Holbrook almost to Flagstaff. At one time the Hashknife had 60,000 head of cattle. The large number of cattle made rustling a problem.

Why was branding needed in Arizona? Ranchers ran their cattle on public lands. Cattlemen who used the same range worked together at roundup time. Each calf was branded like the mother cow. When disputes arose, the brand was the only proof of ownership.

Starting in 1887 all ranchers had to register their brands at the county courthouse. Each brand was burned on a piece of

Roundup in southern Arizona, 1906.

tanned leather. Ten years later a brand book for the whole Territory of Arizona was started.

At one time there were over 17,000 brands listed. With so many brands in the book, it was hard to make up new brands.

The brand language uses shapes like box,

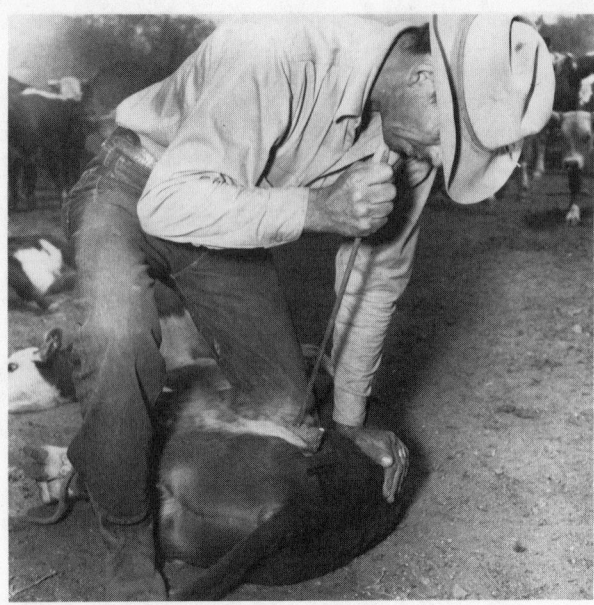

Branding.

How to Read a Brand.

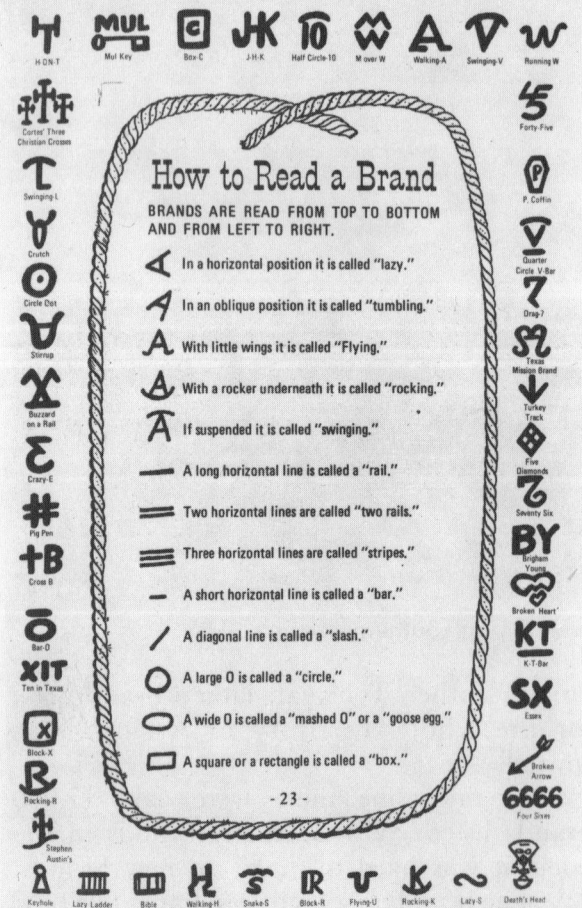

circle, diamond, bar, triangle, or cross. There are rules for reading brands. If a brand has one figure above another, read the top one first. If two figures are side by side, read them from left to right. If one figure is inside another, read the outside figure first.

When a letter is written instead of printed, it is said to be "running." A letter that is slanting or tipping over is said to be "tumbling." If the letter is lying down, it is "lazy."

There are many character or picture brands. The hearts are still popular. Others are the rocking chair, umbrella, tepee, half-moon, coffee pot, anvil, violin, and many Mexican designs.

Some brands are chosen because of where the ranch is. The pair of dice brand, for example, is used in Paradise Valley. Initials are common. One rancher used the ICU brand. Some cowpoke with a sense of humor caught one of the ICU calves. He added a number to make the brand read ICU2.

There is a trick to branding. The iron has to be right. If it is too narrow and sharp, it cuts and goes in too deep. A wide brand holds the heat better. Some cattlemen use a "running iron" and draw the brand on a calf. When the branding iron is cherry red, it doesn't have to be held against the calf very long. With a little salve spread over the brand, the burn heals in a week or so.

The cowboy, fact and fiction. Very little of the cowboy's work was romantic. His life was lonely. He worked long hours and often seven days a week. He dug holes for fence posts and repaired fences. He cleaned corrals, cared for sick stock, shoed horses, fixed windmills, and hauled salt. He even milked cows. Branding was a hot, dirty job. Most of the early day cowboys were drifters. They had little learning. Their pay was low.

But the American image of the cowboy is quite different. It was the cowboy—not his rancher boss—who became a folk hero. Western magazines and movies showed the cowboy as a slim, young, outdoor man of action. He

Cowboys at Holbrook, 1887.

was free as a bird, big-hearted, and happy-go-lucky. By his code, life was a struggle between good and evil. Though shy with strangers, he would fight to protect the weak. The cowboy is looked upon as an "all-American" hero.

SHEEP INDUSTRY

The Navajo and Hopi Indians had sheep in the 1850s. They learned to raise sheep from the Spaniards.

About the only other sheep in Arizona at that time were passing through on their way to California. Thousands were driven from Mexico and the Rio Grande Valley in New Mexico.

Juan Candelaria was the first sheep rancher in Arizona during the American period. In the 1860s he started a ranch near present-day Concho in Apache County. Candelaria and his brothers raised fine Spanish Merino sheep.

Northern Arizona saw the biggest growth in the sheep industry. Many sheep were driven into Arizona from California in the 1870s. A drought was the reason. The California sheep carried alfilaria seed in their wool. The "filaree," as it is called, started growing in Arizona. Today it is a valuable plant on the sheep ranges.

During the 1870s and 1880s sheep were raised mainly for wool. Getting the wool to market was a problem before railroads were built in Arizona. Some wool was hauled by steamboat down the Colorado River.

Flagstaff became the center of the sheep industry. In 1875 John Clark brought 3,000 head from California. The Daggs brothers

Sheep on the Navajo Reservation.

were big operators. At one time they owned 50,000 head near Flagstaff. Their purebred Merinos won many blue ribbons at fairs.

The Babbitt brothers also ran a lot of sheep. They had lands from the Grand Canyon to Springerville. There was a joke about the number of Babbitt sheep. It was said that the sound coming from thousands of northern Arizona sheep was "Baa-ab-itt, Baa-ab-itt."

Sheep drives. In the 1880s sheepmen began a new practice. When frosts hit the mountains, the sheep were driven to winter pastures. The sheep slowly ate their way through the public grazing lands down to the Salt and Gila valleys.

Cattlemen protested. They said the slow moving sheep ate too much grass. The U.S. Forest Service solved the problem. Driveways were marked off through the forests. Sheepmen had to take their sheep over these routes. They had to move at least five miles a day.

Today most sheep are moved to winter pastures by truck or trains to save time.

A sheep bridge over the Salt River.

Ostrich farm near Phoenix.

Basque sheepmen. Many early day sheep ranchers hired Basque herders from Spain. The Basques were used to the lonely job of tending sheep. Today a large number of Arizona sheep ranchers are of Basque descent. They have been active as officers in the Arizona Wool Growers' Association.

OSTRICH INDUSTRY

Ostrich farms were thriving near Phoenix and Yuma in the early 1900s. Ostrich feathers were in demand. They were used in women's hats, scarfs, and feather dusters.

The feathers were plucked every eight months. Each bird yielded up to two pounds a year. The market price for feathers was between $20 and $30 a pound. At those prices ostrich raisers made money. It took only about a fourth of an acre of alfalfa to support a bird.

Some ostrich farmers also made money raising chicks. One company in Tempe sold six-months-old chicks for $100. A pair of four-year-olds were worth at least $800. Ostriches sold for more than cattle and ate less.

On the bigger ostrich farms, eggs were gathered in the pastures by the wagonloads. The eggs were incubated. They also made a delicious food. One ostrich egg was equal to thirty hen eggs. A big joke on ostrich farms was to ask guests at breakfast if they wanted one egg or two.

A flock of ostriches was called a "troop." An ostrich-boy knew how to handle the 300-pound, eight-feet-tall birds. With a shepherd's staff he could hook the neck of an ostrich and bend it down. The bird was then harmless. But the birds were not easy to catch. They took giant strides and ran very fast.

The ostriches could not be moved like cattle. One troop of ostriches took off in all directions when men tried to drive them from Buckeye to Chandler. What should have been a one-day job turned out to be a week-long circus.

The ostrich industry did well in Arizona until World War I started in 1914. Feathers then went out of style. It was not patriotic to spend money on luxuries in wartime.

Farmers in the Salt River Valley were

Ostrich ranch near Tempe in 1900.

stuck with 8,000 ostriches. Many birds were killed and buried in trenches. The last 2,600 were sold at $7 each. They were used for fertilizer in California.

Words and Terms to Know

longhorn
range
public land
overgrazed
yearling
to rustle
alfilaria
purebred
to incubate

Match the words above with the following definitions.

1. A young animal past its first year.
2. A breed of cattle with long horns.
3. A type of animal which has not mixed with another breed for generations.
4. To steal, especially cattle.
5. To hatch an egg by artificial heat.
6. A wild plant of the geranium family that is used as forage for sheep.
7. Land that belongs to all the people in the nation.
8. Land over which cattle or sheep roam and graze.
9. The condition of grassland after too many cattle have been feeding on it.

Finding the Facts

1. _____ _____ drove cattle from Texas to supply beef to Army posts and Indian reservations in Arizona.
2. Arizona's grasslands began to erode after too many _____ were turned loose to graze.
3. Cattle were driven to the _____ area to fatten on alfalfa.
4. The _____ was the brand of the Aztec Land and Cattle Company.
5. A _____ _____ is used to draw a brand on a calf.
6. The folk hero of the cattle industry was the _____, not his rancher boss.
7. The _____ brothers and the _____ brothers were prominent sheepmen in the Flagstaff area.
8. Many of the sheepherders are _____ from Spain.
9. Ostrich _____ were used in women's hats.
10. Arizona's ostrich industry ended with the outbreak of _____ _____ _____.

14. FARMING

An irrigated farm in the Salt River Valley.

Only water is needed to turn Arizona's dry desert valleys into good farmland. The valleys are not sandy wastes like the Sahara Desert. The soil in the valleys is deep and fertile.

The Hohokam Indians were the first people to irrigate crops in Arizona. They dug canals in the Salt and Gila valleys to water their fields.

In later times, the Pima Indians, the Spaniards, and the Mexicans farmed along the Santa Cruz River south of Tucson. Some Pima farmers lived along the Gila River. The Gila Pimas sold food to people who came from the States in the 1840s, 1850s, and 1860s.

The Salt River Valley around Phoenix became a major farming region after the Civil War. Jack Swilling led the digging of the first non-Indian canal in this valley.

Swilling was in the Southern army for awhile during the Civil War. In 1867 he was living in the mining town of Wickenburg. The miners there were paying high prices for food. There was little farming in Arizona then. Most food had to be hauled in by wagon. Swilling wanted to solve these problems.

Town of Phoenix. Swilling started a canal company to bring water to farms in the

Jack Swilling.

Painting of the legendary Phoenix bird by Paul Coze in the Phoenix air terminal.

Salt River Valley. With the help of hard working men from Wickenburg he dug a canal. The canal was called Swilling's Ditch. It was on the north side of the river. By the summer of 1868, some farmers were irrigating crops on the land that is now east Phoenix. Soon other canal companies were digging ditches on both sides of the river.

A village of adobe houses grew up near Swilling's Ditch. The village was named after the Phoenix bird. This legendary bird lived 500 years. The bird then burned itself in a fire and was born again from the ashes. Phoenix was a good name for the town. Why? Because Phoenix farms were located on lands once farmed and deserted by Hohokam Indians.

William Hellings started a flour mill near Swilling's Ditch. Heavy mill machines were bought in San Francisco. They were hauled by boat to Ehrenberg on the Colorado River. The machines were then loaded in big wagons for the trip to Phoenix.

Washington Street, Phoenix, 1872.

Captain Wm. A Hancock, the "Father of Phoenix."

A pioneer Mormon family.

The Hellings flour mill produced tons of good flour each day. The wheat by-products—bran and shorts—were fed to hogs. Soon Hellings had the first meat-packing business in Arizona. He sold hams, bacon, and lard to stores all over the Arizona territory.

Townsite of Phoenix. There were only 240 people in the Salt River Valley in 1870. In that year a new townsite for Phoenix was chosen. It was located where downtown Phoenix is today. The blocks were surveyed and divided into lots by William Hancock. The first lots sold for an average of $40 each. Can you guess what they would be worth today?

Mormon farmers. In 1877 Mormon families settled at Lehi east of Phoenix. The Mormon pioneers came from Utah in wagons. With the help of Pima Indians, they built a canal from the Salt River.

The next year a second group of Mormons settled at Mesa. Very soon Mesa was an orderly farming community. The Mormons laid out farms. They dug the Mesa Canal and built their homes.

The Mormons settled on farms along the Little Colorado River near Joseph City. They started many farming towns in northern and eastern Arizona. Among the Mormon towns were Littlefield, Pine, Heber, Taylor, Snowflake, Springerville, Eager, St. Johns, Pima, Thatcher, and St. David.

Why was Roosevelt Dam built? All the farmers in the Salt River Valley were troubled by an uncertain water supply. The river would flood in the spring after snows melted in the mountains. Then in the summer the water level of the river would drop.

A huge dam was needed to hold water in lakes upstream. Water could then be stored in wet years for use in drier seasons.

There was plenty of water. It just needed to be stored. In 1891, for example, the Salt River flooded. The river was eight miles wide in some places. The Tempe railroad bridge was washed out. People in parts of Phoenix had to leave their flooded homes.

In the 1890s there was a long dry spell. Armed men patrolled canals to protect their water rights. At least a third of the farmland had to be deserted for lack of water. Orchards became firewood. Families moved away. Then the rains came again. Dirt and rock dams were destroyed by a flash flood. The water rushed down the river. It was wasted.

Roosevelt Dam made it possible to control water in the Salt River. A better place for the dam could not have been chosen. It was built between steep canyon walls. The dam rests on a tough sandstone foundation. It is 284 feet high and 170 feet thick at the base.

The dam was dedicated by ex-President Theodore Roosevelt in 1911. People went to this ceremony on horseback, in buggies, on bicycles, and in cars.

Cotton has been a crop in Arizona for a

Horse and buggy crossing the Salt River at Tempe about 1900. There were no dams across the Salt River then to hold back the water.

Train wreck at Tempe. The railroad bridge was weakened by a flood. It collapsed on October 30, 1902.

Roosevelt Dam.

long time. When Columbus sailed to the New World in 1492, the Pima Indians were raising cotton.

The Pimas wove the cotton fiber into cloth. They also ground the cotton seeds with mesquite beans to make flour. Sometimes the Indians dried the seeds and ate them without grinding. Cotton seeds are high in protein.

Cotton was never grown on a large scale, however, until after Arizona became a state in 1912. Arizona farmers learned to grow a cotton with long fibers. It was called "long staple" or "Pima" cotton.

This long staple cotton was much in demand in 1917. In that year the United States entered World War I. Arizona's cotton was needed for cloth used on airplane wings. It was also needed for cotton cord in car tires. The Goodyear Tire and Rubber Company took the lead in planting cotton near Phoenix.

Until the 1920s, horses and mules were used to pull plows on Arizona's cotton farms. The mules were replaced by tractors. By the early 1930s most tractors had rubber tires.

Arizona now has many large cotton farms. But many farmers started on a small scale. Diwan Singh was a good example. Born in India, he came to America in 1906. Singh was a common laborer when he came to Casa Grande.

A citrus orchard in the Salt River Valley.

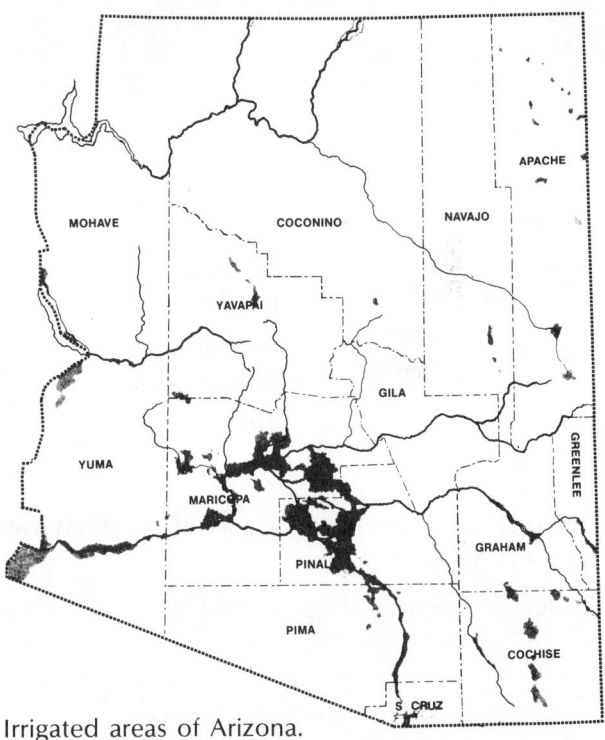
Irrigated areas of Arizona.

Cotton farming near Marana, 1979.

Singh wanted to farm but had no money. The only land he could get had hard alkali soil. With only a horse and a mule, he plowed up 80 acres and planted cotton. Singh did well. By the 1940s he was farming 9,000 acres of land.

125

Other crops. Cotton is Arizona's number one farm crop. But farmers also raise a lot of vegetables, fruit, alfalfa, and grains. By the 1920s large crops of lettuce, cantaloupes, carrots, and citrus fruits were being produced.

The climate is ideal for *lettuce.* It is so important to Arizonans that it is called "green gold." It is grown in the Salt River Valley, Yuma, Willcox, and other places. The winters are mild. Little rain falls to damage the lettuce. There is plenty of irrigation water.

Yuma is the leading *cantaloupe* producing region. Deep orange-colored *carrots* are grown in the Salt River Valley. These carrots are rich in Vitamin A.

Citrus has been grown in Arizona since the 1880s. Navel oranges and grapefruit trees have done well. Valencia oranges are grown in the warmer parts of the state. They were planted to supply the need for fresh oranges during the spring season. Another citrus tree, the Lisbon lemon, does best in the warm Yuma climate.

Farming is one of Arizona's most important industries. It is one of the major sources of Arizona income.

Words and Terms to Know

irrigate   patrol
Phoenix bird   dedication
townsite   alkali
Mormons   citrus

Match the words above with the following definitions:

1. Members of a church who settled on farms in Arizona.
2. To guard an area with an armed person.
3. Place where a town is surveyed.
4. A legendary bird which was reborn from its own ashes.
5. A kind of fruit tree.
6. The ceremony that is held after a new building or dam is finished.
7. A kind of mineral salt found in some desert soils.
8. To supply with water.

Finding the Facts

1. Only _____ is needed to turn Arizona desert valleys into farmland.
2. The _____ Indians were farming along the Gila when the first whites came to Arizona.
3. _____ _____ deserves credit for the first non-Indian canal in the Phoenix area.
4. _____ _____ started a flour mill in what is now east Phoenix.
5. _____ _____ surveyed the townsite of Phoenix.
6. The Mormons settled at _____ and _____ in the Salt River Valley.
7. Roosevelt Dam was finished in _____.
8. Cotton with _____ _____ was in demand during World War I.
9. _____ is "Arizona's green gold."
10. The Yuma area is a leading producer of _____ _____ trees and _____.

15. THE FIRST SCHOOLS

The Casa Grande school in 1896.

There were few schools in Arizona during pioneer days. People were too busy trying to stay alive.

PRIVATE SCHOOLS

The first school in Arizona was the San Xavier mission school near Tucson. It was started by two Mexican Catholic priests from California. In 1864 the first legislature of the territory gave the mission school $250. The money was used to buy books, paper, and furniture.

The first legislature also gave $250 to S. C. Rogers for a private school in Prescott. But there was a catch! Rogers had to raise another $250 from the people of Prescott. He did.

PUBLIC SCHOOLS

The first public school district in Arizona

The first school in Prescott.

was organized in Tucson in 1867. It is still known as Tucson School District 1.

The first Tucson school board rented an old adobe building with a dirt floor. They hired Augustus Brichta as teacher. Brichta, a former New Yorker, was Arizona's first public schoolteacher. He taught 60 Mexican

This replica of Brichta's schoolhouse is at Old Tucson. It is seen by many visitors.

Governor Safford.

John Spring in his Union Army uniform.

Josephine Brawley Hughes, Arizona's first woman public schoolteacher.

boys in 1868. But tax money ran out after six months. The school had to be closed.

Governor Anson P. K. Safford is known as the "father of Arizona public schools." Safford became governor in 1869. At that time there were nearly 2,000 school-age children in Arizona. But there was not one public school.

Governor Safford got the legislature to pass a *public school law* in 1871. Money for schools was to come from taxes on property. When a school started, it had to remain open "for at least three months each year."

The 1871 law listed the subjects to be taught. These were reading, arithmetic, spelling, grammar, geography, and health.

Tucson started the first public school under the new law. It opened in 1872. The teacher was John Spring, a former soldier in the Union Army. Spring's schoolhouse was a one-room adobe building on Meyer Street. The dirt floor had to be sprinkled to hold down the dust. The crude furniture was very rough and splintery.

The students were all boys. They ranged

in age from 6 to 21. Most of them were Mexican-American. The first thing they had to do at the school was learn English. Their parents wanted Mr. Spring to be strict. He was given ash sticks to whip unruly students.

One of the pupils taught by Mr. Spring was Ignacio Bonillas. This boy was the son of a blacksmith. Governor Safford took a personal interest in Ignacio. He gave the boy a part-time job so he could remain in school.

Ignacio later attended college in the East. He then moved to Mexico and did well. At one time he was ambassador from Mexico to Washington, D.C. Ignacio Bonillas never forgot the little adobe school in Tucson. He often praised Governor Safford for his work with schools.

Girls in Tucson could attend St. Joseph's Academy. This was a private school. The teachers were Catholic nuns.

It was 1873 before a free public school for girls was opened. The schoolhouse was an old brewery building. The teacher was Mrs. Josephine Hughes. Her husband was editor of the *Arizona (Daily) Star* newspaper. He was later governor of the territory.

The first graded school. In the earliest schools, all grades were in one room. The first graded school was built in Prescott in 1876. The people in Prescott went into debt (sold bonds) to build a two-story brick schoolhouse. This school was the pride of Prescott.

The Prescott school had several teachers. The students were separated by grade. The principal was Moses Sherman. He came from Governor Safford's home state of Vermont. Sherman later became Arizona's first superintendent of public instruction. Do you know who holds that job today?

What were the early schoolhouses like? Governor Safford made trips in his buggy to nearly every part of Arizona. He tried to get schools started wherever there were children.

Schools were opened in many kinds of places. At least two—Ehrenberg and Tempe—were in old adobe saloons.

The first teacher at Ehrenberg was Mary

The first schoolhouse in Phoenix, built in 1873.

"Little adobe schoolhouse." This school is a replica of Mesa's first school in 1880. This one was built in 1976 by students in Mesa. It is one of the exhibits of the Mesa Museum.

Elizabeth Post. She rode the stagecoach from San Diego to Yuma. Her trip from Yuma to Ehrenberg was on a steamboat.

Miss Post later wrote that old miners would wander into her school, not knowing it was no longer a saloon. But her main problem was to learn Spanish so she could teach English to her Mexican students.

After leaving Ehrenberg, Miss Post taught for nearly 40 years at Yuma. Her first school building was an old adobe courthouse of three rooms. One room had once been a jail.

The first school in Phoenix was also held in a courthouse in 1871. The first teacher, J. R. Darroche, did not have to move far in his next job. He was appointed county recorder.

The first schoolhouse in Phoenix was built of adobe in 1873. It was located on Center (now Central Avenue) in what is now downtown Phoenix.

The first school building in Bisbee was an old miner's shack. It had no doors, no windows, and only a dirt floor. Desks were made by laying boards on packing boxes. The seats were planks placed on old nail kegs.

The first teacher at Bisbee, Clara Stillman, used a flour barrel for her desk. After four weeks in the shack, the teacher and pupils were moved to the Miners' Union Hall. It was located in Brewery Gulch. This was the most famous street in Bisbee.

Arizona's pioneer schools had few books. Most of the desks were too rough to write on. The students often used slates. These slates could be erased and used over and over. Blackboards were made from smooth boards. The boards were nailed together and painted black.

There was usually a water bucket in the room. Everybody drank from the same dipper. A pot-bellied stove was used to keep the room warm on cold days. Toilets were outdoor privies.

UNIVERSITIES AND COLLEGES

Two of Arizona's three public universi-

Training school class at Tempe Normal (now ASU) in the early 1900s.

First building of Tempe Normal School (now Arizona State University).

Old Main, first building at the University of Arizona, under construction.

ties were started in 1885. That was the year of the *13th territorial legislature.* The members of this group met at Prescott, which was then the capital. They spent a lot of money. Something was given to nearly every major town. Most of the projects were good for Arizona.

Tempe wanted and got a teacher's college. It was called the Arizona Territorial Normal School. The name was later changed to Tempe Normal School and then to Arizona State College. Now it is Arizona State University.

Tucson was given the University of Arizona. Some people in Tucson were angry. They wanted either the capital or the insane asylum. Why? Because the legislature voted only $25,000 for the university the first year. The asylum was given $100,000.

The University of Arizona has been very important to Tucson. It sets a high cultural standard. It also brings millions of dollars into the city.

Phoenix was given the asylum. Four years later, in 1889, the capital was moved to Phoenix from Prescott.

Other four-year colleges. A second teacher's college was opened in 1899. It was in Flagstaff. Today this college is named Northern Arizona University. Like the universities in Tempe and Tucson, NAU is funded mainly by state taxes.

The only private four-year college in Arizona is Grand Canyon College. It is run by the Southern Baptist Church.

Community colleges. Arizona has many two-year community colleges. These junior colleges are owned by the public. They are tax-supported.

Words and Terms to Know

private school   normal school
public school   slate
one-room school community college
graded school

Match the words above with the following definitions:

1. A school where students learn to be teachers.
2. A school that is divided into grades with different teachers.
3. A school which has all grades in the same room with one teacher.
4. A school that is supported mainly by taxpayers.
5. A school that is sponsored by a church or a non-public group.
6. A two-year public school that offers education above the high school level.
7. A thin sheet of rock that is used as a tablet for writing on with chalk.

Finding the Facts

1. The first school in Arizona was the _____ _____ _____ _____ near Tucson.
2. The first public school district was organized in _____.
3. _____ _____ was the first public schoolteacher in Arizona.
4. The "father of Arizona public schools" was _____ _____ _____ _____.
5. The first law in Arizona to provide for tax-supported public schools was passed in _____.
6. _____ _____ was a student in John Spring's school.
7. Arizona's first graded school was built in _____ and _____ _____ was the principal.
8. The first schools in Ehrenberg and Tempe were housed in old _____ _____.
9. Arizona's pioneer schools had few _____.
10. Arizona State University and the University of Arizona were founded in 1885 by the _____ _____ _____.

16. TRANSPORTATION

An automobile on Roosevelt Road (now Apache Trail) in 1911.

The burro has long been used for transportation in Arizona.

Transportation means the moving or hauling of people or goods from one place to another.

The first people in Arizona had to travel on foot. They did their hunting on foot. The killed game was carried home on their backs.

The Spaniards brought the horse and other animals that could be used for transportation to Arizona. The little burro and the mule did most of the packing and pulling. Some wagons and carts were used in Spanish times.

ROADS

The Mormon Battalion made the first wagon road across Arizona. These men crossed southern Arizona during the Mexican War. The road which they blazed was not graded. It was little more than a trail. But it was used by many people going to California after the war.

The Leach wagon road was the first road built across southern Arizona. Jesse B. Leach was the contractor. He built the road for the U.S. Department of Interior in 1858.

The Leach road ran from El Paso to Yuma. It did not run through Tucson, the main town. Instead it followed the San Pedro River to the Gila. It went along that river to Yuma.

Lieutenant Edward F. Beale.

The road was 18 feet wide on straight stretches. It was widened to 25 feet on curves. Little work was done on the roadbed. Brush, rocks, and trees were cleared. Water wells and tanks were built along the road. That was it.

The Beale wagon road was the first road across northern Arizona. It was built in 1857. Like most roads in the West in those days, it was built by the Army.

The man in charge was Lieutenant Edward Beale. His work crew smoothed out the wagon road. They also built some bridges. The Beale road was used by many people going to California from the Eastern states.

Beale was given another job—a *camel experiment*. Secretary of War Jefferson Davis wanted to find out all he could about camels. He thought this animal might be used to haul freight and mail in the west.

Beale liked the camels. He said they carried heavy loads. They walked long distances without water. But there was a problem. The strange-smelling camels scared the horses and mules. They would stampede when camels

Beale's camel caravan stops to camp.

came close. So nothing came of the camel experiment.

Hi Jolly, one of the camel drivers, later lived in Arizona. He worked as a scout for the U.S. Army and married a Tucson girl. His grave near Quartzsite is marked with a copper camel on a stone pyramid.

Toll roads. In the 1860s some private toll roads were built in Arizona. One of the most used toll roads ran between Prescott and the Colorado River steamboat landings. The charge was four cents a mile for a wagon. A rider on horseback paid two and a half cents a mile.

Army roads. Some first class wagon roads were built by the U.S. Army in the 1870s. These roads connected the army posts.

Arizona did not have a good highway system, however, until the 20th century. The invention of the automobile made good roads a necessity.

MAIL AND PASSENGER LINES

The San Antonio and San Diego Mail Line began in 1857. It was the first mail and passenger company to serve Arizona.

Mules were used to pull coaches. But coaches were not used in some of the desert country. Passengers had to ride muleback part of the way. In fact, the company was called the "Jackass mail."

The largest station between El Paso and San Diego was at Maricopa Wells. It was south of present-day Phoenix. Maricopa Wells had an adobe station hut and a brush corral. Most of the stations were worse. They were only camping places.

The San Antonio and San Diego Mail Line made forty trips along the full length of the route. It then went out of business.

The Butterfield Overland Mail was the first good stage line to serve Arizona. It ran from the railroad terminal near St. Louis to San Francisco. The route dipped south like an ox yoke. That is why it was called the "Oxbow Route."

The Butterfield line began service in 1858. Stages ran twice weekly each way. The trip one way took 25 days.

Stations were about 20 miles apart. Most of the Arizona stations were built of adobe. A wall gave protection from attacks by Indians or outlaws. Each station had fresh horses or mules. There was a supply of hay and corn on hand. Food for passengers and drivers was provided too. But no one was known to brag about the food or cooking.

Diorama of the first eastbound Butterfield Overland Mail stage in 1858.

An old celerity wagon. This stage once carried passengers and mail between Solomonville and Sheldon.

Tombstone newspaper ad of an Arizona stage line.

Fancy Concord coaches were used mainly on the east and west ends of the Butterfield route. The Concord had an oval-shaped body resting on leather straps. It rolled rather than bounced over bumps.

In desert country the lightweight "Celerity Wagon" was used. It was pulled by mules. The wooden seats could be folded down for beds—that is, when the wagon was not crowded.

John Butterfield's orders to his drivers were simple and direct. He said, "Remember, boys, nothing on God's earth can stop the U.S. Mail." The mail was late only three times on the Butterfield route.

In 1861 the Butterfield line was shifted north through Utah. But for a brief time southern Arizona had stage service. Arizona was a link on the greatest overland stage venture ever undertaken.

ARIZONA STAGECOACH LINES

There was no public transportation in Arizona in 1863. That is the year Congress made Arizona a territory.

By the late 1860s, however, both Prescott and Tucson had stage service to California and to eastern cities.

Hundreds of small stage lines were started in the 1870s and 1880s. They served

A "feeder stage" from San Simon on the Southern Pacific Railroad to Paradise in southeast Arizona. After the hot 28-mile ride, passengers would take a drink of spring water, sit in the shade, and say, "Well, this is Paradise."

the needs of towns and mines in all the territory. Many of the stage drivers came from California. In that state railroads were replacing stages.

The local stagecoach business picked up for awhile when the railroads reached Arizona. This was in the 1880s. Why? The Southern Pacific and Santa Fe railroads carried hundreds of passengers to Arizona. These people rode stages to places not on the railroad.

By the early 1900s, however, the railroads reached out-of-the-way places. The stagecoaches became relics of Arizona's colorful past.

Travel on stagecoaches was slow and hard. Not all the stagecoaches were fancy Concords like the ones on western TV shows. In fact, there were more buggies and buckboards in use.

Passengers usually sat on hard seats. They were crowded together like sardines. There was the bad odor of cigar smoke and unbathed people. The roads were rough and dusty. The average speed was five miles an hour. Stage holdups were common.

Stage stations served poor food. A common menu was jerky or salt pork, stale bread, bad coffee, and beans.

The story is told about one salesman who would not eat the beans at one Arizona stage stop. He demanded better food. But a local man in western clothes put a Colt's revolver in his face and said, "Stranger, eat them beans!" And he did.

WAGON FREIGHTING

Wagon freighting was an important business in territorial days. Before the railroads were built, everything had to be hauled in wagons. It took a long time to get goods from the States.

Albert Steinfeld, a pioneer merchant in Tucson, often spoke about the problem. He said it took two to three months to get goods for his store from San Francisco. Goods from the East were as long as six months in coming.

Freight was hauled in high-sided wagons. The bigger wagons had wheels that were eight feet across. Sometimes 20 to 30 mules were hitched to pull three or four big wagons.

Mules cost more than oxen. But they were faster and needed less water. The smartest pair of mules were put in front. The strongest pair were next to the wagon. They were called the "wheeler" mules.

The driver rode the left wheeler mule. He guided the team with a single rein. This

Freight wagons and teams in Pinal County, 1897.

rein ran to the left lead mule. A steady pull meant "move to the left." A number of jerks on the rein was the mule's signal to move to the right.

The driver had to work the brakes on the wagons. He could do this with a rope. Braking was hard when going down hill with heavy loads. Men were sometimes hired to help the driver. They were called "swampers." Their job was to handle the brakes and do other chores.

Some drivers owned their own rigs. But most of them worked for freighting companies. All major towns had freight depots. There were also blacksmiths to repair wagons. Harness shops and wagon builders did a good business.

Wagon freighting was still a good business after the railroads reached Arizona. Wagons were needed to haul freight from the railroads. Trucks were not used much until the 1920s. Use of trucks and better roads came to Arizona at about the same time.

RAILROADS

One of the biggest events of pioneer days was the arrival of the railroads.

The first railroad in Arizona was at Clifton. During the 1870s it ran uphill five miles to the Longfellow mine.

The first major railroad in Arizona was the Southern Pacific. It reached Yuma from the California coast in 1877. Chinese workers

One of the first engines used on the Southern Pacific through Tucson.

Ore wagons at the Silver King mine.

Blacksmith shop in Phoenix in the 1880s.

The first railroad engine at Yuma, 1877.

137

did much of the hard labor on the S.P. They laid tracks east of Yuma. At Casa Grande, the railroad stopped building for awhile because of hot weather. Many workers were laid off. Some of the Chinese went to Phoenix to live.

In March, 1880, a locomotive finally whistled into Tucson. A spike made from Tombstone silver was driven as a crowd of people looked on.

The Southern Pacific Company then built east across Texas to New Orleans. A lot of stations along the railroad became important towns. Some of these were Casa Grande, Benson, and Willcox.

An important railroad ran across northern Arizona. The Atlantic and Pacific (now the Santa Fe) was built into Arizona from the east. The first train tooted into the new town of Winslow in November, 1881.

The line was delayed west of Winslow. It took six months to build a bridge across Canyon Diablo. This canyon was 225 feet deep and 550 feet across.

A big delay came at the Colorado River. Several bridges were started and washed away

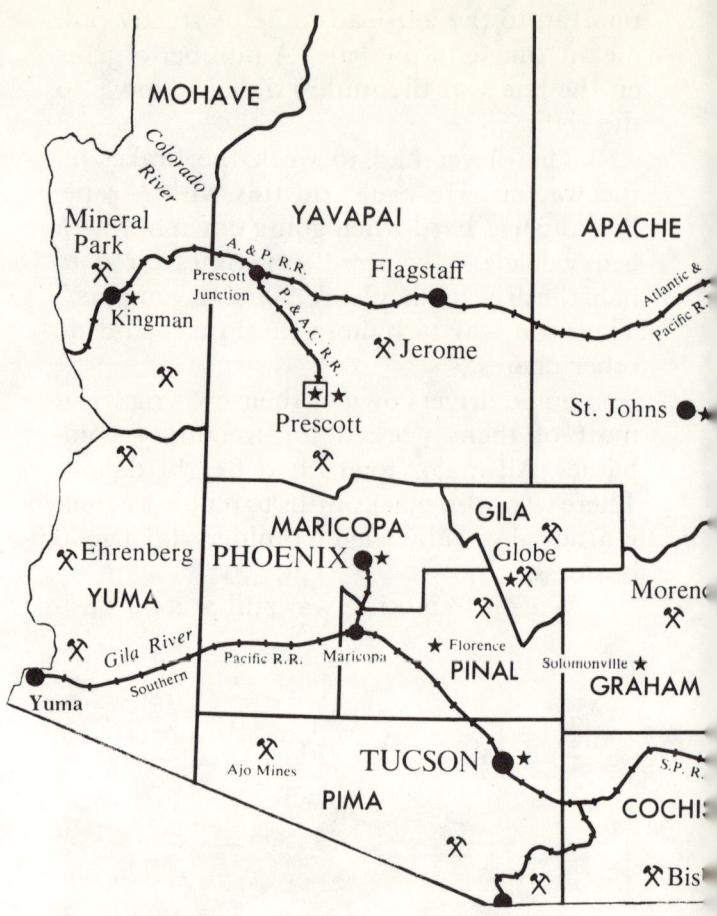

Arizona Railroads in 1887.

In the 1880s the sawmills made wood ties for the railroads. Later logs and lumber were hauled by trains such as this one.

by high water. Finally, a bridge was completed in August, 1883.

The A and P had one big advantage over the S.P. There was more timber in northern Arizona to make railroad ties.

Important towns grew up along the Atlantic and Pacific railroad. Among them were Winslow, Holbrook, Flagstaff, Williams, Ash Fork, Seligman, and Kingman.

Most of these towns had a Harvey House restaurant. Passengers on trains could get a good meal there. The service was good too. Fred Harvey hired young ladies from the East as waitresses. They were called Harvey Girls.

The railroad company carried these girls free to their jobs. The company also built the restaurants and hauled Harvey's food without charge. Why? The Harvey Houses were good for railroad business.

STEAMBOATS ON THE COLORADO

Steamboats in Arizona? Yes, they once hauled freight and passengers on the Colorado River.

The earliest steamboats were hauled on sailing ships to the mouth of the Colorado River. The steamboats were put together after they were unloaded.

The *Uncle Sam* was the first steamboat to navigate the Colorado River. It was a 65-foot sidewheeler. It could carry 32 tons of freight. Starting in 1852, the *Uncle Sam* hauled freight to Fort Yuma from the mouth of the Colorado.

Gradually, bigger and bigger steamboats were used. The *Cocopah* was 140 feet long. It carried 100 tons. The *Mojave* was launched in 1863. It could haul 193 tons.

Steamboat captains on the Colorado faced many problems. The river channel was always changing because of shifting sand. In places the river spread out. Not even the best pilots could see where the real channel was. The boats often were stuck for hours on a sand bar. And south of Yuma there were four foot waves where the gulf tide met the river current.

The steamer Cocopah was launched in 1859. The Southern Pacific Railroad bridge in the background was built at Yuma in 1877.

Then there was the problem of fuel. The steamboat owners depended on Indians to keep piles of wood near the river banks.

Fifteen miles was as far as a steamboat could go upstream in a day. But land travel along the Colorado River was even slower. After Fort Mohave was built in 1859, it was supplied by steamboat. It took a week and a half for a steamer to get to Mohave from Fort Yuma.

The steamboats became less important after the railroads reached Arizona. The boats could not compete with the faster and cheaper "iron horse." Today it would not be possible to take a steamboat up the Colorado. Bridges and a half dozen dams are in the way.

AUTOMOBILE

First autos. The first "horseless carriage" in Arizona was a steam Locomobile. Dr. Hiram Fenner had it shipped by rail to Tucson in 1899.

The earliest autos were little more than costly toys. It took time for eastern auto

Prescott families go for a ride.

Highway in Oak Creek Canyon in 1931.

makers to produce cars that were more dependable and cheaper. By 1912, however, there were 1,852 cars in Arizona.

The first "gas buggies" were sold as a sideline by bicycle stores and wagon makers. Drugstores sold gas and oil. Stables were changed to garages. Blacksmiths learned how to fix broken auto parts.

Better roads were needed. Once cars became popular, bad roads were a problem. The old wagon routes were not built for autos.

Towns began to make better roads. To bring attention to the need for good roads, Phoenix businessmen held car races. In 1911 an annual race between Los Angeles and Phoenix was started. A driver named Harvey Herrick won the race. His time was 20 hours and 23 minutes.

Maricopa County set a good example. More than 300 miles of concrete farm-to-market roads were built in the 1920s. The roads were only 16 feet wide.

The Arizona highway system got a slow start. The only paved roads in the 1920s were near the big towns.

Motoring in Arizona was not always pleasant in the early days. The roads were bad. The high pressure tires were easily punctured. Engines had little power.

A driver going very far was advised to carry a tool box. It was wise to have a couple of spare tires, a tow rope, wheel-cup grease, an oil can, and a tire repair kit. Most of the cars were open with only a canvas top.

AVIATION

The first airplane flight in Arizona was in Phoenix on February 12, 1910. Charles Hamilton, known as the "Man-bird pilot," was the pilot. He flew a bamboo and silk

This Dodge car was hauled across the Gila River at Florence in 1920. High water washed out an approach to the bridge.

flying machine at the state fairgrounds. He beat a Studebaker car in a five-mile race. But he lost a race to the car the next day.

Hamilton was a barnstormer. He went from town to town to thrill crowds. From Phoenix, Hamilton shipped his plane by train to Tucson. There he reached an altitude of 900 feet and a speed of 40 miles an hour. He had to land the plane in a small field surrounded by a board fence.

A woman daredevil flyer. In 1915 a 19-year-old woman pilot thrilled Tucson fair crowds. She did loop-the-loops and a death-dip. This was a steep dive toward the crowd. Katherine Stinson also flew a sack of "air mail" from the fairgrounds. She dropped it at a downtown post office. Though just a stunt, this was the first "official" air mail flight in Arizona.

Tucson built the nation's first city airport in 1919. It was near the Nogales highway south of town. In 1927 a new airport was opened. It was named Davis-Monthan and was dedicated by Charles Lindbergh. He was greeted at the airport by 12,000 people. Only four months earlier Lindbergh became the first pilot to solo across the Atlantic.

Commercial air service began in Ari-

Charles Hamilton at Tucson, 1910.

zona in 1927. The Aero Corporation flew planes between Los Angeles and Tucson with a stop in Phoenix. Fokker monoplanes were used. The flight took 7 hours and 10 minutes. How long would it take in today's jet planes?

There were other pioneer airlines in Arizona. One of the most interesting was Scenic Airways. During 1928 this airline carried more than 5,000 passengers to view the Grand Canyon. Ford tri-motor planes were used. These planes were called "the gooses."

Scenic Airways also built an airport in Phoenix. The city of Phoenix took it over in 1935. Today this airport is called Sky Harbor.

The first transcontinental air mail service through Arizona was in 1930. Winslow

Charles Lindbergh at Tucson in 1927.

was a stop on the TWA northern route. Phoenix, Tucson, and Douglas were on a southern route. Each town celebrated the arrival of the first plane. In Phoenix the postmaster took 15,000 air mail letters to the plane at Sky Harbor. He rode in an old horse-drawn stagecoach.

From stagecoach to airplane—Arizona's transportation had come a long way!

Words and Terms to Know

transportation
contractor
terminal
buckboard
blacksmith
locomotive
sandbar
"horseless carriage"
"gas buggy"
barnstormer
commercial

Match the words above with the following definitions:

1. The moving or hauling of people or goods from one place to another.
2. The end, such as the last station on a stage or railroad line.
3. A man who repairs or shapes iron with a forge, anvil, and hammer.
4. A ridge of sand formed in a river by the action of currents.
5. An engine that can move by its own power.
6. A person who agrees to do certain work for a stated amount of money.
7. A person who tours the country to entertain the public.
8. Made or done primarily for sale or profit.
9. A carriage with a seat that sits on long boards which rest directly on the axles.
10. Two nicknames for the early automobiles.

Finding the Facts

1. The ___ ___ ___ was the first road built across southern Arizona.
2. The ___ ___ ___ was the first road built across northern Arizona.
3. ___ ___ was a camel driver.
4. A person had to pay to travel on a ___ road.
5. Passengers sometimes had to ride ___ on the San Antonio and San Diego Mail Line.
6. The ___ ___ ___ was the first dependable stage line in Arizona.
7. The driver of a long freight team usually rode on the ___ ___ ___.
8. The first major railroad in Arizona was the ___ ___.
9. Northern Arizona lumber mills made railroad ties for the ___ ___ ___ Railroad.
10. The ___ ___ was the first steamboat to navigate the Colorado River.
11. The only ___ roads in Arizona in the 1920s were near the bigger towns.
12. Arizona's first transcontinental air mail service came to Arizona in the year ___.

17. COMMUNICATION

A Phoenix telephone installer in the early 1900s. He carried phones over his shoulders and tools around his waist.

Communication is important to us. What is it? It is the giving and receiving of information between people. A conversation is a form of communication. The telephone lets us talk to people far away.

A letter is one way to communicate. In the old days, bags of mail were hauled by coaches, wagons, or on horses. Now mail is carried by airplanes, trains, and trucks. The mailman brings mail to homes or stores.

Communication also has to do with reporting news. The radio, TV, and newspapers bring us news from around the world.

How did the early Indians in Arizona communicate? Indians who knew the same language could talk to each other. If the Indians did not understand each other, they used sign language. The hands, face, arms, or legs were used to express thoughts.

The Indians also had ways to communi-

143

cate over long distances. They sent smoke signals into the air. These signals could be seen for miles. Indian runners carried messages from place to place.

NEWSPAPERS

Most pioneer towns in Arizona had newspapers. In fact, there were many good ones.

The first newspaper in Arizona was printed at Tubac. This paper was the *Weekly Arizonian*. It was a neat little four-page, four-column newspaper. The first issue was dated March 3, 1859.

The *Weekly Arizonian* was a small history of frontier Arizona. In the news columns were stories about mines, cattle rustling, horse stealing, Apache raids, and local gossip.

One issue had a story about a soldier at nearby Fort Buchanan. He was found guilty by the Army of stealing a horse and deserting. His punishment was severe. He was given fifty lashes with a whip on his bare back. The soldier's head was then shaven. The letter "D" was branded on his head with a red-hot iron.

Edward Cross, the editor of the *Weekly Arizonian,* fought a bloodless duel with Sylvester Mowry. Cross did not think the region was ready to be organized as the Territory of Arizona. Mowry was for it. After bitter arguments, the duel took place on July 8, 1859. The weapons were Burnside rifles at forty paces. Luckily, it was a windy day. Neither man hit his mark.

Mowry later bought the *Arizonian.* He moved the printing press to Tucson.

Other newspapers. The U.S. Congress created the Territory of Arizona in 1863. The next year the first territorial officers came to Fort Whipple. In one of the wagons there was a printing press.

Secretary Richard C. McCormick began publishing the *Arizona Miner* at Fort Whipple in March, 1864. The press was soon moved to the new town of Prescott. A June issue of the *Miner* told about the "Governor's Mansion" that was to be built in Prescott. Today

Richard C. McCormick.

this log building is part of the Sharlot Hall Museum.

In 1867 Arizona's "capital on wheels" was moved to Tucson. By that time McCormick was governor. He financed another newspaper on the side. His Tucson paper was called the *Arizona Citizen.* It was started in 1870. McCormick was a good politician. By owning a newspaper he always got good publicity.

Today the *Citizen* is Tucson's evening newspaper.

Arizona's first daily newspaper was the *Bulletin* in Tucson. It was a daily, however, for only four weeks in 1877. It then became the tri-weekly *Star.*

What was unusual about the *Bulletin* and the *Star*? The paper had a news service. News came over a desert telegraph line from San Diego. Today the *Star* is Tucson's morning newspaper. It is now called the *Arizona Daily Star.*

Press used by the *Salt River Herald* after 1878.

Wyatt Earp.

Phoenix's first newspaper was the *Salt River Herald*. It began in 1878. The name was soon changed to *Phoenix Herald*. In 1899 the *Herald* became part of the newspaper that is now named *The Arizona Republic*.

The *Phoenix Gazette,* an evening paper, was started in 1880. It was then called the *Arizona Gazette*.

There were many newspapers in territorial times. Among these papers were the *Arizona Sentinel* (Yuma) and the *Arizona Silver Belt* (Globe, later Miami). Flagstaff's *Arizona Champion* became the *Coconino Sun*.

In the early 1880s the boom town of Tombstone had three dailies. The *Epitaph* was the most famous. One of its editors, John Clum, sided with the Earp brothers in their feuds. Wyatt Earp was the U.S. Deputy Marshal in Tombstone. He quarreled with Sheriff John Behan, the Clantons, and others. The Earps had a famous shoot-out with the Clanton gang. This fight was in the street near the O. K. Corral.

Most of the early newspapers were very partisan—either Democrat or Republican. The editors did a lot of name calling. They often called rival editors and politicians "liars." If editors did the same thing today, they might be sued for libel.

TELEGRAPH

The telegraph is a system of sending messages over an electric wire. Each letter of the alphabet is made by a set of dots and/or dashes.

The Deseret Telegraph Company of Utah built the first telegraph line into Arizona in 1871. The line ran to a station at Pipe

Stanwix Station, on the Gila River, was one of the first telegraph stations.

Spring. This Mormon settlement was north of the Grand Canyon. The telegraph gave Pipe Spring communication with Mormon towns in Utah.

Today Pipe Spring is a national monument. It is preserved by the U.S. government.

The first long telegraph line in Arizona was built by the U.S. Army. In 1873 a wire was strung on poles from San Diego. It ran to Fort Yuma and then to Maricopa Wells. Branch lines were built to connect army posts. One line ran from Maricopa Wells by way of Phoenix, Wickenburg, and Prescott to Camp Verde. The telegraph operator at Phoenix was Morris Goldwater. He was the uncle of U.S. Senator Barry Goldwater.

Another branch line gave telegraph service to Florence, Tucson, and army posts in eastern Arizona. Florence got on the line by giving the telegraph company a lot of telegraph poles.

The military telegraph made the Army in Arizona better. The scattered forts could get quick messages. Civilians could use the telegraph too.

A soldier at Camp Grant was married over the telegraph line in 1876. Corporal William Storey could not get leave to marry his sweetheart in San Diego. So the bride came by stagecoach to Camp Grant. Her preacher in San Diego read the wedding vows to a telegrapher. He sent the words over the wire to Camp Grant. Each "I do" came back and the preacher pronounced the couple man and wife.

The army telegraph lines were torn down after the railroads reached Arizona. Why? Because Western Union telegraph lines were built along the railroads.

TELEPHONES

The Territory of Arizona was not far behind the nation in getting telephones. The telephone was invented by Alexander Graham Bell in 1876. Five years later the first telephone switchboard in Arizona was installed in Tucson.

Tucson. The Tucson switchboard was in a stage station and post office building on Congress Street. Charles H. Lord, president of the Arizona Telephone Company, was also the postmaster.

In 1888 the Tucson switchboard was moved to the second floor of City Hall. This wood building looked like a Dutch windmill. It was called Bell Tower. Why? Because the town fire bell was on the third floor. The switchboard operator rang the bell when a fire was reported.

Phoenix. The first two phones in Phoenix were connected in 1882. S. D. Lount strung a wire between his home and his ice factory. Only private phones of this type were in Phoenix until 1891. In that year, Sunset Telephone and Telegraph Company installed a switchboard.

In the early days Phoenix always had more than one telephone company. As late as 1912 there were two companies. Phoenix residents had to buy a phone from each company. That way they could talk to all phone owners in town.

In 1908 the Consolidated Company started the *first long distance telephone service* between Phoenix and Tucson.

Two years later the Overland Company installed an *automatic dial system* in Phoenix. It was the first in Arizona and one of the first in the nation.

Prescott, like Phoenix, had more than one telephone company. The Prescott Electric Company did two things. First, it sold electricity. The company also ran a switchboard for about fifty phone customers. The company's owner, Frank Wright, did some unusual things. Once he hired a two-man orchestra to play music to his phone subscribers.

Wright's company and the Sunset company did Prescott an extra service. They alerted the town when a fire started. Their switchboards were busy on July 4, 1900. On

Prescott Electric Company switchboard in 1900. Operators dreaded rainstorms. Lightning that hit open wires around town would crack their eardrums.

that day a great fire raced along Whiskey Row on Montezuma Street. This street was famous for its saloons, dance halls, and gambling rooms.

Mountain States Telephone and Telegraph Company. This company brought all the small companies of Arizona together. The Mountain States company came from Colorado. Its first phone service in Arizona was at Bisbee and Douglas. It then grew to give Arizona one system.

The Mountain States company used the latest Bell Telephone System equipment. Arizona was tied into Bell's national and international network.

All the mergers and improvements took time. But they were done by 1912. That is the year Arizona became a state.

In 1912 there were 6,051 telephones in the whole state. By contrast, the Mountain States Company had 1.4 million phones in 1976. That was the centennial year of the telephone.

RADIO

The radio was a great invention. It made possible long-distance communication without wires.

The nation's first commercial radio station was KDKA of Pittsburgh. It began broadcasting in 1920. Soon the airwaves were filled with the squawking of big and little stations. Two networks — NBC and CBS — were formed in the 1920s.

In 1927 Congress passed a law to control broadcasting. Stations had to get a license.

The first amateur radio station in Arizona was 6BBH. It went on the air in 1921. Young Barry Goldwater was one of the operators for 6BBH. Listeners used crystal sets in the 1920s. The first sets had earphones, not speakers. Later, 6BBH became KOY.

Arizona's first licensed commercial radio station was KFAD in Phoenix. The call letters were later changed to KTAR. This station was once owned by a Phoenix newspaper. The call letters stood for "Keep Taking the

The first radio transmitter at ASU, early 1930s.

Arizona Republican."

Arizona's next two radio stations were in Tucson. KTUC began in 1926. KVOA (now KCUB) started three years later.

October 24, 1924 was a big day for Arizona radio listeners. They heard President Calvin Coolidge speak in Washington, D.C. The speech was picked up from radio stations in Fort Worth, Texas and Los Angeles. The *Tucson Citizen* wrote about a "week of wonders." A few days before the speech, people in Tucson saw the *Shenandoah*. This blimp was the first of its type to cross and recross the country.

The radio quickly became popular. By 1930 nearly one-fifth of Arizona's families had a radio. That was progress. Young people had fun at "radio parties."

Public address systems were sometimes used as a service to people without radios. In 1927 some 10,000 people stood in the rain on Central Avenue in Phoenix. They heard the Tunney-Dempsey boxing fight broadcast.

The fight news came over the telegraph wires to the *Arizona Republic*. The newspaper then told the news over the public address system. Radio owners who stayed home heard the same news over KFAD.

At first, Arizona radios could only pick up local broadcasts. Then, in 1930, KTAR joined the NBC network. For the first time people could hear national broadcasts live on a local station.

There are dozens of radio stations in Arizona now. Many of them broadcast one kind of music or program.

TELEVISION

TV is a popular communication system today.

The pioneer days of television were not long ago. The first TV station in Arizona was KPHO in Phoenix. It started December 4, 1949. KPHO-TV is now an independent station.

A television license is worth a lot of money. Only a few licenses are issued by the Federal Communications Commission.

Today many Arizona people in small towns receive TV broadcasts through boosters and high towers.

Words and Terms to Know

communication   telegraph
conversation   switchboard
publicity   international
libel   centennial

Match the words above with the following definitions:

1. The giving of information from one person to another person.
2. Any information which brings a person or event to the attention of the public.
3. A system of sending messages over an electric wire by using a code of long and short signals.
4. The equipment that connects one telephone line to another line.
5. A written or printed statement that injures a person's reputation.
6. A talking together of two or more people.
7. Between or among nations.
8. The 100th year.

Finding the Facts

1. Instead of speaking, the Indians sometimes used _____ language.
2. Arizona's first newspaper was the _____ _____ at Tubac.
3. Richard C. McCormick started two newspapers, the _____ _____ and the _____ _____.
4. The first newspaper in Phoenix was the _____ _____ _____.
5. Tombstone's most famous newspaper was called the _____.
6. The first long telegraph line in Arizona was built by the _____.
7. The town of _____ had the first telephone switchboard in Arizona.
8. The Overland Company installed Arizona's first _____ _____ _____ in Phoenix.
9. The _____ _____ Telephone and Telegraph Company combined Arizona's smaller companies into one big one.
10. Arizona's first licensed commercial radio station was _____ of Phoenix (now KTAR).
11. The first TV station in Arizona was _____ in Phoenix.

18. LIFE IN PIONEER TOWNS

Flagstaff in 1882.

February 24, 1863! On that day President Abraham Lincoln signed the Organic Act. Arizona became a territory.

At that time the population of Arizona was only about 10,000. This number included 4,000 friendly Indians. The only towns were Tucson, Tubac, Arizona City (Yuma), and La Paz.

Arizona was a territory for 49 years. During that time a lot of people moved west from the States. The population of Arizona grew to more than 200,000 by 1912. Many new towns were started.

In 1863 there was not even a stagecoach to ride. But by 1912 there was a good railroad system. Arizonans owned about 1,800 automobiles. Airplanes were beginning to fly over the territory.

Finally, Arizona became a state. On February 14, 1912, President William Howard Taft signed the statehood proclamation.

Why were new towns started in Arizona? Most of Arizona's towns were founded during territorial days. Some grew and prospered. Others died and became ghost towns.

New towns were started for many reasons. Some grew up near the mines. Tombstone, Bisbee, Globe, Clifton, Morenci, and Jerome were *mining towns.*

Some towns were *farming communities.* Phoenix, Chandler, Safford, Florence, and most of the Mormon settlements were farm towns.

A lot of *railroad stops* became important towns. Some towns grew up for a combination of reasons. It was the railroad, the lumber, and the livestock industry that got Flagstaff and Williams started.

BEATING THE HEAT

Summers were hot in the desert towns. The houses had no cooling in the old days. Both Mexican and Anglo homes had thick adobe walls to keep the heat out. When lumber was available, a wide porch was built to shade the walls. Water was sprinkled on dirt floors during hot summer days.

Most people slept outdoors. Some people had screened sleeping porches. Hotels put cots on an open balcony for the guests.

The Hotel Adams in Phoenix had an unusual cooling system. Huge blocks of ice were placed in pans spaced around the lobby. Electric fans blew air over the ice. Air conditioning did not come into general use until the 1930s.

Ice was made by companies in Tucson and Phoenix after 1879. But it cost too much for many people.

Most families had an outdoor *desert refrigerator*. It was homemade. A wooden frame was covered with burlap on all sides. The burlap was kept damp by water dripping from a bucket on top. The wind furnished the fan. It was surprising how well this desert refrigerator kept milk, butter, and meat.

Arizonans who could afford it left for the summer. Merchants often sent their wives and children to the mountains. Some went to the

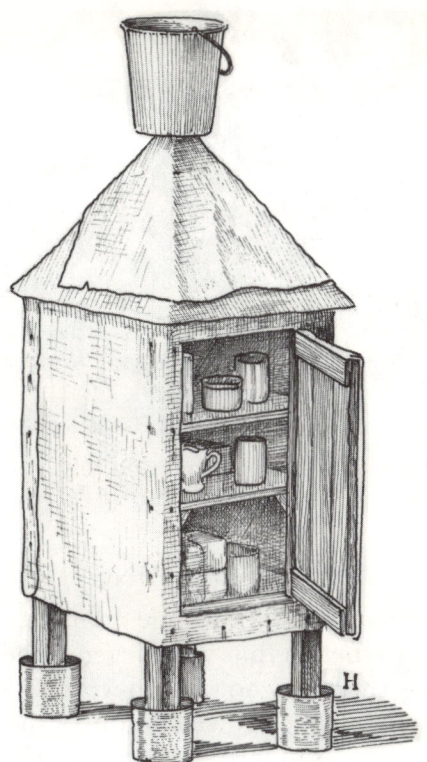

A desert refrigerator.

Adobe bricks, like these at Pioneer Arizona north of Phoenix, were once used in most Arizona houses.

Salt River swimming hole at Tempe, 1923.

California seashore. Some farmers in the Salt River Valley went camping in the cool mountains after the summer harvest was over.

Those who stayed home to sweat it out did what they could to stay cool. Children in Phoenix went swimming in the Salt River. They swam in the canals too.

Part of the Orndorff family and relatives in Tucson, dressed in their Sunday best, 1889.

CLOTHING

The Mexican people adapted to the hot climate better than people from the East. At home the Mexican women wore short-sleeved muslin or calico gowns. Many of the Mexican men wore sandals and light clothes to beat the heat. They also liked the wide-brimmed sombrero (hat).

By contrast, Anglo housewives suffered in long-sleeved dresses with high-ruffled collars. The men usually bought wool "California pants." They wore either boots or shoes with leather spats. Hats came in all sizes and shapes.

LIGHTING

In the early days, homes were lighted by candles. Some people used a burning rag dipped in a saucer of grease.

Kerosene (coal oil) lamps were used during most of the territorial period. These lamps were smoky and dangerous. One started a fire at the Bijou Theater in Phoenix. It was accidentally knocked off the chandelier.

Gas lights came into use during the 1880s. They were used mainly in stores and for street lights. Hutchlon Ohnick, a Japanese, built a gas plant in Phoenix in 1886. Gas was made from crude petroleum. Ohnick's biggest customer was the Crystal Saloon which used fancy gas lamps.

There were some *electric lights* in the 1890s. At first electricity was made by steam engines. Later water power was used to turn generators. One of the first hydroelectric plants was built on the Verde River north of Phoenix in 1910. The water came from Fossil Springs. This water gushed out at the rate of 20,000 gallons per minute.

STREETCARS

At least five towns in Arizona had electric trolleys. They were Phoenix, Tucson, Prescott, Douglas, and Bisbee-Warren.

Some of the towns used mule or horse-drawn streetcars. The first horse cars in Phoenix were pulled along Grand Avenue in 1887. Later, mule-drawn cars ran on Washington Street. The backs of the seats on these cars were reversible. When the car reached the end of the line, the mule team was moved to the other end. The seats were turned to face the opposite way.

Electric trolleys were first used in Phoenix in 1893. The last run on Washington Street was made to the state capitol in 1948.

In Tucson the first trolley ran from downtown to the University of Arizona campus. Student pranksters sometimes took the lightweight cars from the track at night. The cars were pushed to the campus. The trolley company did not think this was very funny.

A trolley car on the line to the Indian School in Phoenix in the early 1900s.

Prescott had a trolley in the early 1900s. It ran along Gurley Street to Fort Whipple.

OUTLAWS

Most Arizona towns had to deal with outlaws in the early days. Tombstone is famous for its gunmen, stage robbers, cattle rustlers, and crooked gamblers.

The rich silver mines brought bad people to Tombstone in the 1880s. Tombstone, however, was not really much worse than other towns. Most of the people in Tombstone were law-abiding. The town had churches and schools.

Sometimes people in the towns took justice into their own hands. The "Bisbee massacre" is a good example. On December 8, 1883, five outlaws robbed the Casteneda and Goldwater store. Joe Goldwater (a great uncle of U.S. Senator Barry Goldwater) was forced to open the safe. Four innocent people on the street were killed. One was a deputy sheriff. One was a woman.

A posse chased and caught the five outlaws one by one. Another man, John Heath, was also arrested. He was not at the robbery, but he was suspected of planning it. Heath confessed. He was convicted of second-degree murder. Heath was sentenced to 20 years at the Yuma prison.

Citizens of Bisbee and Tombstone were angry. They thought Heath was getting off too easy. About thirty men broke into the Tombstone jail. They took Heath to a telegraph pole and hanged him.

The five "Bisbee massacre" robbers were sentenced to death by the court. A crowd of one thousand saw the men hanged at the Tombstone courthouse.

FUN TIMES

There were times for fun in the frontier towns. The 4th of July was usually a special day. Most towns had *parades*. The 1879 parade in Tucson was a mile long. A brass band and soldiers from Fort Lowell took part.

The 4th of July programs had contests.

Grave of John Heath in Boothill cemetery, Tombstone, Arizona.

Chinese parade in Phoenix, about 1900.

There were foot races, burro races, and bronco riding. The *hose team races* were popular in northern Arizona towns. Each team pulled a two-wheeled fire hose cart to a hydrant. The hose was hooked up and the water turned on. The team with the fastest time won. Rivalry between hose teams from Prescott and Jerome was keen. Both towns had been destroyed by fire. The people knew the need for speed in putting out a fire.

In mining towns the *hard rock drilling contest* was a popular event. One man would hold a steel drill. His partner drove it into a block of stone with a sledge hammer. There was danger the holder would get his hand smashed. But the prizes were big. The winners in Bisbee one year got $800. They drilled a record hole of nearly 47 inches.

The hilly town of Bisbee introduced *coaster racing* to the nation in 1911. Boys built their own coasters. They were clocked—one at a time—on a long, steep, curvy, dirt road. Coaster racing is still the highlight of the 4th of July in Bisbee.

Two favorite Mexican holidays were *Cinco de Mayo* (May 5) and the *Fiesta de San Juan.* There was a parade on Cinco de Mayo. A beautiful girl was chosen to reign as queen for a day.

The 1883 San Juan's festival in Phoenix was fun. Some 1,500 people bought huge glasses of lemonade at the booths. Some danced to the music of a six-piece band. There was a bull fight. But most of the fans jeered. Why? Because the horns of the bull were sawed off.

SPORTS

Baseball. Sports were not as well-organized in the old times as they are now. Most baseball games were of the pick-up kind. In Jerome the young miners and merchants would pile on wagons. They rode downhill to a flat spot near the Verde River. A diamond was marked out for a game of baseball.

After awhile mine companies began to provide sports for the workers. They organized baseball. After statehood, both Jerome and Clarkdale won the state baseball championship.

Football became a sport in Arizona high schools in the 1890s. The Phoenix Union High School team was organized in 1898. It played four games, winning three and tying one. Two games were played with Tempe Normal School (now ASU) and two with Phoenix Indian School. The last game with the Indian School ended in a 5 to 5 tie. A touchdown counted five points then.

The players wore canvas suits. At first they had no padding. Handgrips were fastened to the trousers of linemen. Backfield men could grab these grips and be pulled for more yardage. A player could not re-enter the game once he left. Teams were penalized for forward passing over the line of scrimmage.

Hardrock drilling contest in Bisbee, Arizona on the 4th of July, 1902.

The first football team at Arizona State University, called Tempe Normal in 1896. Note the large football.

A play was not dead until the runner with the ball could no longer move or said "down."

THEATER

The theater was a popular form of entertainment in the early towns. Tucson Mexicans enjoyed outdoor plays. A favorite in the 1870s was *Elena y Jorge*. The beautiful Elena had a wicked uncle. He wanted to sell her for gold. But the play ends happily. Elena marries her true lover, the handsome Jorge.

Many traveling groups came to Arizona. They often performed in Tombstone. Schieffelin Hall was the largest theater between El Paso and San Francisco. The Bird Cage Theater was smaller and less highbrow.

The stage play *Uncle Tom's Cabin* was acted at the Bird Cage in 1882. A drunken cowboy got too involved in the plot. He shot the bloodhound that was chasing Eliza. Eliza was the runaway Black slave in the play who crossed the icy Ohio River.

Most towns had a theater of some kind. The Dreamland Theater in Globe doubled as

Nola Forest sang at the Bird Cage Theater.

a skating rink. Globe also had the smaller Majestic Theater. A popular star in the early 1900s was the comedian Fatty Arbuckle. He featured a large group of girl singers and dancers. Arbuckle later became a silent movie star in Hollywood.

MONEY

Paper bills and coins were different in pioneer days. There were 28 national banks in Arizona which could issue paper money after 1882. The *national bank bills* were printed in Washington, D.C. But each bill had the name of the bank and the name of the town where the bank was. The first bank bills were called "horse blankets." They measured 7½ by 3¼ inches. That is bigger than the paper money used today.

There are stories about Arizona bankers who carried uncut sheets of paper money. When they made a purchase, they might ask the clerk for scissors. They cut off the number of bills needed.

Token used by the Palace Saloon in Tucson.

Silver and gold certificates made up most of the paper money issued by the federal government. They could be turned in at the bank for silver or gold coins.

Coins were sometimes scarce. Many saloons and other businesses used *tokens*. The tokens helped to advertise a place of business. The printing on a token told what it would buy or how much it was worth in trade.

Words and Terms to Know

territory	trolley car
adobe	coaster
sombrero	penalize
spat	national bank
generate	silver certificate
hydroelectric	token

Match the words above with the following definitions:

1. Spanish word for hat.
2. A sun-dried brick made of dirt and straw.
3. Paper money that can be cashed for silver.
4. A stamped piece of metal or pasteboard that can be used as a substitute for coins.
5. A bank which had permission from the federal government to operate and issue its own money.
6. A land area in the United States which had a government but no votes in Congress.
7. To produce electricity.
8. A streetcar that is connected by a pole to an overhead electric wire.
9. Having to do with the production of electricity by water power.
10. A vehicle that carries a passenger downhill.
11. To punish for breaking a rule.
12. A covering for the ankle and instep.

Finding the Facts

1. Arizona was a territory from the year _____ to _____.
2. Bisbee is an example of a _____ town.

3. Florence started as a _____ town.
4. In pioneer days most families preserved food in a _____ _____.
5. The Mexican people wore _____ clothes to beat the heat.
6. At least _____ towns in Arizona had streetcars.
7. Some outlaws were attracted to _____ by the rich silver mines.
8. The _____ _____ _____ was usually a fun day in pioneer times.
9. Two favorite Mexican holidays were _____ _____ _____ and the _____ _____ _____ _____.
10. _____ became a sport in Arizona high schools in the 1890s.
11. The _____ _____ Theater in Tombstone was a popular entertainment place.
12. Some pioneer businesses used _____ as a substitute for money.

The town of Williams in 1880.

UNIT 5
ARIZONA AS A STATE

February 12, 1912! On that day Arizona became a state. The people of Arizona were soon involved in national events. They took part in World War I and World War II. The decades between those wars—the 1920s and the 1930s—brought rapid changes.

The 1920s was a time of prosperity for most people. They enjoyed the car, the radio, movies, and appliances.

The 1930s brought the Great Depression. Money was scarce. Many people were out of work. The United States had been in depressions before. But none was so bad or lasted so long.

The depression was ended by World War II. Wars cause destruction and human suffering; but more Americans began to work and make money. The United States spent millions of dollars for air bases and new defense plants in Arizona.

During the war Arizona farmers planted more cotton. They got higher prices. The copper mines operated at full capacity. Merchants and workers of all kinds made money.

In the years since World War II, Arizona has continued to grow. The climate attracts lots of people. Many skilled workers come to work in clean-air factories.

Manufacturing is now Arizona's number one basic industry. Tourism also provides many jobs. Thousands of Arizonans make a living from tourists.

The future growth of Arizona depends on two things. First, new sources of cheap energy must be found. Maybe it will be nuclear or solar energy. Second, people must conserve water, or we must find a way to import water from other states.

Parade in Tempe, early 1930s.

19. ARIZONA IN TWO BIG WARS

Frank Luke, Jr. and his airplane, 1918.

WORLD WAR I (1914-1918)

The United States entered World War I in 1917. The people of Arizona can be proud of the state's record in this war.

Arizona men in the service. An Arizona National Guard unit—the 158th Infantry—fought in France. After the war the 158th was selected as President Woodrow Wilson's honor guard at the peace conference in Paris.

One of America's greatest air heroes was Frank Luke Jr. He graduated from Phoenix Union High School in 1917. Luke was known as the "Balloon Buster from Arizona." In a short time he shot down fourteen German observation balloons and four airplanes.

Shooting down balloons was dangerous work. The pilot had to swoop down close to the ground. His airplane was exposed to gun fire. The Germans also fired aerial bombs, called "onions," from mortars.

Luke was finally shot down. But he refused to surrender. He died defending himself with a pistol.

Mathew B. Juan, a Pima Indian, was the first of 321 Arizona men killed in World War I. Like many Native Americans, he had shown his patriotism by enlisting.

The home front. People who stayed home also helped win World War I. Indians, older boys, and Mexican aliens worked on the farms. Many Arizonans bought war bonds. There were "wheatless" and "meatless" days to save food.

The war in Europe ended on November 11, 1918. Arizona celebrated with the nation. In Phoenix people headed downtown. Cars got in line and made a parade a mile long that honked its way along the streets. Church bells rang. Guns were fired. It was a happy night.

About the time the war was over, a world-wide flu epidemic hit Arizona. The flu virus quickly spread across the state. Public meetings were forbidden. Schools, churches, and movie theaters were closed. The state fair was cancelled in November. People in Phoenix and Tucson were forced to wear gauze masks while on the street. By the end of January, 1919, the flu epidemic was over. The virus somehow changed form. People did not catch the new virus. It began attacking pigs and chickens.

1920s

The decade of the 1920s was a prosperous time. People had money to spend on cars and new gadgets. Arizona life-styles changed.

The automobile brought many changes. Many people were employed to sell or service the cars. New kinds of businesses opened. There were gas stations, garages, motels, and drive-ins. A few new roads were built near the large towns.

The radio was an exciting invention of the 1920s. It added richness to the lives of

World War I soldier with gas mask.

Road building in the early days.

The Fox Theater on Congress Street in Tucson was a popular place.

Refrigerators unloaded in Phoenix in the 1920s.

people. By 1929 one-fifth of Arizona families owned a radio. Families with radios sometimes had radio parties with friends.

Movie-going was a popular pastime in the 1920s. Most large towns had at least one theater. Phoenix had seven in 1929. The fancy Orpheum Theater was opened that year.

The first movies were "silents." The first "talkie" was *The Jazz Singer*, starring Al Jolson. It was shown in Arizona in the late 1920s.

Electrical appliances became popular in the 1920s. But not many people in Arizona had refrigerators or washing machines at that time.

The crash of 1929. The prosperity of the 1920s was not real. Too many Americans borrowed money to buy goods. The demand for goods raised prices. As a result, farmers raised more food than buyers needed. The factories made too many cars and other goods.

Many people gambled on the stock market in the 1920s. They borrowed money to buy more stock as prices went up and up. But the stocks were not worth what people were paying for them. In 1929 the stock market crashed. Stock prices fell. Everyone wanted to sell. Some people lost all they had.

The country went into the Great Depression of the 1930s.

1930s

Hard times fell on Arizona and the rest of the nation in the 1930s.

What did the Great Depression do to Arizona? The closing of eastern factories hurt Arizona's economy. Many copper mines had to shut down. Mine workers lost their jobs. Some of them tried to make a living by looking for gold.

The depression affected almost everyone. Farmers suffered when prices for cotton fell. Cattlemen and sheepmen had trouble making ends meet. Tourism and house building fell off.

WPA workers building a bridge on highway between Nogales and Patagonia, 1936.

School enrollments told the story. Many boys and girls were in and out of school. Their parents moved around the country looking for jobs.

Jobless families had to stop buying. Old clothes were mended. The pioneer practices of "make it over," "make it do," "wear it out," and "eat it up" were followed. At first each family tried to take care of itself.

Before long, churches and charities tried to help. Leaders in the towns raised money to aid the poor. The Arizona legislature used a special sales tax and other state money to help the needy. The United States also began to give relief money to the states.

The New Deal. President Franklin Roosevelt started an aid program called the New Deal in 1933. Federal programs such as the WPA (Works Progress Administration) provided jobs. WPA workers built roads, post offices, sidewalks, bridges, water systems, and other public works.

Thousands of young men were in the CCC (Civilian Conservation Corps). They planted trees in the mountains. Over-grazed ranch lands were reseeded. Canals were lined with concrete to save water. New trails and guard rails were built in Colossal Cave near Tucson.

The Indians also got a New Deal. Two

The Fox Theater in Phoenix was air conditioned in the 1930s.

laws to help Indians were passed by Congress in 1934. One law made it possible for Native American children to go to public schools. The U.S. government paid school districts that would teach Indian children.

Another federal law allowed Indian tribes to adopt their own tribal constitutions. Each Arizona tribe set up its own government. It was usually an elected council and a chairman.

Life went on. Keeping alive was a problem for many people during the depression. But life went on. Not all was gloom and doom. People still drove cars. But they kept them longer. There were still "picture shows." But it was more of a treat to see one. Free baseball games gained more fans.

Even during the depression, the state made progress. The first natural gas pipeline reached Arizona in 1933. Evaporative coolers came into use. The Arizona Highway Patrol was started.

In 1939 Old Tucson was built as a movie set. Columbia Pictures built it to make the movie *Arizona*. This movie was about a girl who was stranded in Tucson when her father died. She made a living baking pies. Later she ran a freighting business. Since 1940 hundreds of western movies and TV films have been made at Old Tucson.

This stadium at the state fairgrounds in Phoenix was built by the WPA.

Before natural gas was piped into Phoenix in 1934, gas had to be manufactured. It was stored in huge high pressure tanks like this Hortonsphere.

The wedding scene in *Arizona*, filmed at Old Tucson.

WORLD WAR II

No other event changed Arizona so much or so fast as World War II!

Copper plants and cotton farms prospered. Huge sums of federal money were spent in Arizona. Army and Air Force bases and defense factories were built here. Thousands of people came from other states to Arizona.

Some 30,000 Arizona men and women did military service during World War II.

USS Arizona battleship. The United States got into World War II when the Japanese bombed Pearl Harbor. That was on December 7, 1941.

One of the ships sunk was the *USS Arizona.* This battleship was launched in New York in 1915. A pretty high school girl from Prescott cracked a bottle of Arizona water over the hull to christen the ship. Today the anchor of the *USS Arizona* rests on a memorial east of the capitol in Phoenix.

The Arizona National Guard was called into service in 1940. That was before the United States entered the war. Formed as the 158th Infantry Regiment, the Arizona guardsmen trained in Panama for jungle warfare. There they took the name "Bushmasters." It was the name of a deadly jungle snake. The 158th soldiers were sent to the Pacific. They fought their way through the islands to the Philippines.

A close up view of the *U.S.S. Arizona* anchor makes the state capitol look small.

The Bushmasters cross a stream during training in Panama.

Mauldin created two soldier characters named Willie and Joe. His cartoons of them were called "Up Front." They gave a good picture of the daily lives of GIs fighting the German army in Italy.

Air Force training. Thousands of pilots, soldiers, and sailors were trained in Arizona during World War II. Davis-Monthan air base in Tucson was the largest heavy bomber training base in the United States.

Fighter pilots were taught at Luke Field and Williams Air Force Base near Phoenix. There were also air fields at Douglas, Kingman, Yuma, Marana, Prescott, and other towns.

Other military bases. Not all the soldiers were in the air force. Thousands of men were trained in desert warfare. They were trained at Camp Hyder near Yuma and Camp Horn

World War II bombers in flight.

Bill Mauldin drawing a Willie and Joe cartoon during World War II.

Bill Mauldin. Other Arizonans fought in Europe. Americans got a glimpse of the war in Europe through the cartoons of Bill Mauldin. He was once a student at Phoenix Union High School.

Many soldiers were trained for desert warfare in Arizona.

near Wickenburg. Black soldiers were trained at Fort Huachuca. The Black 92nd division was sent to Europe. The 93rd division fought in the Pacific.

Arizona's minority groups made a good record during World War II. The most famous Indian hero was Ira H. Hayes. He was a Pima. He was one of six marines who raised the American flag on Mount Suribachi. This hill is on the Pacific island of Iwo Jima.

Mexican-Americans served in all branches of the armed forces. Silvestre Herrera of Phoenix won the Congressional Medal of Honor. He made a one-man assault on two German gun crews which had stopped his platoon. Both his feet were blown off when he stepped on a mine. Herrera was in severe pain. But he kept the Germans pinned down with rifle fire. Meanwhile his fellow soldiers went around the mine field. They rushed in to capture the gun crews.

Japanese-Americans. During the war the United States did not trust its Japanese citizens. Some 112,000 Japanese-Americans were put in relocation camps. Most of these people had been living in California.

Two of the ten camps were in Arizona. One was on the Gila Indian Reservation near Sacaton. The other was on the Colorado River Reservation south of Parker.

The camps were wooden barracks

Pfc. Ira Hayes, age 19, ready to jump at the Marine Corps Paratroop School.

grouped in blocks. Each block had a dining hall, play area, and a washroom.

The Japanese on the Gila Reservation dug canals and grew tons of vegetables. A school was also started at the Gila camp. Faculty members from Arizona State at Tempe taught college classes. They also trained Japanese teachers.

After the camps were closed in 1945, most of the Japanese-Americans went home. But most of their farms and homes in California had been sold. They were only partly paid by the government for their losses.

The uprooting of the Japanese-Americans was unfortunate and unnecessary. They were loyal to the United States. Their young men had a good combat record during the war. The 442nd Regiment won more medals

Japanese-American farmers harvest Daikon, a radish-like vegetable, at the Gila camp.

Part of the Papago POW camp in East Phoenix.

Japanese-American school children in a Harvest Festival parade at the Gila camp, 1942.

fighting in Europe than any unit in the U.S. Army. The 442nd was entirely Japanese-American. Their motto was "Go for broke."

POW Camps. Several thousand German and Italian prisoners of war (POWs) were placed in Arizona camps during the war.

The biggest German POW camp was in Papago Park in East Phoenix. Most of the POWs there were captured German sailors and submarine men. They were shipped to the desert so they would not be near seaports.

There were many escapes from the Papago prison camp. The "great escape" was on Christmas Eve, 1944. Sixty men got out through a tunnel that took months to dig. Most of them tried to reach the Mexican border. They were all caught. The last one was captured in Phoenix. For 35 days he hid in a cave north of town. When he ventured into Phoenix, his German accent gave him away. A policeman returned him to the POW camp.

World War II ended in Europe on May 8, 1945. But the war in the Pacific went on until August. The Japanese leaders signed surrender terms on September 2, 1945.

The rapid growth of Arizona started during World War II. World War II defense contracts gave Arizona factories their first boost. Most of them were near Phoenix.

The Garrett Corporation led the way. It made parts for B-17 bombers. In the 1950s Garrett's AiResearch plant near Sky Harbor Airport began making gas turbine engines. Goodyear Aircraft at Litchfield also made airplane parts.

Alcoa opened the world's largest aluminum plant in West Phoenix. After the war Alcoa sold the plant to the Reynold's Corporation.

Allison Steel was an old Phoenix com-

Aerial view of the Reynolds Metal Company Plant in west Phoenix.

pany. They made portable bridges during World War II. It is now the Marathon Steel Corporation.

During World War II the world discovered Arizona. People who came to the state liked what they found. They liked the climate, the scenic wonders, and the natural resources. After the war people kept coming. By the 1970s Arizona was the fastest-growing state in the nation.

Words and Terms to Know

prosperity
skilled worker
appliance
energy
epidemic
stocks
the economy
council
natural gas
memorial
minority group
relocation camp

Match the words above with the following definitions:

1. A condition of being well-off.
2. A system of producing, selling, and consuming things of value.
3. Certificates that show part ownership of a corporation.
4. A place to which people are moved from their homes.
5. A fuel that can be piped from the earth to the place where it is burned.
6. Power, which usually comes from fuel, for doing work or running a machine.
7. A machine used in the house.
8. The legislative body for a town or Indian tribe.
9. A person who is an expert in some craft or job that requires knowledge.
10. A smaller group which differs from the majority in race, religion, politics, or for some other reason.
11. Anything meant to help people remember some event or person.
12. The rapid spreading of a disease.

Finding the Facts

1. One of America's greatest air heroes was _____ _____ _____.
2. Near the end of World War I a _____ _____ spread across Arizona.
3. The _____ changed the lives of most people and created many new jobs in the 1920s.
4. The Great Depression was in the _____.
5. During the depression many _____ mines had to close down.
6. The _____ _____ was a federal program to help the needy.
7. _____ was the name of the Arizona National Guard unit that fought in World War II.
8. A Phoenix cartoonist who became famous during World War II was _____ _____.
9. _____ _____ was the largest heavy bomber training base in the United States.
10. The Mexican-American soldier who won the Congressional Medal of Honor was _____ _____.
11. Japanese-Americans were relocated at camps on the _____ and the _____ Indian reservations.
12. The biggest German POW camp in Arizona was located in _____ _____ in Phoenix.
13. The _____ _____ manufactured B-17 bomber parts in Phoenix during World War II.

20. ARIZONA'S INDUSTRIES SINCE WORLD WAR II

Lumber was Arizona's first major manufactured product. It is still an important source of income.

POPULATION GROWTH

Figures. During World War II Arizona's population grew. It went from less than 500,000 to over 600,000. Between 1945 and 1960 it more than doubled. It doubled again to two and a half million people by 1980.

Experts figure that Arizona will have over four million people by the year 2000.

MANUFACTURING

Manufacturing means making things by hand or machine.

When the pioneers mixed dirt and straw with water, put the mud mixture in a mold, and dried it in the sun, they were manufacturing adobe bricks. When the miller ground wheat, he was manufacturing flour. Sawmills and copper smelters are also kinds of manufacturing.

In pioneer times most manufacturing was done in the home. Now most manufacturing is done in factories.

Until World War II most income in Arizona came from mining, farming, ranching, and tourists. The growth of manufacturing since the big war has given Arizona another new source of income.

Manufacturing became Arizona's main industry in the 1960s. By that time there were hundreds of factories. They made everything from doughnuts to missiles.

Electronics was the first new large-scale industry in Arizona after World War II.

Motorola led the way. Its first research lab in Phoenix was built in 1948. Now Motorola is the state's largest employer.

General Electric in Phoenix also hires a lot of workers. Dickson Electronics in Scottsdale and Mesa and many other companies make electronic parts.

Products made in Arizona range from small transistors to big computers. Phoenix is fast becoming the electronics capital of the United States.

The electronics industry is good for Arizona. Why? There are two reasons. It provides jobs for all levels of job skills. And it is a clean industry. It does not pollute the air with smoke.

Aircraft parts and missiles. Several aircraft parts companies built plants in Phoenix during World War II. Then, in the 1950s, Hughes Aircraft came to Tucson. Hughes produced Falcon missiles.

Other manufacturers of aircraft parts in the state today are Goodyear Aerospace, AiResearch, Sperry Rand Flight Systems, and Talley Industries—all in the Phoenix area.

Food processing plants hire one-tenth of the factory workers in Arizona.

Cudahy in Phoenix and Swift in Tolle-

A typical assembly line at Motorola's semiconductor plant in Phoenix.

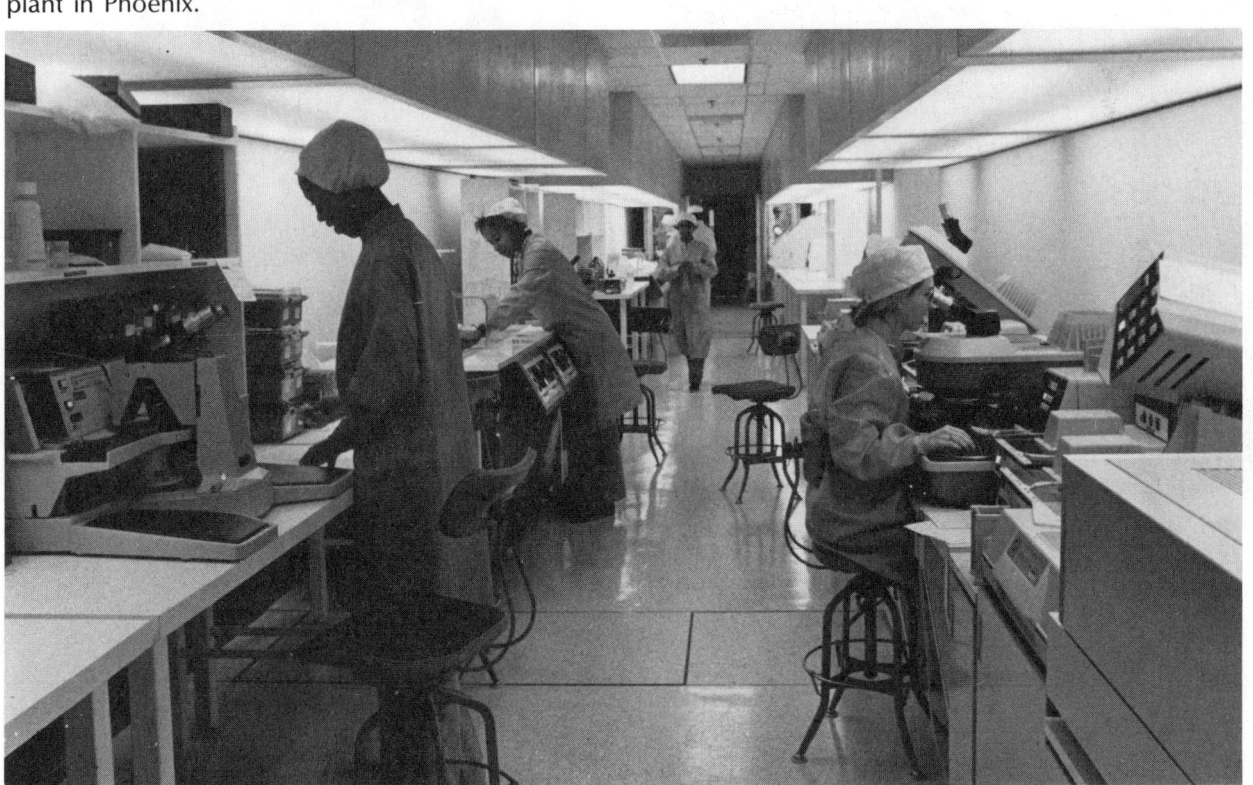

Meat is processed for bacon at Cudahy's Phoenix plant.

Southwest Forest Industries' paper mill at Snowflake, Arizona.

tories, and copper wire mills.

The Western Electric Company in Phoenix has hundreds of workers. They make telephone cable.

Dozens of factories in Arizona make clothes. They make women's dresses, T-shirts, sleepwear, and shirts.

Manufacturing is very important to Arizona. About one-sixth of all job holders in the state work in manufacturing.

TOURIST INDUSTRY

Tourism has been called the "unsung hero" of the Arizona economy. By the late 1970s, nearly 70,000 Arizonans worked in the tourist industry. Another 110,000 jobs depended partly on out-of-state tourists and vacationing Arizonans.

State offices promote tourism. The *State*

Front cover of the first *Arizona Highways* magazine, April, 1925.

son have big meat-packing plants. Spreckels Sugar Company first processed sugar beets at Chandler in 1967.

Two other food processors are the Hayden Flour Mills in Tempe and Rosarita Mexican Foods in Mesa. There are lots more.

Other factories. Many plants in Arizona make products from mine and forest materials. These plants include lumber mills, paper mills, copper smelters, cement and brick fac-

Parks Board builds camps and other tourist places. The *Office of Tourism* (OOT) gives stories and pictures to out-of-state newspapers, TV, and radio.

The *Arizona Highways* magazine does a good job telling the world about Arizona. The Grand Canyon has been the most popular subject. The canyon was on the front cover 25 times from 1925 to 1972. Pictures of the Navajo Indians have been the second most popular.

The *Arizona Highways* is sold all over the world. It is the most successful magazine of its kind.

Modern tourism. By the 1970s "tourism" in Arizona meant many kinds of things. The millions who visit Arizona each year include people on a short vacation, winter visitors, and delegates to conventions. Other tourists are business people, shoppers from Mexico, campers, and local sightseers.

Tourists travel by car, train, bus, or plane. They spend millions of dollars on food, lodging, gas, and other goods or services.

People from Mexico spend lots of money in southern Arizona. Many merchants in Nogales, Tucson, and Douglas do a good business with Mexican citizens.

Tourism is also good for our state because it helps us learn about other people. We can meet and talk to people from other states and even from other countries.

MINING

Arizona is a mining state. Thousands of men work in the mines. Some have jobs in smelters. Lots of people have jobs transporting the ores.

Copper is the most important mineral in Arizona. Our state produces about half the nation's copper.

Nearly all the modern mines have low-grade copper ore. Most of them are open pit mines. They are run by large-scale methods. Explosives are used to blast the ore loose. Huge crushing machines smash large boulders. Gigantic trucks can haul 200 tons in a single load.

Tucson is now the "copper capital of the world." Today 95 per cent of the state's copper is mined in areas close to Tucson. There is a large body of low-grade ore on the west side of the Santa Cruz River.

Mining began there in 1952. In that year the Pima Mining Company began an open pit near Twin Buttes, which is south of Tuc-

Phoenix civic plaza.

Open pit mine at Ajo.

Phelps Dodge reduction works at Morenci.

son. Other companies—Asarco, Duval, and Anaconda—soon opened more mines.

New mines have also been opened north of Tucson. The Magma Copper Company has one of the largest underground mines in the country. It is at San Manuel. Other mines are near Casa Grande.

Mine companies now help protect the environment.

Clean air. By law the mine companies must remove most of the sulfur dioxide from smelter stack smoke. In 1974 Kennecott Copper Corporation was given the first permit to operate. Kennecott's smelter at Hayden met clean air standards.

Sulfur dioxide that used to go up in smoke is now converted to liquid sulfuric acid. Some of this acid is used on farms. It improves soil that is too salty.

Planting around mine dumps. Some mine companies are trying to improve the looks of mine areas. South of Tucson, for example, some land is being reclaimed. Grasses and trees are planted on tailing dumps. These dumps are huge piles of wastes from the mines and smelters. The new plants look nice. They also help to control dust and erosion.

A Black Mesa coal mine on the Navajo Reservation.

Cotton picking machines in the Salt River Valley.

Harvesting lettuce near Phoenix.

Other important minerals. Gold, silver, and molybdenum are found in Arizona. They are mainly by-products of copper refining. Molybdenum is used in alloys and in such things as spark plugs.

Uranium mines are found in northern Arizona. The largest uranium mine in this state is the Orphan Lode. It is in the Grand Canyon National Park. Uranium is also mined on the Navajo Reservation.

Coal is another important mineral. It is mined mainly on Navajo lands.

FARMING

Farming has changed a lot since pioneer days. Farms now are much larger. And fewer people have farm jobs because of machines that save labor.

Cotton-picking is a good example. Until the late 1940s most cotton was picked by hand. A hand picker might pick only 200 pounds a day. Now cotton-picking machines can pick 10,000 pounds in one day.

Only two per cent of Arizona's land is farmed. But this land is very productive. Arizona's sunshine and irrigation really help farming. Crop production has been increased in many ways. Good seeds, fertilizers, and better planting methods are used. Herbicides control weeds and root rot.

Cotton is the major crop. Arizona grows about ten per cent of the nation's cotton.

Alfalfa is the main forage crop. Some of it is used for sheep pasture in the winter. But most of it is cut for hay. It is fed to livestock in feedlots.

Lettuce makes up half of Arizona's vegetable crop. Harvest time for the lettuce is different for different elevations. Yuma's lettuce is cut between December and April. In Willcox, which is about 4,000 feet high, fall lettuce is cut in September and October. Spring lettuce is cut in June.

Lettuce, *carrots, onions,* and other vegetables are grown in the Salt River Valley. The leading *cantaloupe*-raising region is around Yuma.

Citrus is the main fruit grown in Arizona. A few *peaches* are grown above 3,500 feet in southeastern Arizona.

CATTLE INDUSTRY

Before World War II, raising calves on ranches was the main part of the cattle industry. Cattle feeding was only a sideline to the range cattle industry.

Now *cattle feeding* is a big business. Feedlots fatten cattle from Arizona's ranges. They also import livestock from other states and Mexico to feed.

Today's ranchers face many problems. The most basic problem is how to get enough *land* for their livestock. Most cattlemen have to lease federal or state lands. Without permits to run their cattle on public lands, most Arizona cattlemen would go broke.

Cattlemen pay higher and higher prices for feed, fence posts, wire, and other supplies. But the price the ranchers get for beef is not certain. If they raise too many cattle, the price goes down. The rancher then loses money.

Most cattlemen are self-reliant. They may have to operate at a loss for a year or two. But somehow they manage to stay in business.

What is the biggest change in the cattle industry since the 1890s? Older cattlemen say it is disease prevention. Modern cowboys carry a hypodermic syringe instead of a six-shooter. They vaccinate cattle to prevent disease.

Words and Terms to Know

manufacturing
transistors
computer
job skill
food processing
tourism
sightseers
low-grade ore
environment
self-reliant

Match the words above with the following definitions:

1. Ability to do a certain job.
2. A person who visits places of interest for pleasure or education.
3. Making something by hand or machine.
4. A machine that stores information and sorts it out according to instructions.
5. Very small devices through which an electric current can flow.
6. Travel which results in income for a business or city.
7. Changing food into more eatable form.
8. Having confidence in one's own abilities.
9. The surroundings.
10. Rock material that does not have much metal in it.

Finding the Facts

1. Manufacturing became Arizona's number one industry in the _____.
2. _____ was the first electronics industry in Phoenix.
3. Hughes Aircraft came to Tucson in the 1950s to make _____ _____.
4. Rosarita Mexican Foods is an example of a _____ _____ industry.
5. _____ has been called the "unsung hero" of the Arizona economy.
6. The _____ _____ magazine promotes Arizona all over the world.
7. Most modern copper mines are _____ _____ rather than underground.
8. _____ is now the "copper capital of the world."
9. By law the copper companies have to remove most of the _____ _____ from smelter stack smoke.
10. _____ and _____ mines are operated on the Navajo Reservation.
11. Only _____ per cent of Arizona's land is farmed.
12. _____ is the major farm crop.
13. _____ _____ is now big business, not just a sideline to the range cattle industry.
14. The cattleman's most basic problem is how to get enough _____.

21. RECREATION

Water skiing is popular on Arizona's lakes.

OUTDOOR FUN

Arizona's great variety of climates makes *many kinds of recreation* possible. Thanks to good weather, many Arizonans can take part in outdoor fun.

People get out-of-doors to camp, hike, or swim. There are thousands of fishermen and hunters in the state. Two kinds of skiing are popular. Some people ski on snowy slopes. Others like water skiing. Many Arizonans are sightseers. Some people are just plain sun worshippers. They like relaxing in lawn chairs.

On weekends, hundreds of Arizonans head for the lakes or tall timber. Many take their boats or motor homes. There are more pleasure boats *per capita* in Arizona than in any other state. Many man-made lakes provide water for boating.

Within Arizona's 114,000 square miles there are *many kinds of scenery*. Millions of tourists visit the national parks and monuments, the national forests, and the state parks. The

Lake Powell near Page.

Shooting the rapids on the Colorado River.

Fishing is a popular pastime in Arizona.

Thousands of visitors at Colossal Cave have walked along stone and concrete trails built by the CCC.

Grand Canyon National Park, of course, is the state's most popular tourist attraction. People come from all over the world to see it.

The parks and monuments are protected by the government so that people will always be able to enjoy them. There is no hunting. People may not pick the flowers or take the rocks. Why not? A story about what happened at one park tells why:

A visitor at the Grand Canyon Park found a small, pretty rock. He wanted it. But the park ranger told him that he could not take it.

"Look," the visitor said, "all I want is this one little piece of rock. What will that hurt? You have tons of the stuff."

The park ranger smiled. "That much would not hurt," he said. "But nearly 3 million people come here every year. Why don't you pick up 3 million pieces that size and pile them together? See how big the pile would be. And that is just for one year!"

The visitor thought it over. He decided he did not want the rock after all.

WESTERN TRADITION

Arizona has a western tradition. There are dozens of horseback-riding stables in the state. Many communities have rodeos and parades. During those times people are en-

Campers in Oak Creek Canyon, 1890s. Camping has been a popular pastime in Arizona for a long time.

Horseback riding is a year-round sport in Arizona that provides a close-up look at the desert and a feeling of the Old West.

Indian cowboys at a Prescott rodeo.

couraged to dress in western clothes.

Tourists can get a taste of the Old West by visiting Tombstone, Old Tucson, or the "ghost town" of Jerome. There are also many museums and Indian ceremonials in the state.

The Arizona Historical Society's museum in Tucson gives visitors a good view of Arizona history. Colorful dioramas and displays show pioneer life. The whole scope of the state's history is shown. There are exhibits of photographs, models, antique furniture, old guns, and old styles of clothing.

COLLEGE AND PROFESSIONAL SPORTS

Baseball spring training. The avid sports fan can see plenty of action in Arizona. The state has great spring baseball weather. A half dozen major league teams do their spring training in Arizona. The "Cactus League" exhibition games draw large crowds.

College sports. *Baseball* at Arizona's universities and colleges is the best in the country. Both Arizona State and the University of Arizona have won the national championship in baseball. Both schools are in the Pacific 10 Conference. They have good teams in all sports.

An Arizona State player slides into home plate to score a run.

Northern Arizona University is in the Skyline Conference. Grand Canyon College in Phoenix is an independent Southern Baptist school. Its athletes excel in baseball and basketball.

Professional sports. The Phoenix Suns *basketball* team brought Arizona its first glory in a major league sport in 1976. The Suns got to the finals of the NBA (National Basketball Association) play-offs.

Professional *golf* tournaments can be seen in Arizona during the winter. The Phoenix and Tucson events are on the PGA (Professional Golf Association) circuit. Top golfers compete for big prize money.

Hockey is another popular sport. Phoenix and Tucson each have a team in the Pacific Hockey League.

Arizona has two *minor league baseball* teams. The Phoenix Giants and the Tucson Toros play in the AAA Pacific Coast League.

Arizona sports fans have many chances to watch some of the best athletes in the world.

Phoenix Suns star Walt Davis, known as "Sweet D", is guarded by a Seattle player.

A golfer's view of the Catalina Mountains north of Tucson.

A Phoenix hockey player heads for the goal.

Words and Terms to Know

motor home
per capita
monument
park ranger
tradition
diorama
avid
exhibition

Match the words above with the following definitions:
1. An official who enforces rules or laws in a public park.
2. Very eager or enthusiastic.
3. A custom or practice which has been going on for a long time.
4. A small house attached to a truck.
5. A stone statue, a building, or an area of land set aside to keep alive the memory of a person or an event.
6. For each person.
7. A museum display—usually on a smaller scale than the real thing—that shows how an actual event or scene looked.
8. A public display or show of such things as athletic talents or art work.

Finding the Facts

1. A variety of climates makes many kinds of _____ possible in Arizona.
2. Arizona has more _____ *per capita* than any other state.
3. The _____ _____ _____ _____ is Arizona's most popular tourist attraction.
4. Tourists can get a taste of the Old West by visiting _____, Old Tucson, or the "ghost town" of _____.
5. The _____ _____ _____ museum in Tucson has many colorful dioramas.
6. The _____ League is made up of major league baseball teams that train in Arizona.
7. Arizona State and the University of Arizona are in the _____ _____ Conference.
8. Arizona's only NBA professional basketball team is the _____ _____.

22. THE ARTS

A Navajo Indian painter.

The fast growth of Arizona's population has enriched the fine arts.

Arizonans can now enjoy live symphonies, rock concerts, or old-time fiddling. Many towns have art exhibits, live theater, and dance programs.

There are Indian ceremonial dances that non-Indians can watch. Arizona has many festivals. There are Mexican as well as Indian ones. Native dances, music, food, and craft exhibits can be enjoyed.

INDIAN ARTS

Arizona is known for Indian art. Navajo and Hopi silversmiths do beautiful work. Many Navajos are excellent painters.

Many reservations have *arts and crafts centers*. Silverwork, jewelry, baskets, pottery, and other Indian works can be bought at these centers.

Many *galleries* in the major cities also exhibit and sell Indian art works. Original

Hopi girl with pottery.

Pima Arts and Crafts Center on the Gila Indian Reservation south of Tucson.

paintings, jewelry, rugs, sculpture, glass work, and pottery are in demand by art buyers.

Indian *turquoise jewelry* is very popular. Today good turquoise is hard to get. Indian artisans are making fine jewelry using other things. They use malachite, shell, coral, ironwood, gold, jet, and diamonds.

PAINTING

Lew Davis was the first Arizona painter to be famous. He grew up in the mining town of Jerome. Davis was the son of a carpenter. He left home at age sixteen to study art in New York City.

Davis worked his way through art school. He came back to Jerome to paint. His paintings of the miners at Jerome helped make him famous.

Davis joined the army during World War II. He was assigned to Fort Huachuca. This fort was then a post for Black soldiers. At Huachuca he painted murals and posters with black instead of white faces. He did a 40-foot mural that was called *The Negro in America's Wars*. Davis also started a newspaper for Black soldiers.

These five 1974 *Arizona Highways* special issues include articles and photos on Indian pottery, weaving, and turquoise jewelry. All five are collector's issues.

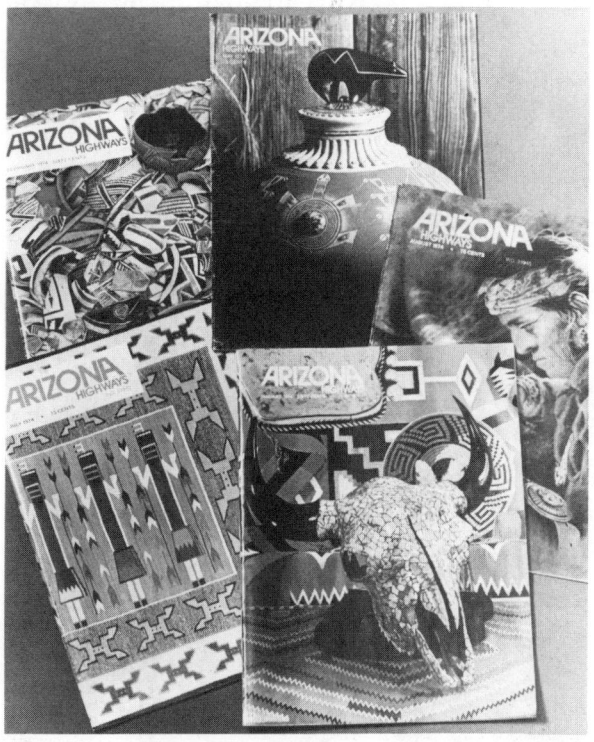

In the 1950s Davis and his wife had a simple home built in the desert north of Scottsdale. He likes to live and paint away from people.

Davis has won many awards for his paintings.

Ted DeGrazia is another famous Arizona artist. He grew up at Morenci. An Italian miner's son, DeGrazia became rich doing what he wanted to do—paint!

DeGrazia went to the University of Arizona for awhile. Next he went to Mexico City. In that city DeGrazia studied with two great Mexican painters. They were Rivera and Orozco.

DeGrazia's painting *Los Ninos* (the children) was chosen for the United Nations Christmas card in 1960. Many of his paintings have been in the *Arizona Highways*.

It is guessed that DeGrazia's paintings have been reproduced ten million times. They are on paperweights, T-shirts, jigsaw puzzles, playing cards, wall plaques, and many other things.

In his older years DeGrazia has painted many children. "Kids are joyful," he said. So he paints them in joyful, bright colors.

Maynard Dixon is another well-known painter. He grew up in California. But his first public paintings were for the Southern

"Wild Range Horses in the Corral," painting by Maynard Dixon.

Pacific railroad station in Tucson in 1909. Later he did several paintings of Indians at the Arizona Biltmore in Phoenix.

In and out of Arizona for years, Dixon at last settled in Tucson to get relief from asthma. He often painted scenes of the Catalina Mountains and the desert.

MUSIC

Live music and singing are heard in schools, churches, clubs, and civic groups all over the state.

Both Phoenix and Tucson have had *symphony orchestras* since the 1920s.

Two of the best-known *singing groups* are the Tucson Boys Chorus and the Orpheus Club in Phoenix. Both have given perfor-

Ted de Grazia painting a mural.

Music Hall at the Tucson Community Center seats 2,400 people.

Papago Indian dancers at the San Xavier Fiesta.

mances in Europe.

Local festivals have music along with the other arts. The Tucson Festival Society, for example, started ethnic programs in the 1950s. Two annual Tucson events are the *San Xavier Fiesta* and the *Fiesta of La Placita*. They show the colorful songs, dances, and customs of Indian and Mexican people.

Flagstaff is a fine arts center. The *Flagstaff Festival* has grown into a full summer of events. Great music, dance, theater, and films can be enjoyed. Big name artists perform at the Flagstaff Festival.

THEATER

Arizona's love of live theater goes back to pioneer days. Traveling actors used to visit mining camps and frontier towns.

Both Phoenix and Tucson had *little theaters* by the 1920s. The first Little Theater play in Phoenix was produced in an old carriage barn.

Today amateur plays and musicals are presented in theaters all over the state. Stars from Hollywood and Broadway perform in the larger cities.

ARCHITECTURE

The growth of large cities has changed Arizona architecture. Many high-rise buildings can now be seen in Phoenix and Tucson. These skyscrapers are modern in design.

Bennie M. Gonzales is one of the best-known architects. He was born in Arizona. Gonzales puts a love of vast space into his designs. He did this in the award-winning Scottsdale Civic Center.

Gonzales also designed libraries in Phoenix, Mesa, Wickenburg, and Nogales. In these buildings a person has a feeling of space and can enjoy panoramic views.

Frank Lloyd Wright designed some well-known buildings in Arizona. Wright believed that a building should look natural in its surroundings.

A good example of Wright's style is the Grady Gammage Auditorium in Tempe. It is a beautiful building. It is designed to give the feeling of a tent in the desert. The sides of the building appear to be raised like the canvas sides of a tent. Two long ramps look like tent ropes tied to stakes. All this is done

The Bird Cage Theatre stands today as one of Tombstone's most authentic tourist attractions.

Scottsdale City Hall, designed by Bennie M. Gonzales.

Grady Gammage Auditorium on the campus of Arizona State University at Tempe.

Arizona Biltmore Hotel in Phoenix.

Arcosanti.

with concrete, steel, and other strong materials.

Wright is sometimes given credit for the Arizona Biltmore in Phoenix. But this beautiful hotel was really designed by Albert Chase McArthur in the 1920s.

Wright was famous for his designs. He drew the plans for buildings all over the world. He did much of his work at Taliesen West in Paradise Valley.

Paolo Soleri studied at Taliesen West with Wright. Soleri wanted to combine architecture with ecology. He made the word "arcology" to name his style.

What is ecology? It is the study of all living things and the environment in which they can best live.

Soleri puts his arcology into practice. In the 1970s Soleri began building a new town called Arcosanti. It is located on a mesa near Cordes Junction between Phoenix and Flagstaff. College students from all over the country come to Arcosanti to work and to learn from Soleri.

In what ways does Arcosanti combine architecture and ecology?

Arcosanti, when it is done, will be a twenty-story city for 2,500 to 3,500 people. Both land and energy will be conserved. The whole city will cover only eight or nine acres.

A greenhouse on the side of the mesa will provide food. Hot air from the sun-warmed greenhouse will be carried through ducts to heat the buildings in the winter.

Roofs over the work areas are located so that they give shade in the summer. They let in the sun's rays in the winter months. The roofs at Arcosanti will catch rain water. The water will be stored in cisterns.

Arcosanti is not like most modern cities. Phoenix and Tucson, for example, are sprawling out. They are building on miles and miles of desert and farmland. But not Arcosanti. It will rise up, saving the land for other uses. It may well be the city of the future.

Words and Terms to Know

symphony orchestra	architecture
gallery	to design
turquoise	panoramic
artisan	ecology
mural	arcology
festival	cistern
custom	to sprawl

Match the words above with the following definitions:

1. A semiprecious stone which is greenish-blue, greenish-gray, or sky blue in color.
2. A picture, usually a large one, that is painted on a wall.
3. The art or profession of designing and constructing buildings.
4. To plan and make sketches.
5. To spread out without a regular pattern.
6. A place where paintings or other art works are on exhibit.
7. A kind of celebration or a series of entertaining events such as singing, plays, dances, or concerts.
8. A large group of musicians who play string, wind, and percussion instruments in harmony.
9. A skilled craftsman.
10. A study of living things and the environment where they live.
11. A combination of architecture and ecology.
12. A storage place for rain water.
13. A wide view in all directions.
14. A usual practice.

Finding the Facts

1. Arizona is a natural center for _____ art.
2. The _____ and _____ silversmiths make excellent jewelry.
3. Indian _____ jewelry is very popular.
4. _____ _____ was the first Arizona painter to earn a national reputation.
5. The paintings of _____ _____ have been reproduced millions of times.
6. _____ _____ has done many paintings of the Catalina Mountains near Tucson.
7. Both Phoenix and Tucson had a _____ orchestra and a little _____ by the 1920s.
8. _____ has an annual summer arts festival.
9. Architect Bennie Gonzales puts a love of _____ _____ into his building designs.
10. _____ _____ _____ designed Grady Gammage Auditorium at Arizona State University in Tempe.
11. Paolo Soleri named his style of architecture _____.
12. _____ is a twenty-story city that is being built between Phoenix and Flagstaff.

23. RAPID GROWTH AND PROBLEMS OF THE CITIES

Aerial view of downtown Phoenix looking north, 1977.

URBANIZATION

Many people are moving to Arizona from other states. Most of the newcomers settle in the bigger cities. Today three-fourths of Arizona residents are in or near Phoenix and Tucson. This movement of people to the cities is called *urbanization*.

Where does the remaining fourth of the people live? Most of them are in growing cities like Yuma, Flagstaff, Sierra Vista, Prescott, Casa Grande, Douglas, Peoria, Nogales, Lake Havasu City, Kingman, Winslow, Globe, Coolidge, Eloy, Avondale, Safford, and smaller places.

Arizona has a small rural population of farmers and ranchers.

Why are Arizona cities growing? The population boom started during World War II. Air bases and wartime industries brought people to the state.

The hot summer sun was a curse to pioneers. Now the heat has been tamed by air conditioning. We can live in comfort the year round.

Today Arizona is one of the fastest-growing states. Arizona's government and business leaders have tried to make it grow. The state has much to offer. A good climate, skilled labor, open spaces, and a growing market for goods attract new industries.

SUBURBS

Much of Arizona's growth is taking place on the outskirts of the cities. Many people left crowded cities in the East to seek wide-open spaces. They want one-family houses with trees and lawns. Most of the houses that meet these conditions are in the new *suburbs* of Phoenix and Tucson. So that is where the new residents go.

Urban sprawl. Phoenix and Tucson have sprawled out over the desert. This *urban sprawl* is taking over desert land and some of Arizona's best farms.

City planners would like to stop urban sprawl. Some want city governments to buy up lands near the cities. *Green belts* would then be made. The green belts would be wide enough to stop new towns being built close to the cities. What do you think about this?

One way to stop urban sprawl is to build high-rise housing in the cities.

Suburban Scottsdale is part of bigger Phoenix. This housing area was once farmed.

Phoenix farm, early 1900s. This land is now covered with houses.

Air pollution over Phoenix in the early 1970s.

A word of caution is offered to city planners. Stopping urban sprawl could make other problems. The inner cities might become too crowded. The crime rate would then go up. There might not be enough parking spaces. Noise pollution might also be a big problem.

Problems caused by urban sprawl. There are problems in urban sprawl too. A good mass transit system is not possible when people are spread out. Arizona cities do not have subway trains, elevated trains, or monorails. Phoenix and Tucson have bus systems but lose money on them.

Heavy traffic on Mill Avenue in Tempe.

An earth fissure east of Mesa. Cracks such as this one are caused by overpumping of groundwater.

Most people use their own car. Cars have some advantages. They are ready when needed. The driver can stop where he pleases. But the car also causes problems. Traffic jams, air pollution and noise are the result of too many cars on the streets.

Freeways can also cause problems. They divide neighborhoods. Some people have to move when their homes are in the way of a new freeway.

Urban sprawl also puts a strain on utilities. Tucson, for example, has a water shortage. All of Tucson's water is pumped from the ground. The city council began urging people to conserve water in the mid-1970s. The council tried to get Tucson residents not to water their lawns or trees at certain times of the day. Prominent people were asked to help. They gave short speeches on TV asking everyone to save water.

WATER

"Arizona grows where water flows." This statement is as true today as in old times.

Arizona's fast growth since World War II has put a strain on the water supply. Now about two-thirds of all water used in Arizona

As water becomes scarce, desert landscaping becomes more popular. Desert plants survive on natural rainfall.

is pumped from the ground. That is too much!

The amount of water being pumped is much more than is put back into the ground by rain and snow. Each year the ground water level goes down and down. In some parts of the state, land is sinking. Along Interstate 10 south of Eloy the land has sunk more than twelve feet.

To keep on growing, Arizona must save water, stop waste, and find *new sources of water*.

There are ways to increase our supply of water. Cleaned sewage water is called effluent. It is now being used by some farmers and mines. In the future, fresh water may have to be taken away from the farms for use in homes and factories. Water may have to be piped in from other states. Someday a cheap way of taking the salt out of sea water may be found.

Granite Reef aqueduct north of Scottsdale and Paradise Valley. The dike will hold back flood waters.

Central Arizona Project.

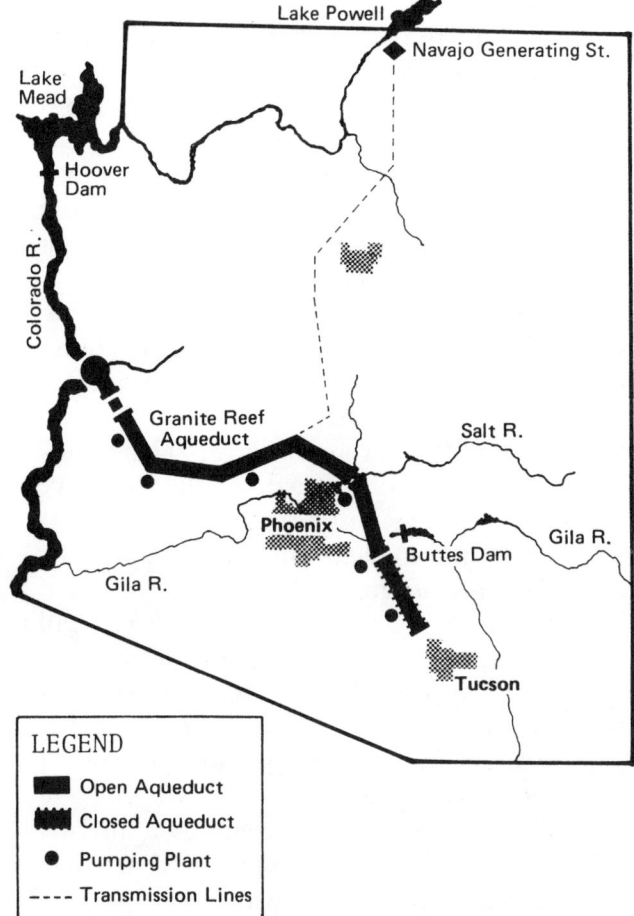

Central Arizona Project. The purpose of the Central Arizona Project is to bring water from the Colorado River to the counties of Maricopa, Pinal, and Pima. This new surface water will help. But it will not replace all the ground water that is being pumped.

The CAP water will be taken from Lake Havasu above Parker Dam on the Colorado River. The water will be pumped to a huge tunnel in the Buckskin Mountains. From the tunnel the water will flow in the concrete-lined Granite Reef Aqueduct (canal) to central Arizona. Two more canals will take some of the water to Tucson.

Arizona's future depends on having enough water.

ENERGY

Low-cost energy helped Arizona to grow. Most *electricity* has come from hydroelectric plants. These plants are at Hoover and other dams. At these dams water power is used to turn huge generators.

A lot of electricity is made at thermal plants. But some of these plants use natural gas and oil to run generators. These fuels are

Part of the Palo Verde nuclear generating plant. (Artist's drawing.)

The Navajo generating plant near Page burns coal.

getting scarce and costly.

Natural gas is piped into Arizona from gas fields in Texas and New Mexico. It is no longer a cheap source of energy.

There was a shortage of natural gas in the 1970s. During the peak-use times, the gas supply to big industrial users had to be cut off. In the future, both industries and homes may have to replace natural gas with other sources of energy.

Nuclear fuel can be used. It comes from uranium. Some people wonder if nuclear energy is safe. Arizona's first nuclear plant will be completed in the mid-1980s. It is the Palo Verde Nuclear Power plant. It is west of Buckeye.

More and more *coal* may be used to replace oil and natural gas. Most of Arizona's coal is at Black Mesa on the Navajo Reservation. This coal is used at the huge Navajo Generating Station near Page. The Black Mesa coal also is burned at the Mohave Power Plant near Bullhead City.

Coal and nuclear fuel will reduce the need for natural gas and oil.

As Arizona grows, more electricity will be needed. The time may come when *solar energy* can be used. It will either make electricity or replace it. But we must learn how to store heat from the sun for a long period of time at a low cost.

The technology of solar energy is already advanced enough that it can be used to warm some homes and to heat water.

Solar cooking. This little girl is saving electricity or gas.

Solar-heated house in Tucson.

THE FUTURE

Arizona has many challenges for the future.

The population will continue to grow. It should reach four million by the year 2000.

On the good side, growth can mean prosperity. How? New people and new industries bring business for merchants. New houses have to be built. More people are working. There are more kinds of jobs. As Arizona grows, the people have more choices. They can choose the kind of job, education, and fun they want.

On the other hand, Arizonans must pay attention to the need for water and energy. Something must be done about traffic jams, air pollution, and the needs of inner cities.

These problems are a threat to the "high quality" of life-style that attracts people to Arizona.

Words and Terms to Know

urbanization	effluent
suburb	hydroelectric
urban sprawl	generator
green belt	thermal
subway	nuclear
pollution	solar
conservation	technology
ground water	

Match the words above with the following definitions:

1. The spreading out of a city.
2. A residential area on the outskirts of a city.
3. The movement of people to the cities.
4. Water that is found below the surface in porous rock.
5. Having to do with the generating of electricity by water power.
6. The protection or care for natural resources such as water.
7. A machine that changes mechanical energy into electrical energy.
8. A kind of underground electric railroad found in some thickly-settled cities.
9. Having to do with the sun.
10. Having to do with heat.
11. Having to do with the central part of an atom which can be split to release energy.

12. An unsettled zone around a city.
13. The cleaned outflow from a sewage tank.
14. The condition of being dirty or impure—air, for example.
15. The science of practical arts.

Finding the Facts

1. Three-fourths of Arizona people live in in the urban areas of _____ and _____.
2. Arizona has a small _____ population of farmers and ranchers.
3. Some city planners want _____ _____ around the big cities to stop urban sprawl.
4. Most Arizonans depend on the _____ for transportation.
5. The amount of water pumped in Arizona is much more than the recharge from _____ and _____.
6. The purpose of the _____ _____ _____ is to bring water from the Colorado River to the central part of the state.
7. In the past Arizona's electricity came mainly from _____ plants.
8. _____ _____ is piped into Arizona from Texas and New Mexico.
9. _____ is replacing oil and natural gas in plants which generate electricity.
10. _____ energy is used in Arizona to warm some homes and to heat water.
11. The growth of Arizona means a greater variety of _____.
12. It is estimated that Arizona will have _____ million people by the year 2000.

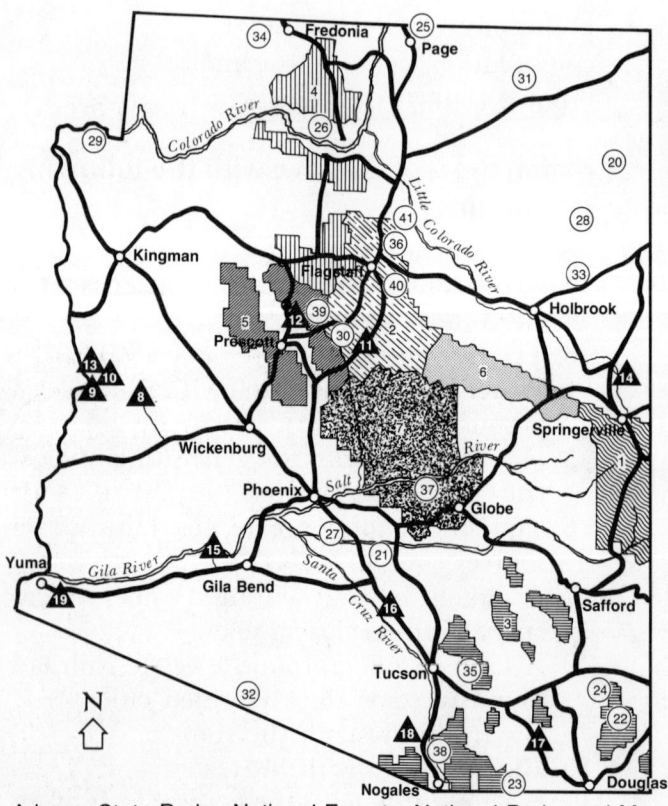

Arizona State Parks, National Forests, National Parks and Monuments

UNIT 6
ARIZONA COUNTIES

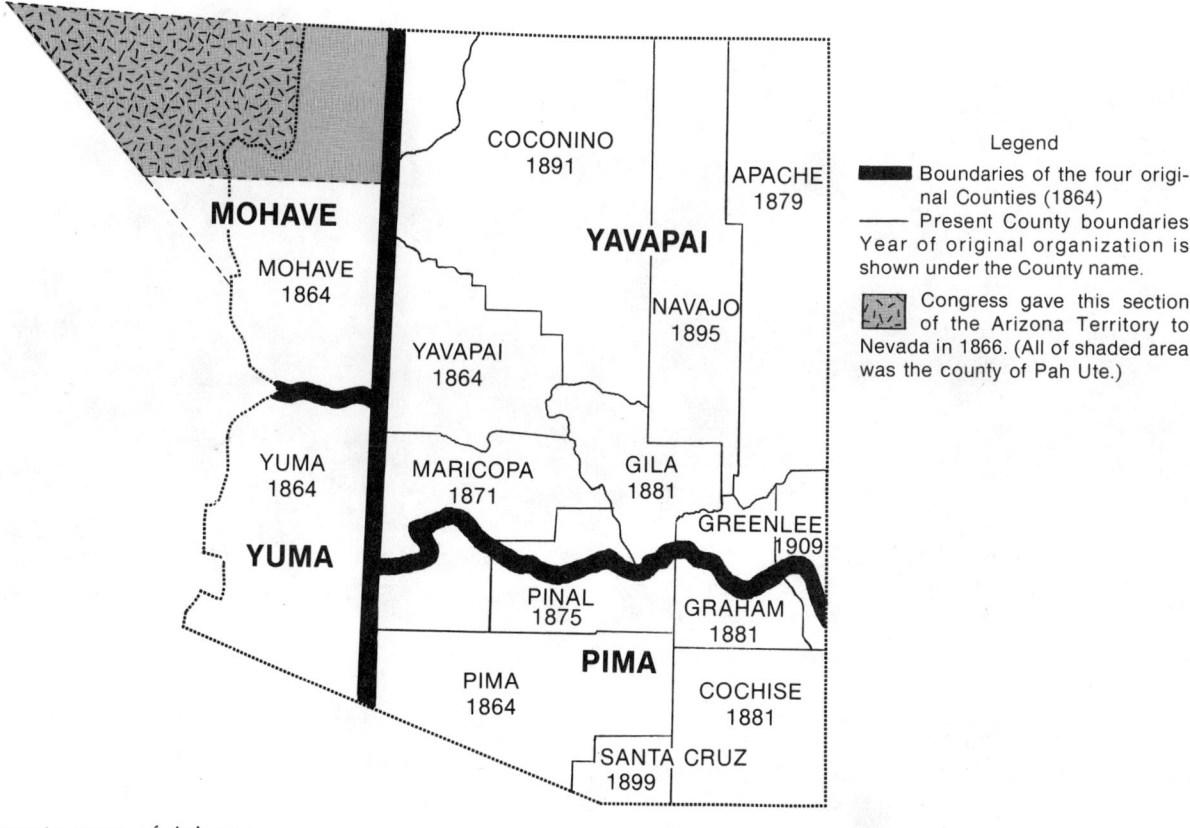

County map of Arizona.

The first legislature in 1864 divided the Territory of Arizona into four counties. During the next 45 years these four counties were split into fourteen. The last county, Greenlee, was created in 1909. That was just three years before Arizona became a state.

Each county has a county seat. It is the head city. Officers are elected to run the county. They work in a building that is usually called a courthouse.

Arizona has no "typical" county. The counties are all different. They vary in size, population, and scenery. They vary in the ways that people make a living.

Coconino County is the largest county in size. It is nearly fifteen times the size of Santa Cruz. Santa Cruz is the smallest county.

Maricopa County has more than half the people of the state. Greenlee has the fewest people. Less than one-half of one per cent of Arizonans live in Greenlee County.

24. THE FIRST COUNTIES

Some of the first officials of the Territory of Arizona. Seated (left to right): Associate Justice Joseph P. Allyn, Governor John N. Goodwin, and Secretary Richard C. McCormick. Standing (left to right): the Governor's private secretary, Henry W. Fleury; U.S. Marshal Milton B. Duffield; and U.S. District Attorney Almon P. Gage.

Arizona was divided into four counties in 1864. The first territorial legislature named each county after an Indian tribe: Pima, Yuma, Yavapai, and Mohave.

Only Yuma County has the same boundaries now. The other counties were split up. There are now 14 counties.

YUMA COUNTY

Yuma was the smallest of the first four counties. It was located along the Colorado River in southwestern Arizona.

La Paz was the first county seat of Yuma County. La Paz was a small mining town. Gold placers were discovered there in 1862 by Pauline Weaver and others. At one time La Paz had 1,500 people. They lived in tents and brush houses.

The first courthouse in La Paz was a house on Weaver Street. It was rented from Michael Goldwater. The rent was $40 a month.

In 1871 the county seat was moved to Arizona City. Arizona City is now called Yuma. The county officers and records were brought down the Colorado River on the steamboat *Nina Tilden*. That was an unusual way to move a desert county seat.

A small adobe courthouse was built in Arizona City. It was not fancy. Curtains separated the courtroom from the offices of the sheriff and the county recorder. The jail was an iron cage surrounded by wide adobe walls.

Judge William T. Howell.

PIMA COUNTY

Pima County, in 1864, had all the land south of the Gila River that was not in Yuma County.

Pima County was the best-known part of Arizona. The Spaniards, the Mexicans, and the first American pioneers from the States settled there.

Tucson has always been the county seat of Pima County. At first, county business was done in rented rooms. The federal district court was also in a rented house. Judge William T. Howell was the first federal judge to hold court in Tucson. After less than one year he quit. Howell said he could not be a judge in an adobe shack with a dirt floor. He only had a box for his bench.

Courthouses. The first courthouse in Pima County was built with adobe blocks. The wood that was used in the building came from mesquite trees.

A second courthouse was built in the early 1880s. It was a two-story brick building. A wing on each side gave this courthouse the shape of a cross. The center part had a cupola on top. This building served Pima County until the late 1920s.

The dividing of Pima County. Pima County was slowly split up by the legislature. Cochise, Santa Cruz, and parts of three other counties were carved out of Pima. But it is still a big county.

Pima County's second courthouse.

YAVAPAI COUNTY

Yavapai was the largest of the first four counties. It covered 65,000 square miles. It was larger than any state east of the Mississippi River.

The Spaniards explored this region. But there were no Spanish or Mexican towns in northern Arizona. The first Americans were mountain men looking for beaver. Then came American miners in the 1860s. They were searching for gold in the mountains south of present-day Prescott.

Prescott was founded in 1864. It was the capital of the Territory of Arizona for awhile. Prescott has always been the county seat of Yavapai County.

Prescott was unusual for an early Arizona town. In the first place, it was built mostly of wood, not adobe. The style of building was eastern rather than Indian or Mexican. Prescott had very wide streets. They were 100 feet wide.

The first Yavapai County officers did their work in a log cabin. It was later known as "Fort Misery."

Courthouses. The first courthouse had walls made of logs twelve inches thick. It had

195

Prescott, early 1880s.

Buckey O'Neill Monument in Prescott.

two stories. The courtroom was on the second floor. It was used for more than court trials. Methodists held church there. Clubs and other groups had meetings in the courtroom.

A two-story brick courthouse was built in Prescott in the late 1870s. It was Victorian in style. The front porch rested on columns. On the roof there was a cupola. It had a clock facing each direction.

The present courthouse was built during World War I. But the statue in front honors a hero of another war. Buckey O'Neill was a Rough Rider. He served in the Spanish-American War. He was killed in Cuba in 1898. The O'Neill statue was done by the famous sculptor Solon Borglum.

Yavapai County is called the "mother of counties." Four counties (Apache, Navajo, Coconino, and Gila) and parts of five other counties were carved out of Yavapai County. But it is still larger than some states.

Yavapai County's second courthouse.

MOHAVE COUNTY

Mohave County was the least known and explored of the original counties. It was located along the Colorado River north of Yuma County. In 1864 Mohave County included the southern tip of present-day Nevada.

The Mohave County seat was changed often. First it was at Mohave City. This town was close to Fort Mohave. The "county seat on wheels" was moved to Hardyville. Later it was Cerbat and then at Mineral Park. Last of all, it was in Kingman in 1887.

In the first three county seats, the county leaders did their work in rented buildings. But in Mineral Park they bought a building. It was made into a courthouse and jail. Mineral Park became a ghost town after the people of Mohave County voted to move the county seat to Kingman.

The location of the county seat tells the economic history of Mohave County. At first steamboating was the most important industry. The first county seats were places on the Colorado River.

Then came mining and mine town county seats. Next the railroad was built. Kingman was a railroad town. Lewis Kingman was the engineer who started the town. It was named after him.

Kingman is the only county seat of Mohave County that survives today.

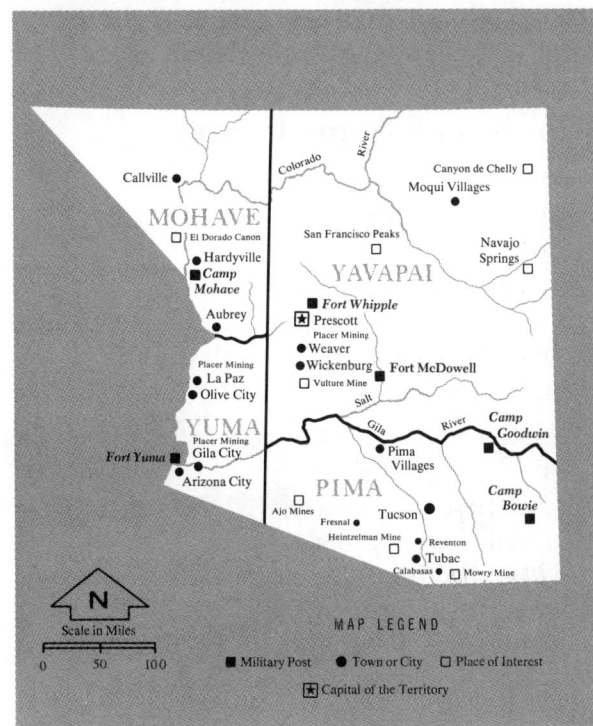

Arizona in 1865 before Pah-Ute County.

PAH UTE COUNTY

Pah Ute was the first new county. It was created in 1865 out of the northern part of Mohave County. Why? The main reason is that farmers were rapidly settling by the Colorado River. So the legislature formed a new county there.

Pah Ute was named for the Indian tribe of that region. At first the county seat was at Callville. This Mormon town was founded by Anson Call. A mail route connected Callville to the capital at Prescott. Later the county seat was moved to St. Thomas.

"Lost county of Pah Ute." In 1866 the United States Congress gave parts of Pah Ute and Mohave counties to Nevada. This land was west of the Colorado River. It became the southern triangle of Nevada. The most important town there now is Las Vegas.

The little towns of Callville and St. Thomas did not last long. Now the sites of these towns are under the waters of Hoover Dam.

The land that was given to Nevada is known as Arizona's "lost colony."

Words and Terms to Know

county
county boundaries
county seat
courthouse
cupola
Victorian architecture
site

Match the words above with the following definitions:

1. A division of a state which has a government.
2. A town or city that is the center of a county government.
3. The building that houses the offices of a county government.
4. The style of architecture when Victoria was queen of England.
5. A small dome on a roof.
6. The borders of a county.
7. A plot of ground set aside for a town or some other use.

Finding the Facts

1. _____ County is the only one of the four original counties which has the same boundaries today.
2. The first county seat of Yuma County was _____ _____.
3. Yuma County records were moved to Arizona on the steamboat _____ _____.
4. _____ County was the best known of the four original counties.
5. The county seat of Pima County has always been _____.
6. _____ and _____ _____ counties were carved out of Pima County.
7. _____ is sometimes called the "mother of counties."
8. At one time _____ was both the capital of the territory and the county seat of Yavapai County.
9. A famous statue of _____ _____ is in front of the Yavapai County courthouse.
10. _____ County once included the southern tip of Nevada.
11. The county seats of Mohave County were _____ _____, _____, _____, _____ _____, and _____.
12. _____ has always been an important railroad town.
13. _____ _____ County was created from the northern part of Mohave County.
14. The towns of _____ and _____ were county seats of Pah Ute County.
15. Part of Pah Ute County was given to the state of _____.

25. THE FOURTEEN COUNTIES

ARIZONA POPULATION STATISTICS

	1940	1950	1960	1970	1978
STATE TOTAL	499,261	749,587	1,302,161	1,775,399	2,449,200
The Counties					
Apache	24,095	27,767	30,438	32,304	49,000
Cochise	34,627	31,488	55,039	61,918	79,500
Coconino	18,770	23,910	41,857	48,326	72,200
Gila	23,867	24,158	25,745	29,255	34,300
Graham	12,113	12,985	14,045	16,578	22,200
Greenlee	8,698	12,805	11,509	10,330	11,200
Maricopa	186,193	331,770	663,510	971,228	1,346,500
Mohave	8,591	8,510	7,736	25,857	46,200
Navajo	25,309	29,446	37,994	47,559	65,000
Pima	72,838	141,216	265,660	351,667	474,100
Pinal	28,841	43,191	62,673	68,579	89,900
Santa Cruz	9,482	9,344	10,808	13,966	18,800
Yavapai	26,511	24,991	28,912	37,005	59,700
Yuma	19,326	28,006	46,235	60,827	80,600
Leading Cities					
Phoenix	64,414	106,818	439,170	582,500	690,100
Tucson	35,752	45,454	212,892	262,933	309,600

Source: Bureau of the Census, except 1978 data which is a preliminary estimate from the Arizona Department of Economic Security. Tucson figures for 1978 are by the Tucson City Planning Department. Phoenix figures are by the Phoenix City Planning Department.

Arizona population statistics.

Arizona now has fourteen counties and fourteen county seats. The counties are different in size and number of people. The ways of making a living are determined by climate, resources, and population. Tourism in the northern counties, for example, is best during the cool summer months. But in the southern counties, the peak of tourism is in the warm winter and early spring.

About a million people have jobs in Arizona. The kinds of jobs change from county to county. Statewide about a fifth of the employed people work in a wholesale or retail business.

The next largest number of job holders work for the government. They may work for the federal, state, or local government. Other workers are in the service trades. Some have jobs in the factories and mines. Other people work on farms and ranches.

APACHE COUNTY

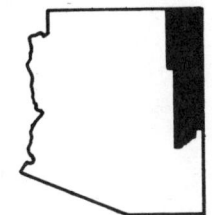

LAND AREA
7,151,000 acres (11,171 square miles)

POINTS OF INTEREST
Petrified Forest National Park, Canyon De Chelly, Four Corners, Window Rock, Big Lake, Hawley Lake, Sunrise Lake and Ski Area.

PRINCIPAL INDUSTRIES
Lumbering, tourism, livestock, government, utilities.

POPULATION
1970 Census 32,304
1978 Estimate 49,000

Apache County.

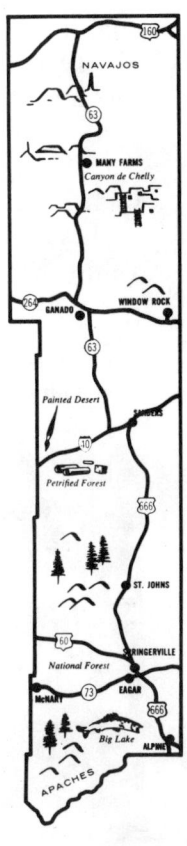

Apache County was formed out of Yavapai in 1879. Many of the early people were Mormons.

Apache County was much larger at first. But parts of Gila and Graham counties were carved out of Apache in 1881. Apache County was split again in 1895 when Navajo County was formed.

County seats. *Snowflake* (now in Navajo County) was the first county seat of Apache County. But after a few months, the people voted to move the county seat to *St. Johns*. It was then moved to *Springerville* for a short time and then back to St. Johns.

Apache County has three main parts. Apache is a narrow county. It is over 200 miles from north to south. It has three geographical sections.

The *northern part* of the county is Navajo Indian land. The basic industries in this section are sheep raising, mining, and tourism.

The Little Colorado River runs through the *central part* of Apache County. This central section is mainly cattle country. But the big coal-fired Coronado Generating Station now gives the town of St. Johns a new source of income. Part of the Petrified National Forest is in the central section.

The *southern part* of Apache County is high mountain country. Mount Baldy is the highest point. It rises to 11,590 feet in the White Mountains.

One of Arizona's famous "lost gold

Spider rock is in Canyon De Chelly on the Navajo Reservation.

mines" is in this region. It is somewhere in the triangle between Mount Baldy and the towns of Springerville and Alpine. The lost mine is known as "Adams Diggings."

Most of the southern part of Apache County is covered with timber. The ponderosa pine and spruce trees are two big sources of lumber. This section also has many trout streams. Thousands of tourists come to fish.

Part of the Fort Apache Indian Reservation is in the southwest corner of the county. The Apaches have good forests. They now have campgrounds and ski runs for tourists.

Land ownership. Only 17 per cent of Apache County is private land. Indian reservations cover 62 per cent of the county. The rest of the land is owned by the U.S. or Arizona governments.

The Hubbell Trading Post on the Navajo Reservation near Ganado.

COCHISE COUNTY

LAND AREA
4,004,000 acres (6,256 square miles)

POPULATION
1970 Census 61,918
1978 Estimate 79,500

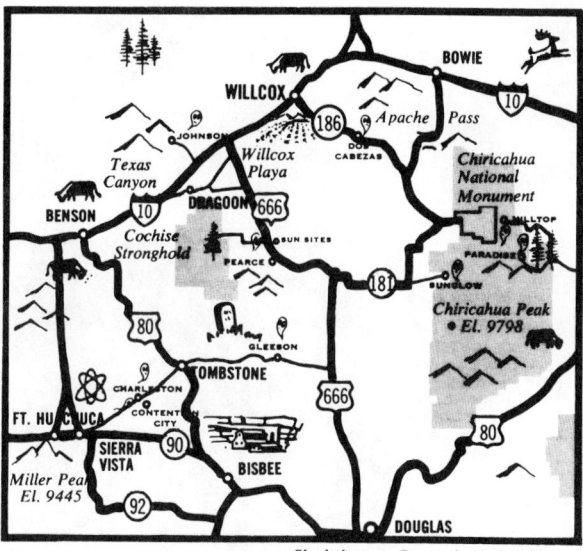

Shaded areas: Coronado National Forest

PRINCIPAL INDUSTRIES
Farming & ranching, tourism, military (worldwide communications center and electronic proving grounds).

POINTS OF INTEREST
Old Fort Bowie, Lavender Pit (open pit copper mine), Tombstone, Chiricahua National Monument, Coronado National Memorial.

Cochise County.

Cochise County was created by the legislature in 1881. It was carved out of Pima County.

County seats. *Tombstone* was the first county seat. The old Tombstone courthouse is now a museum. There is a gallows in the courtyard. It is a reminder of the old days when the sheriff did the hanging.

The people voted to move the county seat to *Bisbee* in 1929. By that time the Bisbee mines were producing lots of copper. The town was named for Judge DeWitt Bisbee.

The old Tombstone Courthouse.

It was given his name even though he was never there. He was a part owner of the Copper Queen mine.

The Copper Queen is no longer worked. But tourists can take tours through the old underground mine. The old Lavender Pit mine can also be seen. A visitor can imagine how Bisbee was in frontier times by walking along Brewery Gulch. A lot of the old buildings are still there.

Other towns. The town of *Douglas* was founded in 1901. It had a smelter for copper mines. Today Douglas is a retail trade center. It has some small factories. Ranching and farming are also important to Douglas.

Willcox is the leading farming town in Cochise County. Willcox has long been known for cattle ranching. Now farming is important too. Lettuce and other crops are grown on irrigated farms.

Willcox was the home town of Rex Allen. He was a famous western movie star. "Rex Allen Days" is an annual event in Willcox. People enjoy the rodeo, parade, western music, and square dancing

Tourists wear mining outfits in the Copper Queen Mine. They walk into the mine. The narrow gauge mining car, shown here, brings them out.

Benson is a transportation center on the Southern Pacific Railroad. The Apache Powder Company is a major industry.

Sierra Vista is the largest town in the county. It is a modern town. It was not incorporated until 1956.

Many of Sierra Vista's residents work at nearby *Fort Huachuca*. This fort is an electronics proving ground. Communications equipment is tested there. Huachuca is the worldwide communications center for the United States Army. A museum at the fort has displays of old U.S. Army uniforms and weapons.

The Chiricahua National Monument is one of the amazing places in Cochise County. It is southeast of Willcox. This monument is a "wonderland of rocks." During millions of years, the rains eroded volcanic lava and made beautiful rock formations. The Chiricahua monument was once the hunting ground of Cochise and the Chiricahua Apache Indians.

The history of Cochise County is closely tied to Arizona's history. The county was the home of the state's first people. The first hunters killed elephants by the San Pedro River. "Cochise man" is the name given to people who were the link between the elephant hunters and later Indians.

Tourists get an idea about what Arizona's frontier days were like by visiting Tombstone, Bisbee, and ghost towns in the county.

Cochise County is still largely rural. Cattle ranching, farming, and mining are important. The towns are small, quiet, and unhurried.

COCONINO COUNTY

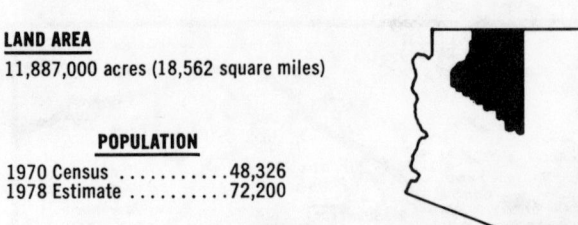

LAND AREA
11,887,000 acres (18,562 square miles)

POPULATION
1970 Census 48,326
1978 Estimate 72,200

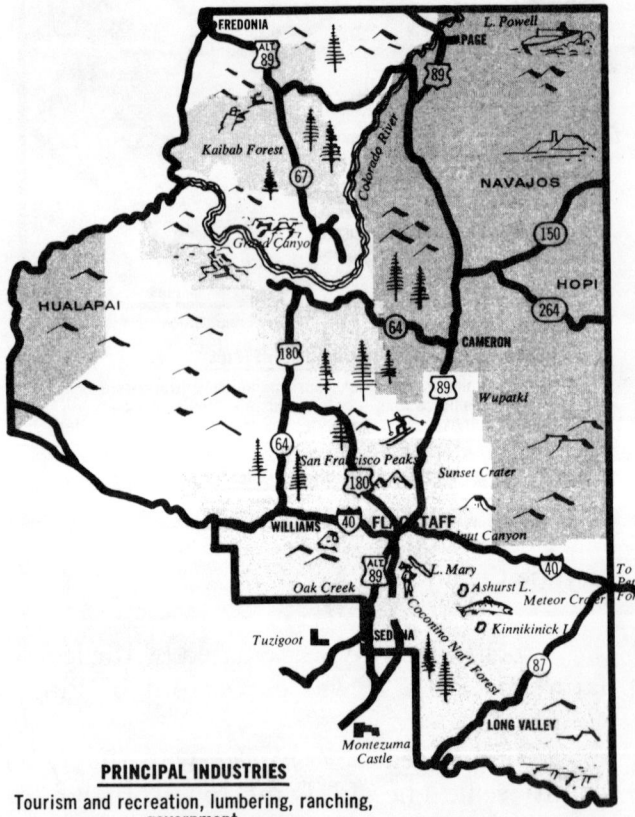

PRINCIPAL INDUSTRIES
Tourism and recreation, lumbering, ranching, government.

POINTS OF INTEREST
Grand Canyon National Park, Sunset Crater National Monument, Walnut Canyon National Monument, Wupatki National Monument, Oak Creek Canyon, Lowell Observatory, Meteor Crater, Glen Canyon Dam, Snow Bowl, Mormon Lake.

Coconino County.

Coconino is the largest county in Arizona. It has 18,562 square miles.

Coconino County was formed by the legislature in 1891. It was carved out of the northern part of Yavapai County. At one time "Frisco" was considered as a name for the new county.

The people voted to have the county seat at Flagstaff. A courthouse was built on land given by the Atlantic and Pacific Railroad. The two-story courthouse was built of native stone. It is still in use today.

The main industries of Coconino County are lumbering, cattle and sheep ranching, and tourism. Millions of tourists visit the county. They come to sightsee, ski, hunt, or fish. The Snow Bowl is north of Flagstaff. It is a popular place in the winter time. The number one attraction any time of the year is the Grand Canyon.

Towns. *Flagstaff* is the largest city. It depends on all the above industries. It is the most important trade center in northern Arizona. Flagstaff is the home of Northern Arizona University. Lowell Observatory is there too. Astronomers working at this observatory discovered the planet Pluto.

Williams started as a lumber, ranching,

Aerial view of Flagstaff.

Chapel of the Holy Cross near Sedona in Oak Creek Canyon.

and railroad town. Tourism is now a major industry too. Williams is sometimes called the "Gateway to the Grand Canyon." The headquarters for the Kaibab National Forest is in Williams. Nearby is Bill Williams Mountain. Annual dog-sled races are held there in February.

The town of *Page* is located near Glen Canyon Dam and Lake Powell. This huge lake is man-made. It draws tourists and water sportsmen from all over the world. The Navajo Power Plant near Page is a big producer of electricity.

The town of *Sedona* is in the beautiful red rock country of Oak Creek Canyon. Some retired people live there year-round. Sedona is a popular place for summer homes. Many artists and writers live there.

Land ownership. About a third of Coconino County has been set aside by the federal government for *national forests and parks*. Part of the world's largest stand of ponderosa pine trees is in the county.

Coconino County is Indian country. *Indian reservations* have 37 per cent of the land. An Indian powwow is held in Flagstaff each summer.

The *State of Arizona* owns 9 per cent of Coconino County. *Private* owners have 14 per cent.

GILA COUNTY

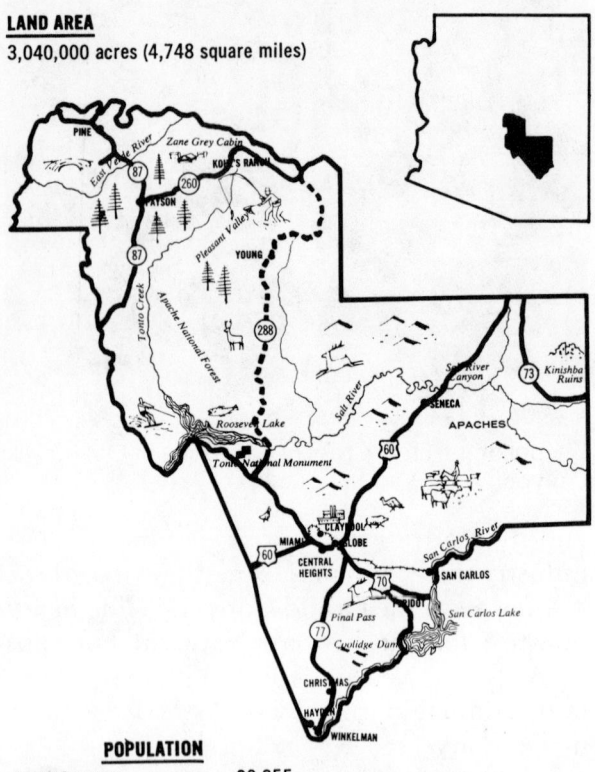

LAND AREA
3,040,000 acres (4,748 square miles)

POPULATION
1970 Census 29,255
1978 Estimate 34,300

PRINCIPAL INDUSTRIES
Copper mining & smelting, ranching, timbering, tourism & recreation.

POINTS OF INTEREST
Salt River Canyon, Tonto National Monument, Coolidge Dam, Roosevelt Dam and Lake, Kinishba Ruins.

Gila County.

Gila became a county in 1881. It was enlarged eight years later. The legislature allowed Gila County to buy 1,500 square miles from Yavapai County. This added land is now the northern part of Gila County. It includes the Payson, Pine, and Pleasant Valley areas.

Mining and other industries. Silver mining brought the first white settlers to Gila County in the 1870s. Later, copper ores were found beneath the silver.

The mining town of Globe became known as a place with a "silver crown and a copper bottom." Large copper mines were also found at Miami, Hayden, and Christmas.

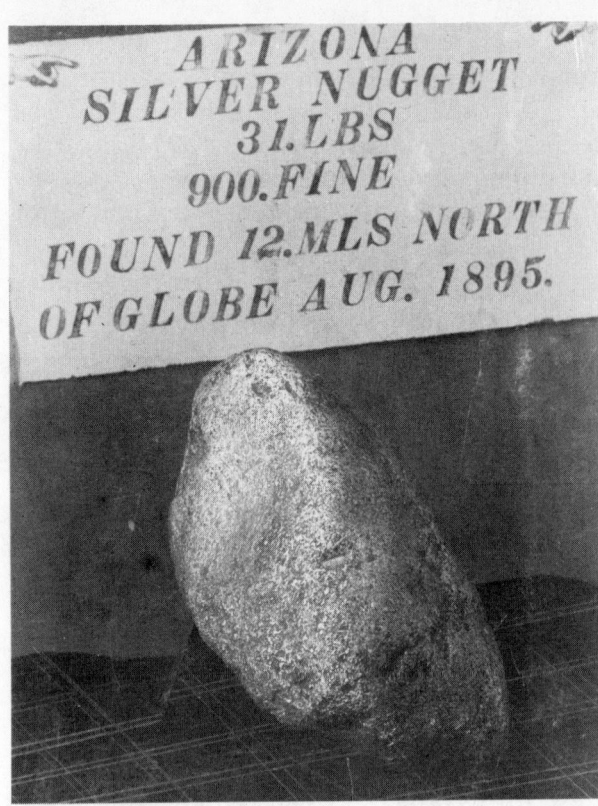

Silver nugget north of Globe in 1895.

Other industries in Gila County today are ranching, lumbering, tourism, and recreation.

Globe has always been the county seat of Gila County. A new courthouse was built in Globe in 1976. It was designed by a woman architect. Her name is Anne Rysdale. The courthouse blends into Globe's history and environment. It has a copper roof, brick walls, and shaded archways in front.

George W. P. Hunt came from Globe. He was one of Arizona's most famous politicians. As a young man, Hunt rode into town on a burro. By hard work he became a rich merchant. But as governor Hunt spoke for the common man. He is sometimes called "George VII" because he was elected governor seven times.

Three parts of the county. Most of Gila County is rugged country. It stretches from the Gila River and Coolidge Dam on the south to the Mogollon Rim on the north. In

Salt River Canyon.

between are mountain ranges and valleys. There are many kinds of scenery in Gila County.

In the *southern part* the country near Winkelman is cactus-covered desert and rocky mountains.

The best-known places of the *central part* are the beautiful Salt River Canyon and Roosevelt Lake.

The high *northern part* is covered with pine trees.

The Graham-Tewksbury feud was an exciting event in Arizona's history. The feud took place in Pleasant Valley east of Payson. The Graham and Tewksbury families were once friendly ranchers. But a feud started when they quarreled over cattle which they had stolen together.

The feud really heated up when the Tewksburys agreed to protect some sheep in Pleasant Valley. The sheep belonged to the Daggs brothers of Flagstaff. The Grahams did not want sheep in the valley. The fussing and shooting went on until all the Graham males were killed.

Zane Grey was a world famous writer. He wrote about the Graham-Tewksbury feud. He lived on a ranch near Payson. Some of the novels he wrote were *To the Last Man, Riders of the Purple Sage,* and *Under the Tonto Rim.*

Some of Grey's stories were about hunting in the early 1900s. There is still a lot of wildlife in Gila County. Hunting, fishing, and camping bring many people to the mountains, forests, streams, and lakes.

Land ownership. Only 3 per cent of Gila County is privately-owned. The Tonto National Forest is in the north and west parts of the county. It takes up 56 per cent of the land.

Indian reservations cover 38 per cent of Gila County. They are in the eastern part of the county.

Another 3 per cent of the county is owned by governments.

GRAHAM COUNTY

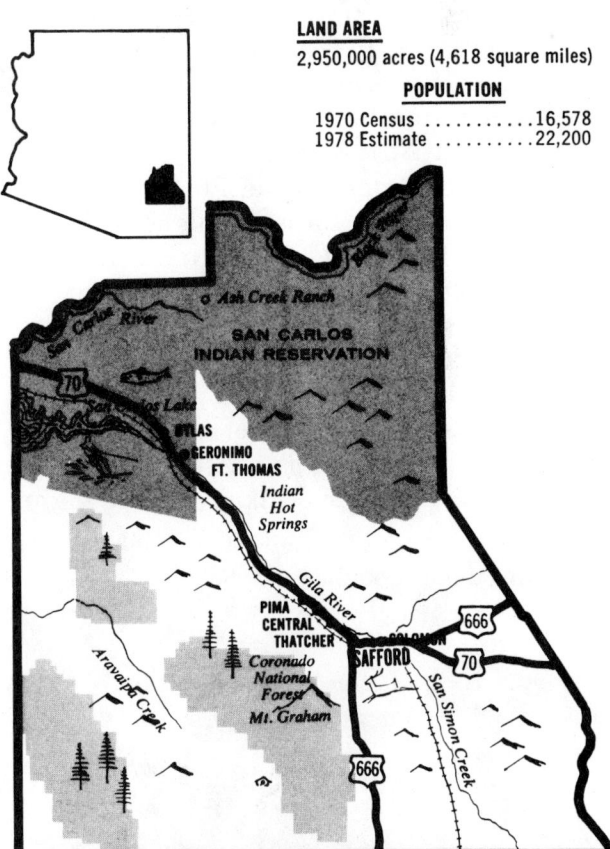

LAND AREA
2,950,000 acres (4,618 square miles)
POPULATION
1970 Census 16,578
1978 Estimate 22,200

POINTS OF INTEREST
Mt. Graham, San Carlos Lake, Aravaipa Canyon, San Carlos Indian Reservation.

PRINCIPAL INDUSTRIES
Farming and ranching, tourism and recreation.

Graham County.

Graham County was created in 1881. The county seat has been at Safford except from 1883 to 1915. During that time Solomonville was the county seat.

Until 1909, Graham County included the land that is now in Greenlee County.

Industries. Farming and ranching have always been major industries in Graham County. Cotton and sorghums are the main crops. Barley and alfalfa are also raised.

The most famous ranch in Graham County is the Sierra Bonita. It was started by Henry Hooker in the Sulphur Springs Valley.

Mining will someday be important in Graham County. The Phelps Dodge Company is making an underground copper mine north of the Gila River.

Towns. The town of *Safford* was named for Governor A. P. K. Safford. The town depends on trade as well as farming. Safford is the trade center for much of eastern Arizona and western New Mexico.

Safford is close to the Pinaleño Mountains. Mount Graham is the highest peak in this range. It is 10,717 feet high. In the summer, people go to the cool pine country on Mount Graham.

Thatcher is located three miles west of Safford. The Gila River provides water for crops, fruit, and pecans. Beef cattle are raised on ranches. Dairying is another important industry in Thatcher. Milk processing plants and cotton gins are there. Thatcher is also the site of Eastern Arizona College.

Pima is an important farming town by the Gila River. Pima was founded by Mormons in 1879. At first it was called Smithville.

Land ownership. Only 10 per cent of Graham County is owned privately. A third of the county is in the San Carlos Apache Indian Reservation. The rest of the land is owned by the U.S. and Arizona government.

Small population. Graham County is lucky in one way. Not many people live there. Graham does not have the pollution and traffic problems that face counties with lots of people.

GREENLEE COUNTY

LAND AREA
1,199,000 acres (1,879 square miles)

POPULATION
1970 Census 10,330
1978 Estimate 11,200

PRINCIPAL INDUSTRIES
Copper mining and smelting, ranching, tourism.

POINTS OF INTEREST
Coronado Trail, Hannagan Meadows, Blue River, Morenci open pit copper mine.

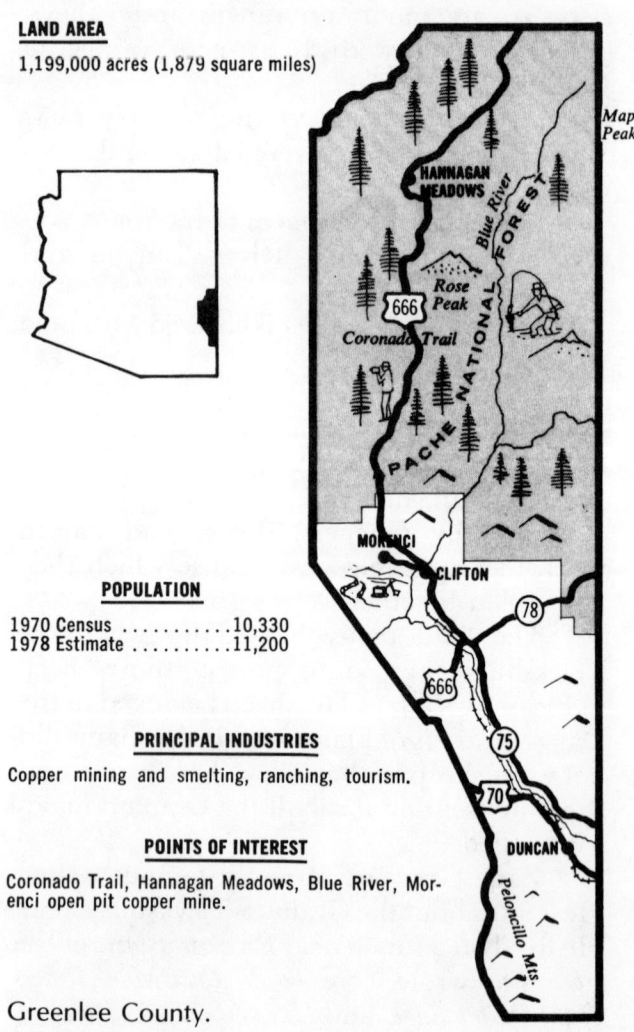

Greenlee County.

Graham County Courthouse at Safford, 1917.

Greenlee was the last county to be formed. It was carved out of the eastern part of Graham County in 1909.

Greenlee County took over the debts of Graham County. This deal was fair because Greenlee got the rich mining districts of Clifton and Morenci.

"**Copper is king**" in Greenlee County. The county is named after Mason Greenlee. He found the first mine. It is north of Clifton. Copper has been mined at Clifton-Morenci since the 1870s. Today two-thirds of the workers in Greenlee County work for the mines.

Towns and industries. *Clifton* is the county seat. This town was once the main mining town. But *Morenci* is now the hub of copper mining in the county. The open-pit mine at Morenci is the second largest in the United States. It is a great sight to see.

Duncan is a farming and cattle shipping town in the southern part of the county. It is by the Gila River. Duncan is sometimes damaged by floods. The town was started in 1883. It was a station on the Arizona and New Mexico Railroad. This railroad connected Clifton with the Southern Pacific at Lordsburg, New Mexico.

Stock raising is important in Greenlee County. The first ranchers came in the 1870s and 1880s.

The Apache National Forest takes in 65 per cent of Greenlee County. The famous *Coronado Trail* runs through this forest north of Clifton. The scenery along the trail is a breath-taking sight anytime of the year.

MARICOPA COUNTY

Greenlee County Courthouse, Clifton.

Gila River flood at Duncan, 1941.

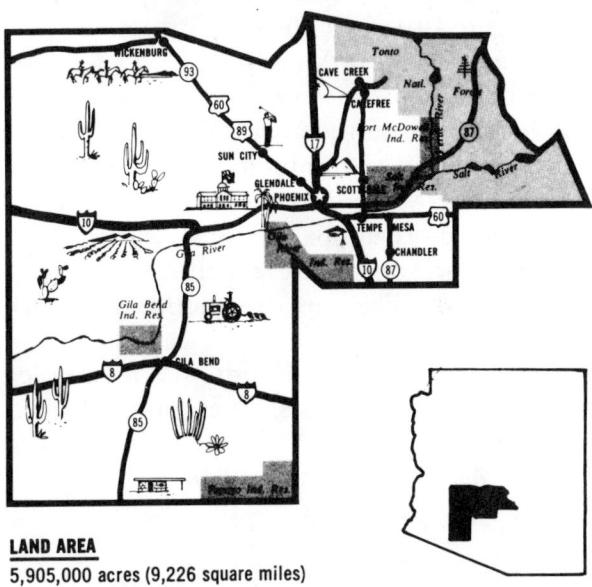

LAND AREA
5,905,000 acres (9,226 square miles)

POPULATION
1970 Census 971,228
1978 Estimate 1,346,500

PRINCIPAL INDUSTRIES
Manufacturing (high technology products), agriculture (largest producer of crops and livestock in the state), tourism and travel (over $1 billion in annual expenditures).

POINTS OF INTEREST
Phoenix Art Museum, Heard Museum, Phoenix Zoo, Pueblo Grande pre-historic ruins, Big Surf, Apache Trail, Arizona Mormon Temple, Desert Botanical Gardens, Phoenix Civic Plaza Center, Valley Bank Center.

Maricopa County.

In 1871 Governor A. P. K. Safford signed a law that made Maricopa the fifth county. The county boundaries were changed several times in the next ten years. Some land was added. Then other land was taken away to form parts of Pinal and Gila counties.

The first county election was in 1871. At the election, the place for the county seat was decided. The two rival towns are both part of present-day Phoenix. The winner was the "Phoenix townsite" where downtown Phoenix is today. The loser was "Mill City." This settlement was near Swilling's ditch in east Phoenix.

The first election for sheriff of Maricopa County was too exciting! One man withdrew from the race after he shot and killed the other candidate. The names of two new candidates were put on the ballot. Tom Barnum was elected the first sheriff.

Courthouses. Maricopa County's first courthouse was in William Hancock's little adobe store. County officers shared the space with the town government, a butcher shop, and a general store.

Two more adobe buildings were rented. Later, a two-story brick courthouse was built in the 1880s. The new courthouse had a 75-foot clock tower.

Today Maricopa County has a complex of county buildings. As the county grows,

Second Maricopa County Courthouse.

The Mormon Temple is a familiar landmark in Mesa.

more buildings are added for new courtrooms and offices.

The rapid growth of Phoenix. Maricopa County is one of the nation's fastest growing places. Over half of the people in Arizona live in the county.

Five of Arizona's six largest cities are in Maricopa County. These cities are Phoenix, Mesa, Tempe, Scottsdale, and Glendale. They are growing fast.

Growth depends on a good water supply. Maricopa County is lucky in this respect. The Roosevelt and other dams on the Salt River supply good surface water.

Maricopa County has become a manufacturing center. The electronics and other industries employ thousands of people.

Many companies now have their national headquarters in Maricopa County. Examples are Ramada Inns, U-Haul, Greyhound bus, and Cudahy meats.

Farming and ranching are still major sources of income in Maricopa County. Tourism does well because of the mild winters. Maricopa County is also a good retirement place. Sun City, a town for retired people, is now one of the largest cities in Arizona.

Phoenix is both the county seat and the state capital. Many people have government jobs. The school districts and the United States government also employ lots of people.

Outlying towns. There are many towns near Phoenix.

Gila Bend is in the southwest part of the

county. Farming is the main industry. Cotton raising and cattle feeding are big sources of income. Gila Bend is also a tourist stop for people going to and from California.

Wickenburg is in the northwest part of the county. It was once known as the "dude ranch capital of Arizona." Tourism is still important in Wickenburg.

Chandler is in the southeast part of the county. It has long been a farming town. It is now a manufacturing center too. Mobile homes are just one product made in Chandler. Other sources of income are tourism and Williams Air Force Base.

Maricopa County has many scenic and historic attractions. There are lakes. They are Pleasant, Bartlett, Saguaro, Canyon, Apache, and Firebird. These lakes make water sports a year-round pastime.

For nature lovers, Phoenix can boast of South Mountain Park. It is the largest city park in the world. Few tourists miss the Japanese flower gardens on Baseline Road. The best place to learn about desert plants is at the Desert Botanical Garden in east Phoenix. Nearby is the Phoenix Zoo. Both native and foreign wildlife are kept there.

Ancient Indian culture can be studied at the Pueblo Grande and the Heard Museum in Phoenix. Indian picture writings can be seen at Painted Rock State Park near Gila Bend.

Japanese flower gardens in south Phoenix. The flowers are sold commercially. They are a popular tourist attraction when in bloom.

Pioneer Arizona is north of Phoenix. It is a living history museum. Some of the old buildings are original. Others are re-created to look like early Arizona buildings.

These attractions, and many more, can keep tourists and Arizona residents busy for days and days.

MOHAVE COUNTY

LAND AREA
8,486,000 acres (13,227 square miles)

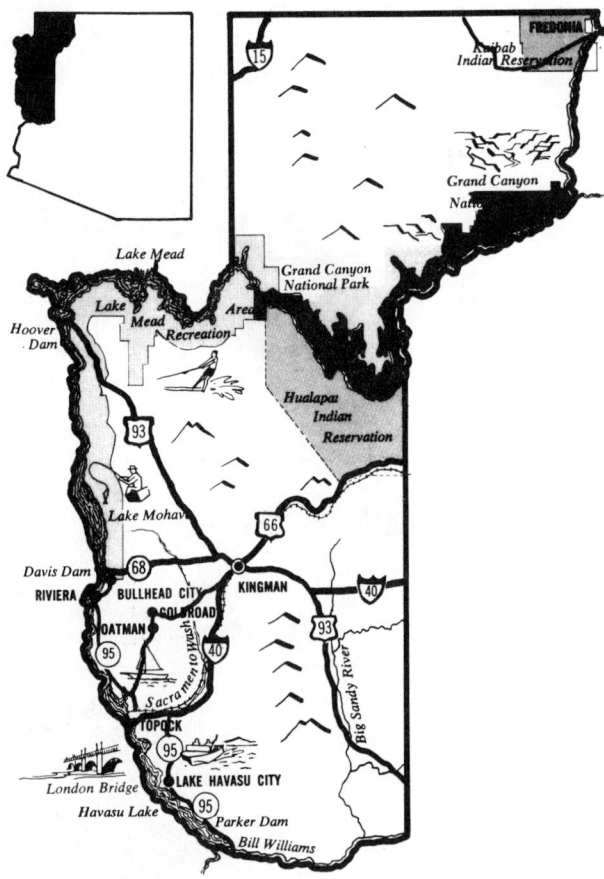

POPULATION
1970 Census 25,857
1978 Estimate 46,200

PRINCIPAL INDUSTRIES
Manufacturing, tourism, ranching, copper mining.

POINTS OF INTEREST
Colorado River, Lake Havasu (London Bridge), Hoover Dam, Lake Mead, Grand Canyon National Park.

Mohave County.

Mohave was one of the first four counties. It is now one of the fastest-growing counties.

In the old days most of the people depended on mining. But now the county has a variety of industries. Many of the early mining centers are now ghost towns.

The Colorado River is a big asset to Mohave County. About a thousand miles of fresh water shoreline are in the county.

Lake Havasu City depends on the river. It was founded in 1963 on the east side of Lake Havasu. This man-made lake is behind Parker Dam on the Colorado River.

Lake Havasu is a water recreational center. It is the scene of big time boat races. There

Beach at Lake Havasu City.

London Bridge at Lake Havasu City.

Davis Dam and Lake Mohave on the Colorado River.

are sailing contests and water skiing. London Bridge is an unusual sight in Lake Havasu City. It was brought, stone by stone, from London and rebuilt.

In addition to tourism, Lake Havasu City has several factories. Chain-saw parts, boats, furniture, tools, clothing, and other things are made there.

Other Colorado River towns are *Bullhead City* and *Riviera*. They are near Davis Dam. Electricity is generated at this dam. Lake Mohave is upstream from Davis Dam. It is a popular place for water sports.

Kingman is the county seat. Today the town does not depend solely on the railroad. Several factories have been built there. Kingman has a good tourist business too. Many travelers on Interstate 40 and people headed for Hoover Dam or Las Vegas stop in Kingman.

Size and land ownership. In size Mohave is the second largest county in the state. It is split into two parts by the Colorado River. The thinly-populated part north of the river is called the Arizona Strip.

Over half of Mohave County is owned by the United States government. One-fifth of the land belongs to private parties. Indian reservations cover 7 per cent of the county. The State of Arizona has 6 per cent of the land in Mohave County.

NAVAJO COUNTY

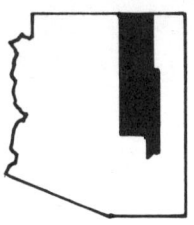

LAND AREA
6,343,000 acres (9,910 square miles)

POPULATION
1970 Census 47,559
1978 Estimate 65,000

PRINCIPAL INDUSTRIES
Tourism, coal mining, manufacturing, timbering, ranching.

POINTS OF INTEREST
Petrified Forest National Park, Painted Desert, White Mountains (hunting and fishing), Hopi Indian villages, Navajo National Monument, Monument Valley.

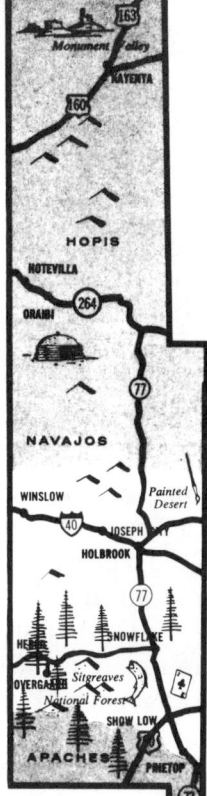

Navajo County.

Navajo County was carved out of Apache County in 1895. The bill to make the new county was passed a few minutes before the legislature adjourned.

Will C. Barnes, a representative from Holbrook, got his way on the new county's name. Some people liked the name "Colorado County." But Barnes wanted an Indian name —Navajo. He wanted Navajo spelled with a "j" and not an "h." All these questions were debated in the legislature.

The land that became Navajo County was already developed. The Atlantic and Pacific Railroad (later called Santa Fe) had been there since the early 1880s. Ranching was important. In fact, the Aztec Land and Cattle Company was the third largest ranch in North America.

The "Painted Desert" northeast of Holbrook.

Two geographic sections. Navajo County is divided by the Mogollon Rim. The high plateau country in the north is arid and desert-like.

The smaller southern part has rugged mountains. It has lots of pine trees.

Holbrook is the county seat. It was founded in 1881 after the Atlantic and Pacific rails reached the Little Colorado River. Holbrook was built two miles west of Horsehead Crossing on the river. During the 1870s some Mexicans lived at the crossing. They ran a store there.

In the old days Holbrook was one of the roughest, toughest towns in the West. Cowboys came to town for a fling. They sometimes got into trouble. It took a good sheriff to control them.

Commodore Perry Owens was the first sheriff of Navajo County. Owens was an unusual man. He had a drooping moustache. Long blond hair fell over his shoulders. He wore twin, long-barreled guns, chaps, and big spurs. Owens was fast on the draw and a dead shot. He had a reputation for killing horse thieves.

Another well-known sheriff was Frank Wattron. He was a Holbrook druggist. Sheriff Wattron is most famous for something he did in 1899. He sent out invitations for a hanging. Wattron was criticized by some people. They thought a hanging should be a serious occasion, not entertainment.

Sheriff Commodore Perry Owens was a good shot with either the rifle or pistol.

The first courthouse in Holbrook was used until 1976. It was built of native stone and brick. At the entrance there are two large petrified logs. These logs come from the Petrified Forest, which is east of Holbrook.

Navajo County is Indian country. Two-thirds of the land is in Indian reservations. The Navajos and Hopis are in the north. The Apaches are in the south.

At one time there were many *trading posts* on the Navajo Reservation. The Navajos brought in blankets, rugs, and fine silver and turquoise jewelry. They traded these items for food and other supplies.

The Petrified Forest east of Holbrook.

One of the early trading posts in Navajo County was at Kayenta. It was started by John Wetherill.

The Indians traveled to the posts in wagons or on horseback. Now they use pickup trucks. They drive to Holbrook or Winslow to shop.

Wagon freighting was a pioneer business. Food, farming tools, and other supplies reached Holbrook by rail. Then big freight wagons hauled the goods 90 miles to Fort Apache and places in between. Snowflake, Taylor, and Woodruff, and Show Low were some of the towns on the wagon route.

Mud was the freighter's worst problem in the high country. Melting snows eroded the wagon trails. The wagons often were stuck in mud holes. Bridges made of poles or planks were built over some of the worst washes.

Pioneer Mormons settled along the Little Colorado in the 1870s. There were four settlements along the river west of present-day Holbrook. Only Joseph City survived floods that washed away crops.

Joseph City was founded in 1876. It is the oldest Mormon town in Arizona. Today it is a quiet little town. It has good farms and dairies. The big Cholla Power Plant is east of the town.

Winslow is the largest town in Navajo County. Like Holbrook, it started as a railroad town. The Santa Fe Railroad still employs many people in Winslow. But the town has some small industries too. Lumber and wood products are made there.

Times have changed. Navajo County is not what it was in 1895. The railroad, highways, radio, and television have brought in the outside world there. The population is growing. Prospects for the future look good.

PIMA COUNTY

LAND AREA
5,914,000 acres (9,240 square miles)

POPULATION
1970 Census 351,667
1978 Estimate 474,100

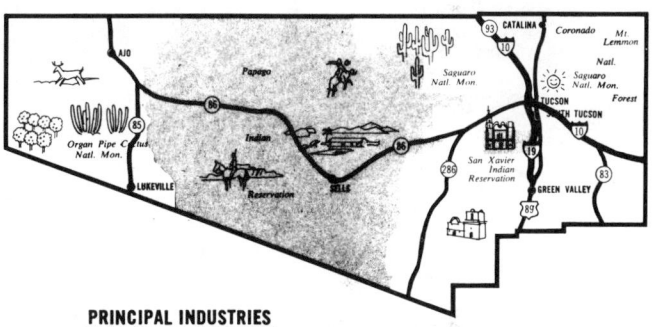

PRINCIPAL INDUSTRIES
Copper mining, manufacturing, tourism.

POINTS OF INTEREST
San Xavier Del Bac Mission, Arizona-Sonora Desert Museum, Kitt Peak National Observatory, Old Tucson, Colossal Cave and Park, Organ Pipe Cactus National Monument, Sabino Canyon, Mount Lemmon, Tucson Community Center.

Pima County.

Pima County has great contrasts in scenery. The elevation ranges from 1,200 feet up to 9,185 feet on Mount Lemmon. The top of this mountain is both a summer and a winter resort.

Mount Lemmon is in the Santa Catalina Mountains. They are northeast of Tucson. The Catalinas and other mountain ranges form a rim around Tucson. On the east of the city are the Tanque Verde Mountains and the Rincons. To the west are the Tucson Mountains.

213

Downtown Tucson. The civic center is in the lower right hand corner.

Old Tucson.

Tourism is big in Tucson. Pima County has few people except in Tucson. Tucson is the second largest city in Arizona. It is 2,390 feet high. That makes it slightly cooler than Phoenix. Many sun-seekers visit Tucson in the winter. The climate makes tourism a big industry.

Historical and scenic attractions. Pima County has many reminders of a colorful historical past. One historic attraction is the *San Xavier mission*. It was built when Arizona was under Spanish rule.

The *Arizona Historical Society* in Tucson is a great treasure of old records and exhibits. In front of the building are copies of two famous statues. They are of Father Kino and John Greenway. The originals are in the capitol in Washington, D.C.

Old Tucson was built in 1939 as a movie set for the filming of *Arizona*. Many movies have been made at Old Tucson. These films include some of John Wayne's great westerns.

The *Arizona-Sonora Desert Museum* is close to Old Tucson. It has many live desert animals and plants.

Colossal Cave is southeast of Tucson. It is visited by both scientists and tourists. Crystal

Saguaro National Monument near Tucson.

Part of the University of Arizona campus at Tucson.

formations in the cave were formed millions of years ago.

The *Saguaro National Monument* is two separate wilderness areas. One is east and one is west of Tucson. Both parts have many giant saguaro cacti.

The *Kitt Peak National Observatory* and the *Organ Pipe Cactus National Monument* are in the big desert west of Tucson.

Pima County has many kinds of industries. *Tourism* has long been important. Tucson's Sunshine Climate Club took the lead in bringing tourists to Arizona. This club was the first Arizona group to advertise in national magazines.

Copper mining is a big source of income in Pima County. The mines are mainly in the Santa Cruz Valley south of Tucson and at Ajo. The town of Ajo is over 100 miles west of Tucson.

Manufacturing is now important in Tucson. Lots of companies followed Hughes Aircraft to Tucson. Motorola, IBM, and other companies now employ many people.

Farming. Most of the farms in Pima County are in the Santa Cruz Valley. Fields are irrigated south of Tucson and to the north beyond Marana. Cotton is the main crop. Other crops are grains, alfalfa, vegetables, pecans, and citrus.

Cattle ranching has done well in Pima County since Spanish days. There are many large and small ranches. One of the most famous is the old Empire Ranch. It is near Vail.

Pima County has a strong ranch tradition. Only horse-drawn vehicles are permitted in the annual rodeo parade. This grand parade is said to be the largest of its kind in the world. The rodeo week is called "La Fiesta de los Vaqueros." The Spanish word "vaquero" means "cowboy."

Education and the air base. The University of Arizona is located in Tucson. Davis-Monthan Air Force Base is also found there.

Land ownership. About 42 per cent of Pima County is in the Papago and San Xavier Indian reservations. Private persons own 14 per cent of the county. The U.S. and Arizona governments control most of the rest.

PINAL COUNTY

LAND AREA
3,442,000 acres (5,386 square miles)

POPULATION
1970 Census 68,579
1978 Estimate 89,900

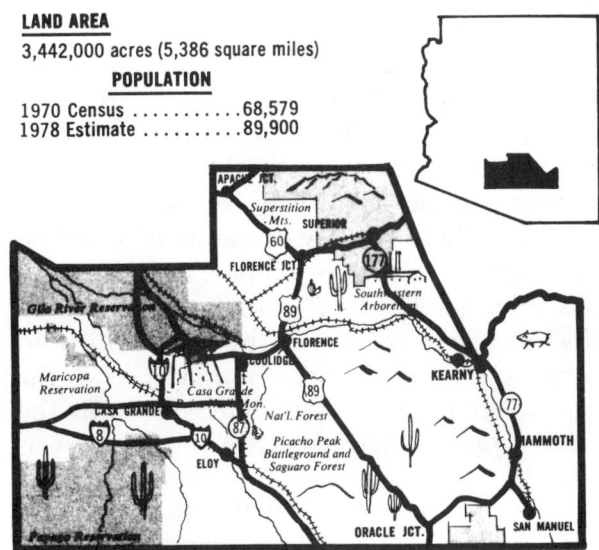

POINTS OF INTEREST
Superstition Mountains, Casa Grande Ruins National Monument, Picacho Peak, Pinal Pioneer Parkway, Southwestern Arboretum.

PRINCIPAL INDUSTRIES
Farming & ranching, copper mining, tourism, manufacturing

Pinal County.

First Pinal County Courthouse in Florence.

View of Boyce Thompson Southwest Arboretum near Superior, Arizona. About 10,000 species of desert plants can be seen there.

Pinal County was created in 1875. It was carved out of Pima and Maricopa counties.

Florence has always been the county seat. Florence was founded by Levi Ruggles in 1866. It is a farming town. The first houses were built of adobe. Ceilings were made of cottonwood logs. Thick mud was put on top of the saguaro ribs. The floors were dirt.

The *first courthouse* was built of thick adobe. It is now used as a museum. The jail was a separate building. It had no windows. There was no door in the doorway. Prisoners were chained to a big boulder.

The *second courthouse* is still used for some county offices. It is a two-story red brick building. The cupola on top has four clocks. No one knows why each clock is set exactly at sixteen minutes to twelve o'clock.

The Pinal County economy is based on the four C's. They are copper, cattle, cotton, and climate. The first mines produced silver. Fortunes were made from the Silver King and Silver Queen mines near Superior. After the top layers of silver were removed from the Silver Queen, a large body of copper ore was found.

Several towns in Pinal County depend on copper mining. These include Superior, Mammoth, and the newer towns of Kearny and San Manuel.

The farming town of Casa Grande began booming in the 1970s when nearby copper mines were developed. Casa Grande is the largest town in the county. Small factories provide jobs for many people. A big attraction is Francisco Grande west of town. The San Francisco Giants baseball team trains there.

Cattle ranching is important in Pinal County. There are many large ranches along the San Pedro. Large *cattle feeding* pens are near Stanfield and Maricopa.

The large cattle feeding center near Maricopa is called "Cowtown USA." The cattle are given feed crops grown nearby. Cottonseed meal and sugar beet pulp are also used to fatten the cattle. Cowtown is on the main line of the Southern Pacific Railroad.

Cotton is Pinal County's main farm crop. Some farmers get irrigation water from San Carlos Lake behind Coolidge Dam. A lot of groundwater has to be pumped too.

Coolidge and Eloy are important towns in the cotton belt. In fact, Eloy was once named Cotton City.

Ideal *climate* is the fourth "C." It brings many winter visitors to Pinal County.

Pinal County has had a colorful past. The Hohokams irrigated farms along the Gila River hundreds of years ago. They built the

Superstition Mountains.

four-story Casa Grande near Coolidge. The Pima Indians were farming the same place when the Spaniards came.

A small Civil War battle was fought near Picacho Peak. Lieutenant James Barrett and two Union privates were killed there.

Pinal County has ghost towns too. Adamsville was started by Charles Adams in 1866. Farmers moved in. Soon a flour mill was built. At first the town grew faster than nearby Florence. But by 1920 Adamsville was deserted.

Arizona's most famous lost mine story took place in Pinal County. Thousands of people have gone into the Superstition Mountains looking for the "Lost Dutchman's gold mine."

According to legend, a man named Carlos Peralta found a gold mine near Weaver's Needle in the Superstitions. His father was a rancher in Sonora. He sent a large group of men with pack animals to bring out the gold. But the group was attacked by Apaches. Only two boys escaped.

Later, in the 1870s, a German prospector named Jacob Walz was lost in the Superstitions. He came across three middle-aged Mexicans who helped him. Two of the Mexicans were the ones who had escaped the Apache massacre as boys. Walz killed the three Mexicans after they showed him gold they were mining. Walz then worked the mine himself.

Before Walz died he drew a map of the mine for a friend. But no one has been able to find the mine. It is quite possible that Walz made up the whole story.

SANTA CRUZ COUNTY

LAND AREA
797,000 acres (1,246 square miles)

POPULATION
1970 Census 13,966
1978 Estimate 18,800

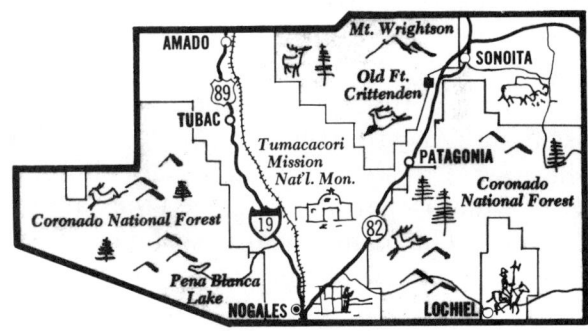

PRINCIPAL INDUSTRIES
Tourism (gateway to Old Mexico), international trade.

POINTS OF INTEREST
Nogales-Mexico, Tumacacori National Monument, Pena Blanca Lake, Tubac, Amado Race Track.

Santa Cruz County.

Santa Cruz is the smallest of the fourteen counties. But it is bigger than the state of Rhode Island.

The name Santa Cruz means "Holy Cross." The territorial legislature considered the names "Papago" and "Grant" before deciding on Santa Cruz. The county was formed in 1899.

Nogales, the county seat, is located on the Mexican border. The first name of Nogales was Isaacson. It was named after Jacob Isaacson. He was a Russian Jew. He started a store in a tent after a branch of the Southern Pacific reached the border in 1880. Railroad men made this store their headquarters.

217

International border crossing at Nogales.

After a few years in his border town, Isaacson moved to Mexico City. For awhile the town was known as Line City. But the U.S. Postal Department changed the name to Nogales. This name means "walnuts."

Nogales is an important port of entry for Mexican farm products. Dozens of produce companies are in Nogales. Many tourists cross the border to shop in Nogales, Sonora.

Some historic places. Tourists sometimes stop at the historic sites north of Nogales. The old Tumacácori mission goes back to Spanish times. Not far away is the old partly-restored Spanish fort of Tubac.

The Pete Kitchen Museum is in the same area. Pete Kitchen was a famous pioneer rancher. His ranch house was built like a fort for protection. Kitchen was one of the few ranchers not driven out or killed by Apaches during the Civil War.

Cattle ranching has long been a big industry in Santa Cruz County. Some of the finest cattle ranches in the state are near Patagonia, Arivaca, Sonoita, and Lochiel. Registered herds of Herefords, Black Angus, Gertrudis, Brahmans, and other breeds graze the grassy hills of Santa Cruz County.

Horse breeding is important on some ranches. Sonoita's annual quarter horse show is a popular event.

Land ownership. The U.S. Forest Service controls 57 per cent of Santa Cruz County. The State of Arizona has 6 per cent of the land. The other 37 per cent is owned by private people.

YAVAPAI COUNTY

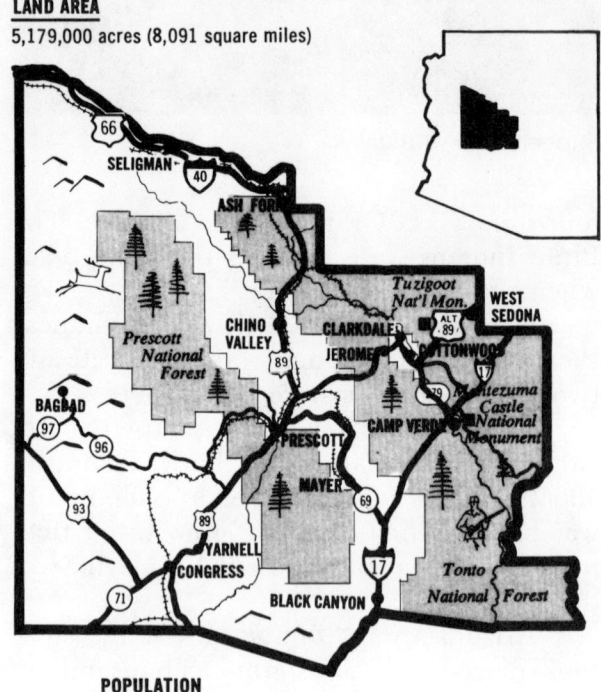

LAND AREA
5,179,000 acres (8,091 square miles)

POPULATION
1970 Census 37,005
1978 Estimate 59,700

PRINCIPAL INDUSTRIES
Tourism and recreation, ranching, manufacturing, copper mining.

POINTS OF INTEREST
Montezuma Castle and Well, Smoki Museum, Jerome ghost town, Tuzigoot National Monument, Granite Dells, Camp Verde Museum, Joshua Forest Parkway, Yarnell Hill.

Yavapai County.

Yavapai County is only about one-tenth of its original size. But it is still larger than the State of New Jersey.

Yavapai County has a variety of towns and scenery. Vast deserts are found in the south. Copper mining keeps the town of Bagdad going in the west.

In the north, good range land supports

Jerome was once the third largest town in Arizona. It has never really been a ghost town.

large herds of cattle. The railroad town of Seligman is a supply center for ranchers. It is also a tourist stop on Interstate 10.

Jerome is a tourist attraction in northeast Yavapai County. Jerome is now a lively "ghost town." It was once a roaring mining town with 15,000 people. It had big buildings and fine homes. One of the homes is the old Douglas mansion. It is now a museum. The famous United Verde mine at Jerome was closed in the 1950s.

Not far from Jerome is the ancient village of Tuzigoot. Another Indian ruin, Montezuma Castle, is in eastern Yavapai County.

In the central part of the county is the Prescott National Forest. There is lots of fishing, hunting, boating, camping, and picnicking in this forest land.

Prescott. In the center of the forest is Prescott. It is the only large city in the county. Prescott is rich in history and culture. The Sharlot Hall Museum is filled with mementos of pioneer days.

Prescott has two well-known celebrations. *Frontier Days* in July has one of the nation's best rodeos. There are also parades, horse racing, and fireworks.

The *Smoki ceremonials* are held at night in August. White men dress as Indians. They perform dances and chant Indian songs. The Smoki pageant takes months of rehearsals.

Prescott is the home of Yavapai Community College. Other private colleges have been there in the past.

Making a living. Many people in Prescott work for the *government*. The U.S. Forest Service is a big employer. Lots of workers have jobs with the county government or in the Arizona Department of Transportation. The Veterans Administration Center at Fort Whipple has a big payroll.

Tourism is also important. Yavapai County's clean air and pine-covered mountains attract lots of visitors.

Cattle and sheep raising are important in the county.

Manufacturing is growing in Prescott. Most of the factories are small.

Land ownership. Half of Yavapai County is owned by the United States government. The State of Arizona has 27 per cent of the land. Private parties own 23 per cent.

YUMA COUNTY

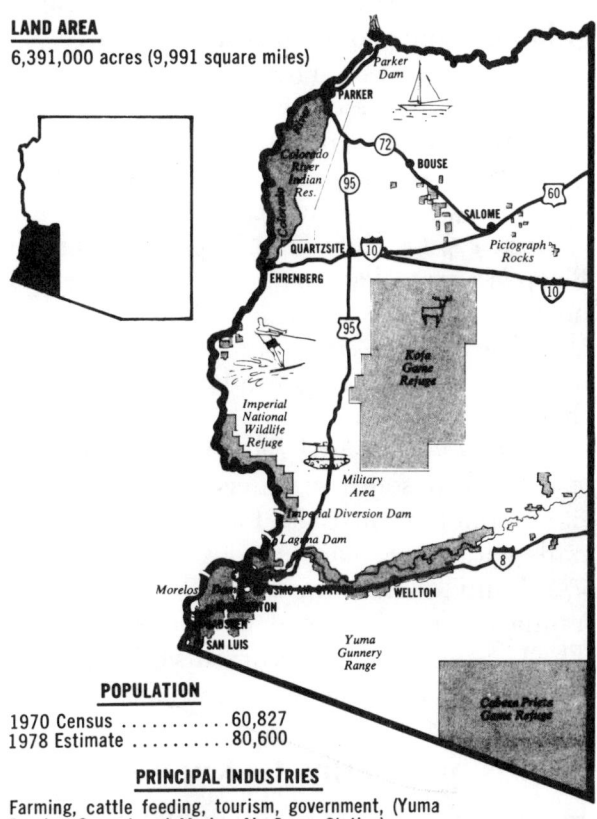

LAND AREA
6,391,000 acres (9,991 square miles)

POPULATION
1970 Census 60,827
1978 Estimate 80,600

PRINCIPAL INDUSTRIES
Farming, cattle feeding, tourism, government, (Yuma Proving Ground and Marine Air Corps Station).

POINTS OF INTEREST
Yuma Territorial Prison, Colorado River, Parker Dam.

Yuma County.

Yuma County is one of the nation's sunniest places. The climate makes farming and tourism the chief industries.

Agriculture. Farming is good in Yuma County. Why? Lots of sunshine, rich soils, and a good supply of irrigation water are the main reasons. Most of the farming is in three places: Yuma-Somerton, Wellton-Mohawk, and Parker.

Citrus is the leading cash crop. Thousands of trees produce good crops of citrus fruits. Lemons do well near Yuma.

Lettuce ranks second to citrus as a cash crop. Bermuda grass seed is also grown. Yuma County raises about 90 per cent of the world's bermuda seed. Other crops are alfalfa, cantaloupes, cotton, barley, sorghum, and wheat.

Cattle feeding is also doing well in Yuma County. The cattle are fattened on winter pastures and in feedlots.

The Colorado River is a popular playground. People come to boat and water ski. Some come to fish. There is camping.

Many people come to Yuma to see the old territorial prison.

The desert is put to many uses. Yuma County has three wildlife refuges. They are Cabeza Prieta, Kofa, and Imperial. Bighorn sheep are protected. So are other animals and birds.

The *Yuma Proving Ground* is north of Wellton. The U.S. Army tests advanced weapons there.

The *Luke Air Force Base Bombing and Gunnery Range* is south of Interstate 8. On this range, pilots from Luke Field practice their skills with space-age weapons.

Land ownership. Only 8 per cent of Yuma County is owned by private parties. The U.S. and state governments own most of the land in the county.

Words and Terms to Know

retail trade
tourism
generating station
private land
gallows
the economy

observatory
trade center
complex
trading post
fiesta
attraction
legend
produce company
registered herd
wildlife refuge
memento

Match the words above with the following definitions

1. Land that belongs to a person or company, not to the government.
2. The selling of goods directly to the consumers.
3. A place to observe the moon, stars, or sun.
4. A store in an unsettled area where goods are traded.
5. An unproved story from earlier times.
6. Anything that serves as a reminder or souvenir.
7. Purebred cattle whose owner has a record of their ancestors.
8. Land that is set aside for the protection of certain animals or birds.
9. Place where electricity is produced.
10. The earning, spending, and investing of money.
11. A town where people go to buy or sell goods.
12. A holiday or celebration.
13. Something that brings people to a certain place.
14. The platform where a condemned person is hung.
15. A business that deals in vegetables.
16. The place where several buildings are grouped.
17. The use of businesses and services to profit from tourists.

Finding the Facts

Draw columns on paper with the following headings. Write down the name of each county and fill in the chart.

County	County seat	Date created by the legislature	Main industries or work	Tourist attractions

UNIT 7
ARIZONA GOVERNMENT

As you can guess, this little Mesa "fire truck" is for display only. The real thing is behind it.

"Government" is a word that is often used. People talk about "the government." They may be talking about city, county, state, or federal government.

What is government? A government may have officers, lawmakers, and judges. They serve and control the people. They are guided by a constitution and laws. When these laws are enforced, people can live safely in society.

Why do we need government? We must have government to do the things we cannot do alone.

First, we must have *peace* and *order*. Government protects our lives and property.

Second, we all want *justice*. We have courts. In these courts, disputes can be settled peacefully.

Third, the government can *improve the lives of people*. It provides schools, streets, public parks, and services.

Fourth, we need a way to pay for services. The *government can tax* us. When we pay taxes, we help pay the costs of the services.

Why do we study government? In a democracy, the government is "of the people, by the people, and for the people."

The people have *political rights*. They have the right to vote. They may hold public office. Citizens may belong to a political party. They may petition the government to do or not to do something.

Voting is important. Voters decide who is elected. Voting is the main way most people take part in government.

Everyone pays taxes of some kind. We must make sure our tax money is spent wisely. This is a good reason to study government.

26. HOW GOVERNMENTS CONTROL, HELP, AND PROTECT

Emergency Medical Service helicopter aids an accident victim.

Any group, large or small, needs rules. People in the group should know the rules. They should know their rights and duties.

Legislatures. Rules in a nation or state are called *laws*. The laws are made by representatives of the people.

Executive officers enforce the laws. The nation has a president to do this. Arizona has a governor. Each county has elected officers.

Governments control, help, and protect. The national government works for all the states. Arizona's government is concerned with just this state. A county or city deals with local concerns.

What do governments control? For the good of all, many things have to be controlled.

Take cars, for example. To save lives we must drive safely. Traffic laws must be enforced. You must know these laws to get a driver's license.

Controlling traffic is the job of police, the sheriff, and state highway patrol. Can you

Highway Patrolman.

Sheep grazing on the Coconino National Forest south of Flagstaff.

imagine how bad it would be if all drivers went as fast as they wanted?

Another kind of control has to do with wildlife. The Arizona Game and Fish Department decides how many fish we can catch. They set a limit on the number of permits issued to hunters. Fishing and hunting licenses are required. This keeps us from killing all the animals.

Can anyone work as a doctor or lawyer? Of course not. These jobs and many others take special training. Those who do them must have a license. Standards are set by state law.

National forests are set aside for the benefit of all the people. But someone has to control the use of the forests. The U.S. Forest Service controls how many trees can be cut down. It limits the number of cattle and sheep that can graze in these forests.

Can you think of other kinds of government control? Some laws apply to all the states in the nation. Other laws are just for the people of Arizona. A county or town may have laws. These are only for that local place.

How does the government help people? In return for our taxes, many things are done for us that we can not do ourselves.

The government builds and maintains our *streets and highways.* We have city street departments and the Arizona Department of Transportation.

Arizona's interstate highways cost millions of dollars. They were built with the help of the U.S. government. The money had to come from the people in the form of taxes. It took a lot of people to pay enough taxes to build the highways.

What about *education?* The local school board is a government. The board helps children by providing schools. Some of the cost is paid by local property taxes. State and federal taxes also help. In fact, the largest share of our state taxes goes to public schools.

The state and U.S. governments help in other ways too. There is welfare and health care for the needy. People who lose their jobs may get government money for awhile. There

Phoenix policemen search a suspect as a police helicopter hovers overhead.

Interchange for I-40 and I-17 South highways of Flagstaff.

Tempe fire department truck.

are many government agencies which help people in some way.

How does the government protect people? It may begin right at the school. Some school boards hire guards. They protect boys and girls when they cross the street.

The main job of protecting us is in the hands of the police or sheriff, firemen, and the armed services.

The *police* arrest lawbreakers. They direct traffic. In some Arizona cities a helicopter is used to locate traffic jams and accidents. Two-way radios are used in squad cars to call ambulances.

Fire has always been one of the greatest dangers to towns and cities. Small towns may have to get by with volunteer *firemen*. But big city fire departments need lots of men. They need huge fire trucks. Firemen now do more than put out fires. They can perform first aid.

Arizona has a *National Guard*. The governor can call out the Guard in times of emergencies. An emergency might be a flood which leaves many people homeless.

In a democracy the people have choices. They can decide, through their representatives, which controls are needed.

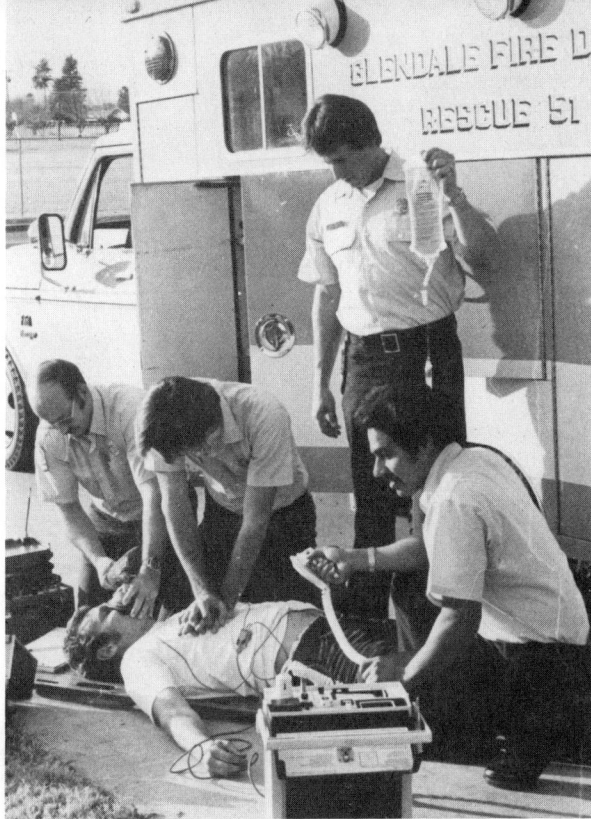

Ready in any emergency, a team of Glendale Fire Department paramedics aids a heart attack victim.

Words and Terms to Know

government	executive officers
justice	controls
political rights	welfare
representative	National Guard

Match the words above with the following definitions:

1. The right to vote and the right to hold office.
2. An elected person in the legislature who speaks for his or her district.
3. The people who enforce the law.
4. The governing body of officers, lawmakers, and judges who are elected or appointed to serve and control the people in a given area.
5. The condition of being fair and right.
6. Help that is given by the government to poor people to raise their living standards.
7. Ways by which people are regulated or forced to do what is expected of them.

Finding the Facts

1. _____ is a system, or governing body, that makes it possible for people to live in a society with others.
3. The government can improve the _____ _____.
3. When we pay taxes we are helping to pay the cost of _____.
4. Voting is especially important in a _____.
5. The rules for the people in a nation or state are called _____.
6. Governments at all levels _____, _____, and _____ the people.
7. There are many things which governments have to _____ for the good of everyone.
8. Government does many things for us that we can not do for _____.
9. The _____, _____, and _____ have the main jobs of protecting us.
10. The governor can call out the _____ _____ in times of emergencies.

225

27. THE CONSTITUTION OF ARIZONA

Members of the Arizona Constitutional Convention, 1910.

In 1910 the U.S. Congress passed the Arizona statehood bill. This bill was called the Enabling Act. It enabled Arizona to become a state. But first Arizona had to hold a convention. The purpose was to write a constitution.

A constitutional convention was held. Delegates were elected by the counties. There were 52 delegates. They met in Phoenix. George W. P. Hunt was chosen president of the convention.

The convention set up three branches of government. These are the legislative, executive, and judiciary.

The delegates tried to give the people a bigger voice in government. How? The initiative, referendum, and recall were put in the constitution.

In one way an initiative is like a referendum. It is a bill which is put on the ballot. The voters pass or defeat it. If passed, the bill becomes a law.

An *initiative* bill starts with the people. They sign petitions to get it on the ballot.

A *referendum* bill comes from the legislature. They have the bill put on the ballot. Then the people vote to pass or defeat it.

Recall allows the voters to remove some-

George W. P. Hunt presiding over the constitutional convention.

President Taft opposed the recall provision in the Arizona constitution.

one from office who is not doing a good job.

The delegates gave the people power in another way. How? They set up the *direct primary election*. This election lets the voters in each party choose a person to run for each office.

The Arizona Constitution was too long. It was four times the size of the U.S. Constitution. Now, many things can be changed only by amending the constitution. That is hard to do. The people have to vote to approve an amendment.

Arizona became a state. After the constitution was done, the people voted on it in 1911. It was passed by more than 3 to 1. But President Taft would not approve it. Why not? Taft opposed the recall of judges.

Another vote was held in Arizona. This time the voters dropped the recall. President Taft then approved the constitution. He signed a proclamation on February 14, 1912. Arizona was a state at last!

After Arizona became a state, the people put the recall back into the constitution.

First elected officials. Arizona's first state leaders were elected before statehood day. George W. P. Hunt was the first governor. Off and on he was to be elected seven times. That is why he has been called "George VII."

On February 14, Hunt walked to the

President Taft signing the Arizona statehood bill in 1912.

George W. P. Hunt.   Carl Hayden.

capitol from his room at the Ford Hotel. He took the oath of office. After his speech there was a parade. At night there was a dance on Central Avenue in front of the Hotel Adams. A brass band from the Indian School played the music.

At first, Arizona had only one member in the U.S. House of Representatives. Why? Because the state's population was so small. The first congressman (as a U.S. House member is called) was Carl Hayden. Before his election Hayden was sheriff of Maricopa County. Hayden took his House seat in Washington D.C. in 1912. He served seven terms in the House and seven terms in the U.S. Senate. All together he served a total of 57 years in Congress. That is a record which may never be broken.

Like all states, small or large, Arizona sent two U.S. senators to Washington in 1912. One of them was Marcus Smith. He was a Tombstone lawyer. The other was Henry Fountain Ashurst of Prescott. Both were Democrats.

Arizona was a Democratic state then. A Republican had little chance of winning a statewide office.

Words and Terms to Know

legislative
executive
judiciary
initiative
referendum
recall
direct primary
amendment
proclamation
capitol

Match the words above with the following definitions:

1. The branch of government that makes laws.
2. The building where the state legislature meets.
3. The branch of government that enforces laws.
4. A public announcement by an official such as the president or a governor.
5. The branch of government that is made up of judges and courts.
6. A system whereby officials may be removed from office by a vote of the people.
7. A bill that is started by people and becomes a law if a majority of voters favor it at an election.
8. A bill that the legislature puts on the ballot for the people to vote on.
9. An election in which each party chooses its candidates for office by direct vote.
10. A change in, or an addition to, a law or the constitution.

Finding the Facts

1. The _____ Act of 1910 made it possible for Arizona to become a state.
2. _____ _____ _____ _____ was elected president of the constitutional convention.
3. An _____ is a bill that the people put on the ballot for the voters to pass or defeat.
4. A _____ is a bill that the legislature puts on the ballot for the people to pass or defeat.
5. Most of the delegates at the 1910 constitutional convention were _____.
6. The delegates favored the _____ _____ whereby each party can choose its candidates.
7. The Arizona constitution is _____ _____.
8. _____ was president when Arizona became a state.
9. Arizona became a state on _____ _____, _____.
10. Arizona's first governor was _____ _____ _____ _____.
11. _____ _____ served a record total of 57 years in the U.S. House and the U.S. Senate.
12. _____ and _____ were Arizona's first U.S. senators.

28. THE THREE BRANCHES OF STATE GOVERNMENT

THE THREE BRANCHES OF STATE GOVERNMENT

EXECUTIVE
Governor
Secretary of State
Attorney General
Treasurer
Superintendent of Public Instruction

POWERS: the executive branch enforces the laws. The governor appoints people to run the state agencies.

LEGISLATIVE

Senate
30 members elected for 2 years

House
60 members elected for 2 years

POWERS: to make laws, appropriate money, and levy taxes.

JUDICIARY

Supreme Court
5 judges appointed for 6 years

Court of Appeals
appointed for 6 years. Two divisions. Division #1 in Phoenix. Division #2 in Tucson. There are 3 judges for each case.

Superior Court
Each county has at least one judge. Serve 4 year term. Elected except in Maricopa and Pima counties. Governor appoints new judges in these counties.

POWERS: to settle disputes.

The three branches of state government.

The state government of Arizona has three parts or branches. They are the legislative, executive, and judiciary.

The *legislative* branch makes our laws. The *executive* branch sees that the laws are enforced. The *judiciary* (courts) settles disputes.

LEGISLATURE

The law-making branch is called the state legislature. It is the most powerful branch. Why? There are two reasons. It decides how much money will be spent. It also decides for what the money will be spent.

The Arizona legislature has two parts. They are the Senate and the House of Representatives. The Senate now has 30 members. The House has 60 members.

Election of the legislature. The state has 30 districts. Each district has about the same population. One senator and two representatives are elected from each district. More than half the legislature comes from Maricopa County.

A legislator in Arizona must be 25 years of age. He or she must have lived in Arizona for at least three years and the county one year.

Members of both the Senate and the House have two-year terms. The legislature meets each year on the second Monday in January.

Salary. Each member makes $6,000 a year. Members also have an expense fund. The

State Capitol in Phoenix.

voters turned down a salary raise to $9,600 in 1978. Serving in the legislature takes a lot of time. Few working people can afford to serve. Campaigning to get elected also takes time and money.

Officers of the legislature. The two houses choose officers. The party that has a majority (more than half) in the House chooses the *Speaker*. The Senate majority elects the *President*. The Speaker and the President preside.

Each party has a person to lead the debate on bills that the party favors or opposes. These officers are called the *majority floor leader* and the *minority floor leader*.

Each floor leader has one or more helpers called a *whip*. The whip's job is to talk to each member and round up as many votes as he can on bills.

How are laws passed? First, a member of either house can make a bill. The bill is given a number. *Committees* study the bill. That is far as most bills go.

Lobbyists talk to legislators. They try to get them to pass or defeat certain bills. The lobbyists work for some special interest. They might work for mine companies, a union, a railroad, or a profession.

If a bill gets out of the committees, it is debated. Some legislators speak for it. Others argue against it. Then a *roll call vote* is taken. If the bill is passed, it is sent to the other house.

When both houses pass the same bill, it goes to the governor. He can *sign the bill* into law. Or he can *veto* the bill. A veto means the bill does not become a law.

EXECUTIVE BRANCH

The governor of Arizona was not given much power by the constitution. The executive duties were divided. There are now five executive officers: governor, secretary of state, attorney general, treasurer, and superintendent of public instruction.

The governor has no power over the other officers. He is simply the "first among equals."

The governor does have some important powers, however. He appoints about 500 persons to boards and commissions.

He can also appoint and fire the director for each "superdepartment." This power was given to the governor when Jack Williams was in office. The legislature grouped dozens of agencies into big departments. The voters approved this change. The director of each superdepartment must now report to the governor.

A big job of the governor is to work with the legislature. He gives a "state of the State" speech at the start of each legislative session. He tells them what laws he would like to see passed.

He has the power to call a *special session* of the legislature. But he has to list the subjects to be discussed at the session.

If the governor dies or quits, the secretary of state takes over. Next in line are the attorney general, treasurer, and superintendent of public instruction in that order.

An example of this happened in 1977. Governor Raul Castro was made ambassador to Argentina by President Carter. Castro resigned. Secretary of State Wesley Bolin became governor.

But Bolin died in March, 1978. So Attorney General Bruce Babbitt became governor. He finished out Castro's term. Babbitt was elected governor on his own in November, 1978.

The secretary of state has many duties. He is the "keeper of the Great Seal of Arizona." This seal is put on offical state documents.

It is his job to have all state laws printed. He also has the *publicity pamphlet* printed. This pamphlet tells the initiative and referendum measures that are on the ballot. People can study the pamphlet before they vote.

The attorney general heads the *Department of Law*. The attorney gives legal advice to state agencies. He or she also helps the 14 county attorneys.

The attorney general handles a few criminal cases. Consumer fraud cases are an example. The attorney prosecutes companies that cheat the public. In the 1970s the attorney took some big bread and milk companies to court. They had agreed to set prices too high. The courts made them pay a lot of money to the state. Then checks were mailed to people who asked for refunds.

Governor Bruce Babbitt.

Former Governor Raul Castro and Jimmy Carter at the Democratic convention in 1976.

231

Attorney General Robert Corbin.

The treasurer is in charge of the state's money. All state tax money goes to the treasurer. He or she also keeps a record of state expenses.

The treasurer can serve only one term.

The superintendent of public instruction heads the Department of Education. He or she is on the state board of education. It works with grade and high schools.

Qualifications and term. The five executive officers each serve a four-year term. They must be 25 years of age. They must be a citizen of the United States for 10 years. They must live in Arizona for five years before taking office.

JUDICIARY BRANCH

The third branch of government is the judiciary. The word "judiciary" is related to the words "judge" and "justice." It has to do with the courts. In Arizona there are four levels of courts.

The Arizona Supreme Court is the highest court in Arizona. It has five judges. They are appointed by the governor for a six-year term. After six years the voters decide if a judge will stay in office another term.

Most Arizona Supreme Court cases are appealed from the lower courts. The Supreme Court makes sure that no error was made in a trial that might cause someone an injustice.

The Court of Appeals was created to lighten the load of the Arizona Supreme

Arizona Supreme Court.

Court. The judges are appointed by the governor. They serve a six-year term. The voters can keep the Court of Appeals judges in office for more six-year terms.

In Court of Appeals cases there is a panel of three judges.

The Court of Appeals can hear any case that comes from the lower courts. There is one exception. A person who has been condemned to death or to life in prison may appeal the case directly to the Arizona Supreme Court.

The Superior Court is the great trial court in Arizona. Each county has at least one superior court judge. No county can have more than one judge for every 30,000 people. The judges are elected except in Maricopa and Pima counties. The governor appoints judges in these two counties.

The term of office for all Superior Court judges is four years.

People who want to sue for more than

Judges of the Court of Appeals, Division 2 at Tucson, 1977. Left to right: Lawrence Howard, James L. Richmond, and James D. Hathaway.

$1,000 must go to the Superior Court. Divorces and juvenile cases are also handled in this court.

Justice of the Peace Courts. All of the above courts keep a careful record of all that is said in the courtroom. But Arizona has two types of courts not of record. They are police courts and justice of the peace courts.

A justice of the peace (JP) is elected for a four-year term. A JP does not have to be a lawyer, but it helps. The JP courts are called "people's courts." A person can sue for any amount under $1,000. But traffic tickets bring the most people in contact with JP courts.

Only persons accused of minor crimes (called "misdemeanors") can be tried in a JP court. There may be a jury, if the accused person wants one. A jury has six persons.

Police courts. Most towns in Arizona have a police court. The judge in this court is called a *magistrate*. He or she is appointed by the city council. The police courts deal mainly with traffic tickets.

Words and Terms to Know

to convene
to campaign
Speaker of the House
majority floor leader
minority floor leader
party whip
lobbyist
special interest
roll call vote
to veto
superdepartment
"state of the State" speech
special session
publicity pamphlet
to prosecute
re-election
qualification
to appeal
felony
misdemeanor
magistrate

Match the words above with the following definitions:

1. To forbid a bill that was passed by the legislature from becoming a law.
2. To come together for a meeting.
3. To talk to voters and advertise in hope of winning an election.
4. To ask that a case be moved to a higher court.
5. To begin and carry on a court trial.
6. The officer who presides over the House of Representatives.
7. A member of the legislature who helps the floor leader and tries to round up enough votes to pass or defeat a bill.
8. Leader of the majority party in either house of the legislature.
9. Leader of the minority party in either house of the legislature.
10. A police court judge.
11. A minor crime.
12. A major crime.
13. A meeting of the legislature that is not held at the regular time.
14. Any group or person which wants favors from the legislature.
15. A person who tries to get legislators to favor some special interest.
16. Annual address given by the governor to the legislature.
17. A way of voting whereby a person says "aye" or "nay" when his or her name is called.
18. A printed summary of initiatives and referendums that will be on the ballot on election day.

19. Any ability, training, or age requirement that fits a person for a certain job.
20. A large grouping of government agencies that have related jobs.
21. The process of being voted into office again.

Finding the Facts

1. The three branches of government are the _____, _____, and _____.
2. The Arizona legislature has two parts: the _____ and the _____ _____.
3. The Senate has _____ members and the House has _____ members.
4. An Arizona legislator has a yearly salary of _____.
5. The person who leads the majority party when the Senate is in session is the Senate _____ _____ _____.
6. After a bill is introduced and given a number, _____ study it.
7. _____ work for special interests and try to influence legislators.
8. The governor can _____ a bill or _____ it.
9. The chief executive officer is the _____.
10. An important duty of the governor is to work with the _____.
11. The governor can call a _____ _____ of the legislature but must name the subjects to be discussed.
12. The _____ _____ heads the Department of Law.
13. Executive officers in Arizona must be _____ years of age.
14. The _____ _____ _____ is the highest court of Arizona.
15. The _____ _____ is the great trial court in Arizona.
16. Persons accused of _____ (major crimes) usually are tried before a jury in the Superior Court.
17. The _____ _____ _____ _____ courts are called the "people's courts."
18. Nearly every town in Arizona has a _____ _____.

29. COUNTY AND TOWN GOVERNMENTS

Tempe city hall.

COUNTY GOVERNMENT

Each of Arizona's 14 counties has a government. Why? There are two major purposes.

The first purpose is to carry out state laws. County officers do many things for the state. They collect some state taxes. They hold court. They arrest people who break state laws. They issue marriage licenses. They keep records of property. They hold elections.

The second purpose of county government is to serve the people in other ways. What are some of these services? The county builds roads. It may have a county hospital. There are county parks and libraries. A county may have a sewage disposal plant.

County officers. Each county in Arizona has the same offices. They are the assessor, county attorney, recorder, sheriff, superintendent of schools, treasurer, a clerk of the superior court, and a board of supervisors.

To hold county office a person must be 18 years of age. An officer must be a U.S. citizen and a voter of the county. He or she must be able to read and write English.

All these county officers serve a four-year term. They are elected in the same years as the U.S. President. That would be 1980, 1984, 1988, and so on.

Yavapai County Recorder's office about 1900.

Phoenix city hall and council chamber.

Board of Supervisors. A county is divided into three or five districts. Each district elects one board member. All the counties have three board members except Maricopa and Pima. By state law, counties with more than 200,000 people have five-member boards.

The board of supervisors approves the county budget. They figure out how much the county will spend. They also figure out how much tax property owners of the county must pay.

Some boards hire a *county manager* to take care of day-by-day details of running the county government.

What are the duties of other county officers?

The *assessor* has to figure the value of property in the county. His office keeps maps that show land and who owns it.

The assessor also registers all cars and trucks. The office issues tags and collects the auto tax on the vehicles.

The *county attorney* must be a lawyer. He or she is the highest-paid county officer. The county attorney's office prosecutes persons accused of breaking state laws. The office will give legal advise to any county official or to schools.

The *sheriff* and his deputies enforce the law outside of towns. They make arrests. They gather evidence for court trials.

The sheriff is in charge of the county jail. He also heads search-and-rescue missions. The sheriff can form a "posse" when needed.

The *recorder* keeps a record of property deeds, mortgages, and other legal papers.

The recorder's second big duty is to register voters. An up-to-date list of voters is kept in his office.

The *county school superintendent* must have a teacher's certificate. He or she must see that all rules of the state board of education are carried out.

The *treasurer* collects taxes for the county. He or she also collects taxes for the state and for cities, towns, and school districts in the county. The treasurer puts the county's money in banks.

The *clerk of the Superior Court* keeps a record of Superior Court cases in the county. The clerk also issues marriage licenses.

TOWN AND CITY GOVERNMENTS

Most of the people of Arizona live in a town or city. The government of a town or city is close to the people. The local government supplies water, repairs streets, and builds parks. It gives police and fire service. It picks up garbage.

The magic numbers. A town with *1,500* people may *incorporate*. That means the town

Fun in Encanto Park, Phoenix.

Phoenix city council in 1979. Mayor Margaret Hance is the third from the right.

legally becomes like a business corporation. It can sue or be sued. It can own land and make contracts. An incorporated town can also get federal funds. The federal money can be used to build sidewalks, streets, sewers, parks and libraries.

When a town has *3,000* people it may call itself a *city*.

A city with *3,500* people may draw up a *charter*. It is like a constitution. The voters must approve it. Charter cities can act more on their own. They can set up the form of government they want.

Arizona has fifteen charter cities. Tombstone was given "home rule" in 1881. That was before Arizona became a state. The other cities and the dates they got a charter are: Phoenix (1913), Yuma (1914), Nogales (1926), Tucson (1929), Glendale and Winslow (1957), Flagstaff and Prescott (1958), Avondale (1959), Scottsdale (1961), Tempe (1964) Chandler (1965), Mesa (1967), and Casa Grande (1975).

Types of government. Most Arizona towns have the *mayor-council plan* of government. The mayor is just a member of the council. He or she has little power.

The *mayor-council-manager plan* is used in towns and cities that can afford it. The council hires a manager to do the day-by-day running of the town or city.

The *strong mayor-council plan* is a third type. Nogales uses this plan. The strong mayor has power to hire and fire city officials.

Words and Terms to Know

to enforce	posse
property tax	charter
to prosecute	mayor-council
incorporated	government

Match the words above with the following definitions:

1. A tax on land and houses.
2. To compel obedience, as to a law.
3. To conduct legal or criminal proceedings in court.
4. The most common type of town or city government.
5. Organized as a legal corporation.
6. A kind of constitution.
7. A body of people who are organized to help the sheriff keep the peace or catch a fugitive.

Finding the Facts

1. One purpose of county government is to enforce _____ _____.
2. All the county officers serve _____-year terms.
3. The annual county budget is approved by the _____ _____ _____.
4. The county _____ handles automobile tags.
5. The highest paid county officer is the _____ _____.
6. The _____ _____ _____ _____ _____ issues marriage licenses.
7. A town with _____ people may incorporate.
8. A town which has _____ people may call itself a city.
9. A town or city with _____ people may draw up a charter.
10. _____ was Arizona's first "home rule" charter city.
11. Most Arizona towns have the _____-_____ plan of government.
12. Many towns and cities have a _____ to do the day-by-day work of running a town or city.

30. ELECTIONS

Some Arizona voters at their polling place.

Elections are part of a democracy. Elections are the means by which the people choose their government leaders. At elections the voters say what they want their leaders to do. The right to vote is one of the most important rights. Without elections and voting there would be no democracy.

Who can vote in Arizona? To vote you must be a citizen of the United States. You must be at least 18 years of age. You must be a resident of the state for at least 50 days before the next election. You must be able to write your name or make your mark.

A convict or an insane person can not vote. But an ex-convict can vote if his or her civil rights have been restored.

Knowing how to read and write English is no longer required for voting.

To vote a person *must register*. The voter fills out a card giving his name, address, and party.

Most people are Democrat or Republican. But one can be a member of a minor party. Some people are in no party. They are

239

listed as "independents."

People may register with the county recorder. There are part-time deputies who sign up voters in their homes or in shopping centers. A justice of the peace can also register voters.

Where do you vote? Each county has voting *precincts*. Each precinct has a *polling place* where people vote. The polling place may be a schoolroom, a church, an American Legion Hall, or some other place.

Some people have to vote by *absentee ballot*. A voter may not be able to go to the polling place. Or a person may have to be out of the county. The voter applies to the county recorder for an absentee ballot. This is done at least 30 days before the election. The ballot will be mailed to the voter. The voter mails it back.

How are candidates nominated? In Arizona the *direct primary* is used to pick people to run. In the primary election, Democrats run against Democrats. Republicans run against Republicans. The winner for each party is called the *nominee*. Each party tries to have a nominee for each office.

Evan Mecham campaigns for governor on the Arizona State campus. Former governor Howard Pyle (right) came along to help Mecham.

To win, a candidate must have a *plurality*. A plurality is to have more votes than any other person.

Arizona has the *closed primary*. That means you vote for persons of your own party only. For example, take the 1978 primary race for governor. On the Democratic ballot there were two names. The voters who were Democrat could vote for Bruce Babbitt or Dave Moss. The Republican ballot had the names of three men. They were Evan Mecham, Jack Londen, and Charles King. The voters who were Republican could vote for one of the three. Babbitt and Mecham were the winners for their parties. They ran against each other in the 1978 general election.

Voters who are "Independent" have no one to vote for in the primary. But they can vote in the general election.

The primary in Arizona is held in September. It is eight weeks before the general election.

A general election decides who will hold office. The party nominees run against each other. Each nominee's name and party is on the ballot. But no party is listed on the ballot for the offices of judge or the school board.

Many voters in Arizona vote a *split ticket*. They vote for some Democrats and some Republicans.

The general election is held on the first Tuesday after the first Monday in November.

How do you run for office? To do this a person must have people sign a petition. They must belong to the same party.

Candidates shake hands with voters and put up signs. They advertise in all the places that they can. A candidate may send letters to voters. He may make telephone calls. People may put bumper stickers on their cars. Sometimes a newspaper will support a candidate. That often helps.

A state law limits how much a candidate can spend on a campaign. All candidates must list their expenses and where they got the money.

Governor Dan Garvey (left), President Harry Truman, and U.S. Senator Ernest McFarland at a train "whistle stop" in Arizona during the 1948 campaign.

An unusual 1920s campaign card. It was made from a thin sheet of copper.

Words and Terms to Know

to register
precinct
polling place
absentee ballot
direct primary
nominee
plurality
closed primary
Independent
general election
split ticket

Match the words above with the following definitions:

1. A place where people vote.
2. A voter who does not belong to a political party.
3. An election where each party selects a candidate to run for each office.
4. An election where a voter can vote only on the ballot for his or her party.
5. To sign up as a voter.
6. A voting district.
7. More votes than anyone else.
8. A person who is nominated to run for an office by his or her political party.
9. The election in which candidates (nominees) of one party run against candidates of other parties.
10. A ballot on which a person votes for candidates of more than one party in the general election.
11. A way of voting by a person who can not be at the voting place on election day.

Finding the Facts

1. The right to _____ is one of the most important political rights.
2. To vote, a person must be a resident of the state for at least _____ _____ before the election.
3. A voter has to be at least _____ years of age.
4. A person must _____ in order to vote.
5. Each voting precinct has a _____ _____.
6. A person who is gone on election day may vote by _____ _____.
7. The _____ _____ is used by political parties to nominate candidates.
8. The _____ _____ is held to determine who will hold office.
9. If a person votes for candidates in more than one party, he or she is voting a _____ _____.
10. Before a person can run for an office, he or she must get signatures on a _____.

ACKNOWLEDGEMENTS AND PICTURE CREDITS

The author wishes to thank the following people who assisted in the making of this book: Gibbs M. Smith of Peregrine Smith, Inc.; Dr. Jimmie D. Merrill who analyzed the manuscript to determine reading level, Richard Firmage who edited, designed and supervised production of the book; Anne Shifrer who assisted in the editing; and Marlene J. Sugden who did the paste-ups and assisted in the book design.

Many people assisted the author in finding pictures and maps for this book. Susan Luebbermann, staff photographer at the Arizona Historical Society (AHS), was especially helpful.

Other people who helped were: Margaret Bret Harte, Donald Bufkin, Stephen Burns, Barbara Bush, Sue Chamberlain, Don Davis, Lori Davisson, Cheryl Dupuich, Walter Fruland, Heather Hatch, Joseph Kennedy, Helen Land, Carol Patrick, Susan Petra, Al Ruland, Paul Schafer, David Strom, Richard Thurm, Bob Wallace, Tom White, and Susan Wilcox.

The specific pictures are credited below. The author and publisher also wish to thank the people who offered photographs that could not be used for lack of space.

Letters beside the numbers designate position on the page: L (left side), R (right side), T (top), M (middle), and B (bottom).

Unit One: 8-9, Peregrine Smith, Inc.; 10, Barry Goldwater, Library of Congress; 11T, AHS; 12, Arizona State Museum, (Helga Teiwes); 13, Ernest Unterman; 14, Library of Congress; 15T, University of Arizona Press (Don Bufkin); 15B, 16T, 16B, 17T, Arizona Office of Tourism; 17B, Tucson Convention and Visitors Bureau; 18T, Arizona Pioneers' Historical Society; 18M, Bureau of Reclamation; 18B, 19, Salt River Project; 20, University of Arizona; 21, Office of Tourism; 22T, 22B, 23, Bureau of Reclamation; 24, 25T, Salt River Project; 25B, Southwest Forest Industries; 26, Salt River Project; 27T, 27B, Office of Tourism; 28T, National Archives; 28B, AHS; 29T, U. of Arizona; 29B, Phoenix Convention and Visitors Bureau; 30, Salt River Project; 31, Arizona Game and Fish Dept. (Ned Smith); 32L, 32R, U.S. Fish and Wildlife Service; 33T, 33M, AHS; 33B, Arizona Game and Fish Dept.; 34, U.S. Fish and Wildlife Service; 35LT, 35RT, AHS; 35LB, 36LT, Arizona Game and Fish Dept.; 36LM, AHS; 36LB, Office of Tourism; 36R, Bureau of Reclamation; 37T, 37B, Arizona Game and Fish Dept.; 38T, AHS; 38B, Arizona Dept. of Library and Archives; 39T, AHS; 39B, Arizona Dept. of Library and Archives; 40L, *The Arizona Republic* (Bud DeWald); 40R, Dana Slaymaker.

Unit Two: 42, Salt River Project (Charles O. Kemper); 43T, Arizona State Museum; 43B, Office of Tourism; 44L, University of Arizona Press (Don Bufkin); 44R, Arizona State Museum (Helga Teiwes); 45T, Charles O. Kemper; 45B, 46T, Arizona State Museum (Helga Teiwes); 46B, Peter Bianchi; 47, Phoenix Chamber of Commerce; 48T, 48B, Arizona State Museum (Helga Teiwes); 49, Museum of Northern Arizona; 50L, Arizona State Museum (Helga Teiwes); 50R, AHS; 51T, 51B, Museum of Northern Arizona; 52, 54, AHS; 55RT, National Archives; 55RM, Museum of Northern Arizona; 55RB, Office of Tourism; 56, AHS; 57T, Museum of New Mexico; 57B, Arizona State Museum (Helga Teiwes); 58T, Smithsonian Institution; 58B, 59LT, 59LM, National Archives; 59LB, AHS; 59RT, 59RB, National Archives; 60, 61T, 61B, AHS; 62T, U. of Arizona Press (Don Bufkin); 62B, U. of Arizona; 63T, AHS; 63B, 64T, Arizona State Museum (Helga Teiwes); 64B, Smithsonian Institution; 65, Office of Tourism; 66L, Smithsonian Institution; 66RT, Arizona State Museum (Helga Teiwes); 66RB, 67LT, 67LB, Smithsonian Institution; 67R, 68, AHS; 69, 70, Smithsonian Institution.

Unit Three: 72, Peregrine Smith; 73, Tim Fuller; 74, Mrs. Jay Datus; 75, Museum of New Mexico; 76L, AHS; 76R, Gerald Cassidy; 77T, 77B, AHS; 78, National Archives; 80, AHS; 81, Peregrine Smith, Inc. (U. of Ariz.); 82L, 82R, 83, 84, 85LT, AHS; 85LB, Tim Fuller; 85RT, AHS; 86, Tucson Convention and Visitors Bureau; 87, National Archives; 89, Goff Dowding; 90L, *Tempe Daily News*; 90R, AHS; 91, Museum of New Mexico; 92, 93, AHS; 94T, Goff Dowding; 94B, Library of Congress; 95, U. of Arizona Library; 96, Library of Congress; 97, Office of Tourism.

Unit Four: 98, Frederic Remington; 99, William Henry Jackson; 100LT, 100LB, Utah Dept. of Fish and Game; 100R, 101, 102, 103L, AHS; 103R, Library of Congress; 105, AHS; 106LT, J. Ross Browne; 106LB, 106RT, AHS; 106RB, J. Ross Browne; 107L; Mesa Museum; 107R, AHS; 108L, 108R, Arizona Public

Service Co.; 109T, Office of Tourism; 109L, 109R, AHS; 110T, Phelps Dodge Corporation; 110B, U. of Arizona Library; 111T, 111B, Phelps Dodge Corporation; 113T, 113B, 114L, 114R, AHS; 115T, Arizona Public Service Co.; 115B, 116T, 116B, AHS; 117T, National Archives; 117B, AHS; 118T, Arizona Dept. of Library and Archives; 118B, National Archives; 119, Tempe Historical Society; 121, Salt River Project; 122T, Arizona Dept. of Library and Archives; 122B, Al Ruland; 123T, 123L, Arizona Dept. of Library and Archives; 123R, National Archives; 124LT, 124LB, Tempe Historical Society; 124R, Bureau of Reclamation; 125L, AHS; 125RT, Salt River Projcet; 127T, Casa Grande Historical Society; 127B, Arizona Dept. of Library and Archives; 128L, *Tempe Daily News*; 128RT, 128RM, 128RB, 129T, AHS; 129B, Mesa Museum; 130T, 130M, Tempe Historical Society; 130B, 132T, 132B, 133T, 133B, AHS; 134, Los Angeles County Museum of National History; 135L, 135RT, AHS; 135RB, U. of Arizona Library; 136, National Archives, 137LT, 137LB, Arizona Public Service Co.; 137RT, 137RB, AHS; 138T, U. of Arizona Press (Don Bufkin); 138B, 139, AHS; 140T, Sharlot Hall Museum; 140B, Arizona Dept. of Transportation; 141T, Casa Grande Historical Society; 141B, 142, AHS; 143, Mountain Bell Telephone Co.; 144, AHS; 145L, U. of Arizona Library; 145R, 146, AHS; 147, Mountain Bell Telephone Co.; 148, Tempe Historical Society; 150, U. of Arizona Library; 151L, Office of Tourism; 151RT, Bob Hale; 151RB, Tempe Historical Society; 152L, AHS; 152R, Arizona Public Service Co.; 153L, National Archives; 153R, Sharlot Hall Museum; 154, 155B, 156, AHS; 157, Arizona Public Service Co.

Unit Five: 158, Tempe Historical Society; 159, National Archives; 160L, Salt River Project; 160R, Arizona Dept. of Transportation; 161LT, AHS; 161LB, Arizona Public Service Co.; 161R, 162B, National Archives; 162T, 163LT, Arizona Public Service Co.; 163LB, AHS; 163R, Office of Tourism; 164LT, Arizona National Guard; 164LB, *Arizona Highways*; 164R, National Archives; 165L, AHS; 165R, 166LT, 166LB, National Archives; 166R, Mr. and Mrs. Larry Jorgenson and Steve Talley; 167, Bureau of Reclamation; 168, Southwest Forest Industries; 169, Motorola; 170LT, *The Phoenix Gazette*; 170LB, Southwest Forest Industries; 170R, Jennings and Thompson Advertising; 171, Phoenix Convention and Visitors Bureau; 172T, AHS; 172B, Arizona Mining Association; 173L, 173RT, Salt River Project; 173RB, Bureau of Reclamation; 175, Salt River Project; 176LT, 176RT, Office of Tourism; 176RB, Tucson Convention and Visitors Bureau; 177LT, AHS; 177LM, 177LB, Office of Tourism; 177R, 178T, *Tempe Daily News*; 178B, Tucson Convention and Visitors Bureau; 179, Phoenix Roadrunners; 180, National Archives; 181LT, AHS; 181LB, Bureau of Reclamation; 181R, Jennings and Thompson Advertising; 182L, 182RT, AHS; 182RB, Tucson Convention and Visitors Bureau; 183LT, 183LB, Office of Tourism; 183R, Bennie M. Gonzales; 184LT, Salt River Project; 184M, McArthur/Biltmore Research Group; 184B, Office of Tourism; 186, 187L, Bureau of Reclamation; 187RT, AHS; 187RB, Salt River Project; 188LT, *Tempe Daily News*; 188RT, Bureau of Reclamation; 188B, Ray Wyatt, Arizona Commission on Agriculture and Horticulture; 189L, Central Arizona Project; 189R, Bureau of Reclamation; 190T, Arizona Public Service Co.; 190B, Salt River Project; 191T, *Mesa Tribune*; 191B, AHS.

Unit Six: 193, U. of Arizona Press (Don Bufkin); 194, U. of Arizona; 195L, Arizona State University; 195R, National Archives; 196T, U. of Arizona; 196B, National Archives; 197L, Arizona Dept. of Library and Archives; 197R, U. of Arizona Press (Don Bufkin); 200L, 200R, 201R, 202L, Office of Tourism; 203L, Landis Aerial Surveys; 203R, Arizona State Dept. of Economic Planning; 204R, National Archives; 205L, Arizona Dept. of Transportation; 206L, 207LT, Arizona State University; 207LB, National Archives; 208L, AHS; 208R, Office of Tourism; 209L, 210T, 210B, 211L, Bureau of Reclamation; 212L, Office of Tourism; 212R, AHS; 213L, 214T, 214B, 215L, Office of Tourism; 215RT, Tucson Convention and Visitors Bureau; 216L, AHS; 216R, National Archives; 217L, Salt River Project; 218L, 219L, Office of Tourism. *The Arizona Statistical Review* (Valley National Bank, Phoenix) for maps and statistical information for each county in chapter 27.

Unit Seven: 221, *Mesa Tribune*; 222, 223LT, Arizona Dept. of Public Safety; 223LB, U.S. Soil Conservation Service; 223R, Al Ruland; 224T, Arizona Dept. of Transportation; 224B, Salt River Project; 225, City of Glendale; 226, 227LT, 227LB, 227RT, 227RBR, U. of Arizona; 227RBL, Arizona Dept. of Library and Archives; 230, Al Ruland; 231T, Dept. of Law; 231B, Governor's Office; 232L, Arizona Republican Committee; 232R, Supreme Court Office; 233, Ray Manley; 235, Salt River Project; 236T, Sharlot Hall Museum; 236B, 237T, Salt River Project; 237B, Al Ruland; 239, *Mesa Tribune*; 240, *Tempe Daily News*; 241T, Arizona State University; 241B, AHS.

INDEX

Adams, Charles, 217
"Adams Diggings," 200
Adamsville, town of, 217
adobe, 151, 168
air conditioning, 187
AiResearch, 166, 169
Air Force bases, 163, 164, 209
Ajo, city of, 112, 172
Alarcón, Captain Hernando de, 77
Alcoa, 166
Allison Steel, 166-67
Alpine, town of, 200
amphibians, 40
animals: See wildlife
Anza, Captain Juan Bautista de, 85
Apache County, 117, 196, 199-200, 211
architecture, 183-85
arcology, 184
Arcosanti, 184-85
Arivaca, town of, 218
Arizona (the movie), 162, 214
Arizona (origin of name), 83
Arizona Biltmore, 182, 184
Arizona Cattle Company, 114
Arizona City, 107, 150
Arizona Daily Star, 129, 144
Arizona Game and Fish Department, 31, 33, 34, 223
Arizona Highway Patrol, 162
Arizona Highways, 170, 171, 181, 182
Arizona Historical Society, 177, 214
Arizona Miner, 144
Arizona Republic, 145, 148
Arizona-Sonora Desert Museum, 214
Arizona State University, 131, 165, 177. *See also* Tempe Normal School
Arizona Strip, 211
Arizona Supreme Court, 232
arts and crafts, 45, 48, 49-50, 57-58, 66-67, 180-85
Ash Fork, 139
Ashurst, Henry F., 228
Atlantic and Pacific (Santa Fe) Railroad, 115, 138-39, 203, 211, 212
attorney general, 231
Aztec Land and Cattle Company, 115, 211
automobile, 139-40, 160
aviation, 140-42
Avondale, city of, 186, 238
Awátovi, 76

Babbitt brothers, 118
Babbitt, Bruce, 231, 241
Babocomari Ranch, 95
Bagdad, town of, 218
Barnes, Will C., 211
Bartlett, John R., 94-95
Basques, 119
Beale, Lieutenant Edward, 133-34
Beale wagon road, 133-34
Behan, Sheriff John, 145
Benson, town of, 202
Betatakin, 49
Bill Williams Mountain, 203
Bird Cage Theater, 155
birds, 34-36
Bisbee, city of, 18, 110, 112, 130, 148, 150, 152, 153, 154, 202
Black Mesa, 190
Black soldiers, 181
Bolin, Wesley, 231
Bonillas, Ignacio, 129
Borglum, Solon, 196
branding, 115-16
Brichta, Augustus, 127-28
Buckeye, town of, 34
Bullhead City, 190, 211
Bushmasters, 163, 164
Butterfield Overland Mail, 134-35

cactus, 24, 27-29
Call, Anson, 197
Callville, town of, 197
camel experiment, 133-34
Cameron, town of, 26
Camp Grant, 146
Camp Horn, 164-65
Camp Hyder, 164
Candelaria, Juan, 117
Canoa Ranch, 113
Canyon de Chelly, 200
capital of Arizona, 131
Cárdenas, Captain García López de, 76-77
Carson, Kit, 57, 103
Casa Grande, city of, 125, 172, 186, 216, 238
Casa Grande National Monument, 47, 216-17
Castro, Raul, 231
cattle ranching, 15, 18, 26, 63, 82, 90-91, 113-17, 161, 174, 202, 203, 204, 206, 207, 215, 216, 218, 219
celerity wagon, 135
Central Arizona Project, 189
Chandler, city of, 150, 170, 209, 238
chaparral, 26
Charles, King of Spain, 84

charter cities, 237-38
Chinese, 137-38, 153
Chiricahua National Monument, 202
Christmas, town of, 204
Cíbola, 74
citrus farming, 126, 173, 220
city government, 237-38
Civil War, 107, 113, 217, 218
Civilian Conservation Corps (CCC), 162
Clark, John, 117
Clarkdale, town of, 154
Clifton, town of, 18, 108, 109, 110, 137, 150, 207
climate, 9, 20-23, 167, 175, 199, 216
Clum, John, 145
coal, 173
Cochise County, 26-27, 44, 195, 199, 201-202
Cochise man, 202
Coconino County, 193, 196, 199, 202-203
colleges, 131, 206, 219
Colorado Plateau, 14
Colorado River, 11, 14, 21, 33, 52, 77, 78, 85, 86, 99-101, 102, 107, 117, 122, 134, 139, 176, 189, 194, 197, 210-11, 220
Colossal Cave, 162, 176, 214-15
communication, 143-49
Concho, town of, 117
Conde, General Pedro, 94
constitution, 226-28
constitutional convention, 226-27
Cooke, Captain Philip St. George, 92, 93
coolers, 162
Coolidge, city of, 186, 216, 217
Coolidge Dam, 204, 216
copper mining, 108-12, 161, 171-72, 204, 207, 215, 216, 218
Corbin, Robert, 232
Coronado, Francisco, 74-78
Coronado National Forest, 78
Coronado National Monument, 78, 201
Coronado Trail, 207
Cortés, Hernán, 71
cotton farming, 124-26, 173, 206, 209, 215, 216
counties, map: 193; 193-98, 199-220. *See also* names of counties
county government, 235-37
county officers, 235-37
Court of Appeals, 232
courts, 232-33
cowboys, 90, 116-17, 174, 177
crash of 1929, 161
Cross, Edward, 144

Daggs brothers, 117-18, 205
Darroche, J. R., 130
Davis, Lew, 181-82
Davis Dam, 211
Davis-Monthan airbase, 141, 164, 215
DeGrazia, Ted, 182
Department of Education, 232
Department of Law, 231
Department of Transportation, 219, 223
depression, 158, 161-62
desert, 18-19, 27-29
Desert Botanical Garden, 209
Dickson Electronics, 169
dinosaurs, 11, 13
Dixon, Maynard, 182
Douglas, 148, 152, 164, 171, 186
Douglas, Dr. James, 110
Duncan, town of, 207

Eager, town of, 123
Earp, Wyatt, 109, 145
earthquakes, 11
Ehrenberg, town of, 122, 129-30
elections, 229, 239-41
Eloy, city of, 186, 189, 216
Empire Ranch, 114, 215
Enabling Act, 226
energy, 158, 184, 189-91
Espejo, Antonio de, 78
Estevan, 73-74
executive branch, 229, 230-32
explorers (Spanish), 73-78, 82-83, 84-85

Farfán, Captain Marcos, 78
farming, 23, 44-45, 121-26, 161, 202, 206, 209, 215, 220
Fenner, Hiram, 139
Firebird Lake, 66
fish, 11, 36-37
Flagstaff, city of, 9, 15, 16, 21, 23, 26, 54, 117, 118, 131, 139, 145, 151, 183, 186, 203, 205, 224, 238
floods, 22-23, 207
Florence, town of, 146, 150, 216, 217
flu epidemic, 160
Fort Buchanan, 144
Fort Huachuca, 165, 181, 202
Fort Lowell, 153
Fort Mohave, 139, 197
Fort Whipple, 102, 153, 219
Fort Yuma, 105, 106, 139, 146
Four Corners, 14, 49
Franciscans, 80, 82, 84-87
freeways, 188

246

Frémont, John C., 103
fur trappers, 98-103, 195

Gadsden Purchase, 95-96, 98
Garcés, Fray, 84-86
Garvey, Governor Dan, 241
General Electric Company, 169
geography, 14-19
geology, 11-13
Geronimo, 62
ghost towns, 202, 210, 217, 219
Gila Bend, town of, 208-209
Gila City, 107
Gila County, 196, 199, 200, 204-205, 208
Gila River, 18, 34, 44, 66, 84, 92, 93, 95, 98, 99, 101, 102, 107, 121, 141, 146, 195, 204, 206, 207
Glen Canyon Dam, 203
Glendale, city of, 208, 238
Globe, city of, 18, 110, 145, 150, 155-56, 186, 204
gold mining, 107-108, 173, 194, 217
Goldwater, Barry, 146, 148, 153
Goldwater, Joe, 153
Goldwater, Michael, 194
Goldwater, Morris, 146
Gonzales, Bennie M., 183
Gonzales, Inez, 94-95
Goodwin, Governor John N., 194
Goodyear Aircraft, 166, 169
Goodyear Tire and Rubber Company, 125
government, 221-41
governor, 231
Governor's Mansion (Prescott), 102, 144
Grady Gammage Auditorium, 183-84
Graham County, 199, 200, 205-206
Graham-Tewksbury feud, 205
Grand Canyon, 9, 11, 15, 55-56, 76-77, 141, 146, 171, 173, 176, 203
Grand Canyon College, 131
Granite Reef Aqueduct, 189
Greenlee County, 36, 193, 199, 206-207
Greenlee, Mason, 207
Greenway, John, 214
Grey, Zane, 205
groundwater, 18-19
Guadalupe Hidalgo, Treaty of, 92-93, 95, 98

Hall, Sharlot, 102
Hamilton, Charles, 140-41
Hancock, William A., 123, 208
Hardyville, town of, 197
Harvey, Fred, 139
Hashknife Ranch, 115
Hawikuh, 76

Hayden, Carl, 227, 228
Hayden, town of, 204
Hayden Flour Mills, 170
Hayes, Ira H., 67, 165
Heard Museum, 209
Heintzelman, Major Sam, 105
heliograph system, 62
Hellings, William, 122-23
Herrera, Silvestre, 165
Herrick, Harvey, 140
Hidalgo, Father Miguel, 89
Hi Jolly, 134
hogan, 57
Holbrook, town of, 16, 115, 117, 139, 211, 212, 213
Hooker, Henry, 113-14, 206
Hoover Dam, 197, 211
horse breeding, 218
Howell, Judge William T., 195
Hubbell, Santiago, 106
Hubbell Trading Post, 200
Hughes Aircraft, 169, 215
Hughes, Josephine Brawley, 128, 129
Humphreys Peak, 9, 21
Hunt, George W. P., 204, 227-28

IBM Corporation, 215
Ice Age, 13
Indian reservations, 54-55; Apache: 61-64, 98, 107, 113, 200, 206; Camp Verde, 56; Colorado River, 165; Fort McDowell (Salt River), 56, 67, 68; Hopi, 212; Navajo, 16, 212; Papago, 68, 215; Pima, 66-68, 165, 166, 181
Indians: Anasazi, 47-49, 64; Apache, 55, 60-64, 87, 90-91; Cochise people, 44; Cocopah, 52, 56; Havasupai, 52, 55; Hohokam, 18, 44-47, 65, 121, 216-17; Hopi, 25, 54, 55, 64-65, 76, 78, 80-82, 85, 117, 180, 181; Hualapai (Walapai), 52, 56; Maricopa, 52, 56, 68; Mogollon, 49-50; Mohave (Mojave), 52, 56, 78, 93; Navajo, 15, 16, 55, 56-59, 60, 64, 117, 171, 173, 180, 200; Paiutes, 56; Papago, 28, 47, 54, 56, 68; Patayan, 52; Pima, 47, 54, 56, 65-68, 82, 83-84, 92, 121, 123, 125, 160; Salado, 52-53; Sinagua, 50-52; Yaqui, 56, 83; Yavapai, 52, 56, 93; Yuma, 52, 55, 56, 77, 85-86; Zuñi, 74, 76, 77
Indians: prehistoric, 42-53; recent, 29, 54-69, 143-44, 162, 203, 205, 211
initiative, 226
Isaacson, Jacob, 217-18

Japanese-Americans, 165-66
Jerome, 18, 78, 110, 150, 154, 177, 181, 219
Jesuits, 80, 83, 84

247

Joseph City, town of, 123, 213
Juan, Mathew B., 67, 160
judiciary branch of government, 229, 232-33
Justice of the Peace courts, 233

kachinas, 65
Kaibab National Forest, 203
Kayenta, 213
Kearny, General Stephen W., 91-92, 103
Kearny, town of, 92, 216
Keet Seel, 49
Kennecott Copper Corporation, 172
Kingman, city of, 139, 164, 186, 197, 211
Kingman, Lewis, 197
Kino, Father, 66, 80, 82-83, 214
Kirkland, Bill, 113
Kitchen, Pete, 113, 218
Kitt Peak National Observatory, 68, 215
kiva, 64

Lake Havasu, 189, 210
Lake Havasu City, 186, 210-11
Lake Powell, 203
lakes, 175, 209
La Paz, town of, 107, 150, 194
Leach, Jesse B., 133
Leach wagon road, 133
legislature: state, 222, 226, 229-30
legislature: territorial (1863-1912), 127, 128, 131, 201, 203, 204, 211, 217
Lehi, town of, 123
Lesinsky brothers, 109
lettuce farming, 126, 173, 220
lighting, 152
Lincoln, Camp, 102
Litchfield, town of, 166
Little Colorado River, 14, 123, 200, 212
Littlefield, town of, 123
lizards, 38-40
lobbyists, 230
London Bridge, 210, 211
Lord, Charles H., 146
Lost Dutchman's mine, 217
Lount, S. D., 147
Lowell Observatory, 203
Luke, Frank Jr., 159
lumbering, 15, 63, 200, 203, 204

mammals, 31-34
mammoth (animal), 12, 13, 43-44
Mammoth, town of, 216
manufacturing, 23, 158, 163, 166-67, 168-70, 208, 215, 216, 219

Marana, town of, 164, 215
Maricopa, town of, 216
Maricopa County, 140, 193, 199, 207-209, 216, 232, 236
Maricopa Wells, 134, 146
Mauldin, Bill, 164
Maverick, town of, 21
McArthur, Albert Chase, 184
McCormick, Richard C., 144, 194
McFarland, Ernest, 241
Mecham, Evan, 240, 241
Mendoza, Viceroy, 73, 74, 75
Mesa, city of, 123, 129, 169, 170, 183, 188, 208, 238
Meteor Crater, 15-16
Mexican Cession, 93
Mexican holidays, 154
Mexican War, 91-93, 103
Mexico, 71, 89-96
Miami, town of, 204
Miles, General Nelson, 62
Mineral Park, town of, 197
Mining, 18, 105-12, 150, 161, 171-73, 202, 204, 215, 219
missionaries, 80-87, 90
Mogollon Rim, 14-15, 26, 204, 212
Mohave City, 197
Mohave County, 197, 199, 209-211
money, 106, 156
Montezuma, Carlos, 67-68
Montezuma Castle, 51, 52, 219
Monument Valley, 15, 16
Morenci, town of, 18, 108, 109, 110, 111, 150, 207
Mormon Battalion, 92, 132
Mormons (Latter-day Saints), 123, 200, 206, 208, 213
Mount Baldy, 200
Mount Graham, 17, 206
Mount Lemmon, 17-18, 213
mountain men: See fur trappers
Mountain States Telephone and Telegraph Company, 148
movies, 16, 161
Mowry, Sylvester, 106, 144
music, 182-83

national banks, 156
national forests, 118, 175-76, 203, 218, 219, 223
National Guard (Arizona), 159, 163, 224
national parks, 175-76, 203, 205
natural gas, 162, 163, 190
Navajo County, 196, 199, 200, 211-13
Navajo National Monument, 49

New Deal, 162
newspapers, 144-45
Niza, Fray Marcos de, 73-74, 76
Nogales, city of, 84, 87, 171, 183, 186, 217-18, 238
Northern Arizona University, 15, 131, 203

Oak Creek Canyon, 140, 177, 203
Oatman Massacre, 93
Ohnick, Hutchlon, 152
Old Tucson, 162, 177, 214
Oñate, Governor Juan de (New Mexico), 78
O'Neill, William O. "Buckey", 196
open pit mining, 171, 172, 207
Oraibi, old village of, 55, 85
Orpheus Club, 182
ostrich industry, 119-20
outlaws, 153
Owens, Commodore Perry, 212

Page, town of, 176, 190, 203
Pah Ute County, 197-98
painters, 180-82
Palo Verde nuclear generating plant, 190
Paradise Valley, 116, 184, 189
Parker, town of, 220
Parker Dam, 189, 210
Patagonia, town of, 218
Patagonia silver mine, 106
Pattie, James Ohio, 100-101
Pattie, Sylvester, 100, 101
Payson, city of, 13, 204, 205
Peoria, city of, 186
Peralta, Carlos, 217
Petrified Forest, 15, 16, 200, 212
Phoenix, city of: beginning of, 121-24. *See also* 18, 22, 54, 114, 119, 129, 130, 131, 140, 141-42, 145, 147, 148, 149, 150, 151, 152, 160, 161, 166-67, 169-70, 178, 182, 183, 185, 186-88, 199, 208-209, 230, 238
Phoenix Gazette, 145
Phoenix Indian School, 154, 228
Phoenix Union High School, 154, 159, 164
Phoenix Zoo, 209
Pierce, President Franklin, 95
Pima, town of, 123, 206
Pima County, 194, 195, 199, 213-15, 216, 232, 236
Pimería Alta, 82
Pinal County, 199, 208, 215-17
Pine, town of, 123, 204
Pioneer Arizona, 151, 209
Pipe Spring, 145-46
plant life, 25-29

Pleasant Valley, 204, 205
Point of Pines, 49
police courts, 233
political parties, 228, 239-41
political rights, 221
Polk, President James K., 91, 93
population, 9, 168, 191, 199, 201, 202, 204, 205, 206, 207, 209, 211, 213, 215, 217, 218, 219
Porras, Fray, 80
Post, Mary Elizabeth, 129-30
Poston, Charles, 105-106
POW (prisoner of war) camps, 166
Prescott, city of, 107, 129, 131, 135, 140, 144, 147-48, 152, 154, 164, 177, 186, 195, 196, 219, 238
prison, territorial (Yuma), 220
publicity pamphlet, 231
Pueblo Grande, 47, 209
Pyle, J. Howard, 240

Quartzsite, 134
Quivira, Gran, 77-78

Radio, 148-49, 160-61
railroads, 109, 137-39, 150-51, 207, 211. *See also* the names of railroad companies
rainfall, 20, 22-23
recall, 226-27
recreation, 63, 175-79, 204, 205, 210-11
referendum, 226
reptiles, 37-40
Reynolds Corporation, 166
Ricketts, Dr. Louis, 111
Riviera, town of, 211
roads, 132-34
rodeos, 176, 177, 215, 219
Rogers, S. C., 127
Romero, Captain José, 90
Roosevelt, President Franklin, 162
Roosevelt, President Theodore, 124
Roosevelt Dam, 124
Roosevelt Lake, 205, 208
Roosevelt Road (Apache Trail), 132
Rosarita Company, 170
Ruggles, Levi, 216
Rysdale, Anne, 204

Safford, Governor A. P. K., 128, 129, 206, 208
Safford, city of, 17, 150, 186, 206
Saguaro National Monument, 215
St. David, town of, 123
St. Johns, city of, 123, 200
St. Thomas, town of, 197

Salt River Valley, 18, 19, 22, 44, 99, 101, 119-20, 121-26, 151, 173, 205, 208
Salt River Herald, 145
San Antonio and San Diego Mail Line, 134
San Carlos Lake, 216
San Carlos Reservation, 49
San Francisco Peaks, 10
San Francisco River, 99
San Manuel, town of, 172, 216
San Pedro River, 44, 75, 90, 92, 99, 101, 133, 202, 216
San Xavier del Bac, 82, 84, 87, 90, 214
Santa Anna, President, 95, 96
Santa Catalina Mountains, 17-18, 84, 178, 182, 213
Santa Cruz County, 193, 195, 199, 217-18
Santa Cruz River (Valley), 82, 84, 90, 105-106, 121, 171, 215
Santa Fe, town of, 101, 103
Santa Fe Trail, 100
Santa Fe Railroad, 135-36, 213. *See also* Atlantic and Pacific Railroad
scalp-hunters, 91
Scenic Airways, 141
Schieffelin, Ed, 108
Schieffelin Hall, 155
Schools, 127-31; school board, 223
Scottsdale, city of, 169, 182, 183, 187, 189, 208, 238
secretary of state, 231
Sedona, town of, 203
Seligman, town of, 139, 219
Sharlot Hall Museum, 144, 219
sheep raising, 15, 57, 117-19, 203, 219, 223
Sherman, Moses, 129
Show Low, city of, 213
Sierra Vista, city of, 186, 202
silver mining, 105-107, 108, 153, 173, 204, 216
Singh, Diwan, 125
skiing, 175
Sky Harbor Airport, 141, 142, 166
Slidell, John, 91
Smith, Marcus, 228
Snaketown, 44, 46
Snow Bowl, 203
Snowflake, town of, 123, 170, 200, 213
solar energy, 190-91
Soleri, Paolo, 184-85
Solomonville, town of, 206
Sonoita, town of, 218
Sonora Exploring and Mining Company, 105-106
Southern Pacific Railroad, 135-36, 137-39, 182, 202, 207, 216, 217

Spaniards, 71-87, 89-90, 117, 195
sports, 46, 154-55, 177-79, 211, 216
Spring, John, 128, 129
Springerville, town of, 123, 200
stagecoaches, 135-36
Stanfield, 216
Stanwix Station, 146
state lands, 200, 203, 205, 206, 211, 215, 218, 219, 220
steamboats, 139, 194
Steinfeld, Albert, 136
Stillman, Clara, 130
Stinson, Katherine, 141
suburbs, 187-88
Sulphur Springs Valley, 114, 206
Sun City, 23, 208
Sunset Crater, 15, 50
superintendent of public instruction, 232
Superior, town of, 111, 216
Superior Court, 232-33
Swift Company, 169-70
Swilling, Jack, 121-22, 208

Taft, President William H., 227
Talley Industries, 169
taxes, 221, 223, 235
Taylor, town of, 123, 213
telegraph, 144, 145-46
telephones, 146-48
television, 149
Tempe, city of, 119, 124, 129-30, 151, 170, 183, 188, 208, 224, 238
Tempe Normal School, 130, 131, 154, 155. *See also* Arizona State University.
Territory of Arizona, 98, 115, 193-98
Territory of New Mexico, 98
Texas, 91
Thatcher, town of, 123, 206
theaters, 155-56, 183
toll roads, 134
Tombstone, city of, 18, 108, 109, 135, 145, 150, 153, 177, 201, 202
tourism, 15, 23, 158, 161, 170-71, 175-77, 199, 200, 202, 203, 204, 208, 210-11, 214, 215, 218, 219
Tovar, Pedro de, 76
town government, 237-38
trading posts, 200, 212
transportation, 132-42
treasurer, 232
trees, 24, 25-26, 27, 29
Tubac, 84, 105-107, 144, 150, 218

Tucson, city of, 18, 54, 85, 90, 92, 95, 96, 127, 129, 131, 133, 135, 141-42, 144, 146-47, 148, 150, 152, 153, 155, 160, 162, 169, 171-72, 177, 178, 182, 183, 185, 186-88, 189, 199, 213-15, 238
Tucson Boys Chorus, 182
Tucson Citizen, 144, 148
Tumacácori mission, 82, 87, 90, 218
Turco, El, 77-78
Tuzigoot, 52, 219

universities and colleges, 130-31, 206, 219. *See also* Arizona State University and University of Arizona
University of Arizona, 131, 177, 215
uranium, 173
urbanization, 186-87
USS Arizona, 163

Vaca, Cabeza de, 73
Vail, 215
Vail, Walter, 114
Verde River (Valley), 51-52, 99, 152
veto, 230
volcanoes, 11, 15
voting, 221, 239-41
Vulture mine, 108

wagon freighting, 136-37, 213
Walz, Jacob, 217
water, 158, 188-89, 208
Wattron, Frank, 212
Wayne, John, 16, 214
Weaver, Pauline, 102, 103, 107, 194

Weekly Arizonian, 106, 144
Wellton, town of, 220
Western Electric Company, 170
Wetherill, John, 213
White Mountains, 21, 200
Wickenburg, Henry, 108
Wickenburg, town of, 121, 122, 165, 183, 209
wickiup, 60
wildflowers, 29
wildlife, 21-40, 220
Willcox, town of, 126, 173
Williams, city of, 150-51, 203
Williams, Jack, 231
Williams, William Shirley "Old Bill", 101-102
Window Rock, town of, 58
Winkelman, town of, 205
Winslow, city of, 54, 139, 141-42, 213, 238
Woodruff, town of, 213
Works Progress Administration (WPA), 161, 162
World War I, 67, 119, 125, 158-60
World War II, 58-59, 67, 158, 163-67, 181, 186
Wright, Frank, 147
Wright, Frank Lloyd, 183-84
Wupatki National Monument, 51

Yavapai County, 194, 195-96, 199, 203, 204, 218-19
Young, Ewing, 99, 101, 103
Young, John W., 114
Yuma, city of, 9, 14, 21, 107, 119, 126, 130, 137, 138, 139, 150, 164, 173, 186, 220, 238
Yuma County, 194-95, 199, 219-20
Yuma crossing, 85, 86
Yuma Massacre, 85-86

Great Seal of the State of Arizona